THE
OERA LINDA BOOK

FROM

A Manuscript of the Thirteenth Century

WITH THE PERMISSION OF THE PROPRIETOR

C. OVER DE LINDEN, OF THE HELDER

The Original Frisian Text

AS VERIFIED BY DR J. O. OTTEMA

ACCOMPANIED BY AN

ENGLISH VERSION OF DR OTTEMA'S DUTCH TRANSLATION

BY

WILLIAM R. SANDBACH

LONDON
TRÜBNER & CO., LUDGATE HILL
1876

[All rights reserved]

In the interest of creating a more extensive selection of rare historical book reprints, we have chosen to reproduce this title even though it may possibly have occasional imperfections such as missing and blurred pages, missing text, poor pictures, markings, dark backgrounds and other reproduction issues beyond our control. Because this work is culturally important, we have made it available as a part of our commitment to protecting, preserving and promoting the world's literature. Thank you for your understanding.

TRANSLATOR'S PREFACE.

THE work of which I here offer an English translation has excited, among the Dutch and German literary societies, a keen controversy in regard to its authenticity—a controversy not yet brought to a conclusion, some affirming that it contains internal evidence of truth, while others declare it to be a forgery. But even the latter do not insist on its being the work of a modern fabricator. They allow it to be one hundred, or perhaps one hundred and fifty, years old. If they admit that, I do not see why they refuse it a greater antiquity; and as to the improbability of the stories related in it, I refer the reader to the exhaustive inquiry in Dr Ottema's Preface.

Is it more difficult to believe that the early Frisians, being hardy and intrepid marine adventurers, sailed to the Mediterranean, and even proceeded farther, than that the Phœnicians sailed to England for tin, and to the Baltic for amber? or that a clever woman became a lawgiver at Athens, than that a goddess sprang, full grown and armed, from the cleft skull of Jupiter?

There is nothing in the narratives of this book inconsistent with probability, however they may vary from some of our preconceived ideas; but whether it is really what it pretends to be—a very ancient manuscript, or a more modern fiction—it is not the less a most curious and interesting work, and as such I offer it to the British public.

In order to give an idea of the manuscript, I have procured photographs of two of its pages, which are bound with this volume.

I have also followed Dr Ottema's plan of printing the original Frisian opposite to the translation, so that any reader possessing a knowledge of the language may verify the correctness of the translation.

In addition to the Preface which I have translated, Dr Ottema has written two pamphlets on the subject of the Oera Linda Book (1. Historical Notes and Explanations; 2. The Royal Academy and Het Oera Linda Bok), both of which would be very valuable to any one who wished to study the controversy respecting the authenticity of the work, but which I have not thought it necessary to translate for the present publication.

There has also appeared in the "Deventer Courant" a series of twelve letters on the same subject. Though written anonymously, I believe they are from the pen of Professor Vitringa. They have been translated into German by Mr Otto.

The writer evidently entered upon his task of criticism with a feeling of disbelief in the authenticity of the book; but in his last letter he admits that, after a minute examination, he is unable to pronounce a positive conviction either for or against it.

His concluding remarks are to the following effect :—

" If the book is a romance, then I must admit that it has been written with a good object, and by a clever man, because the sentiments expressed in it are of a highly moral tendency; and the facts related, so far as they can be controlled by regular history, are not untruthful ; and where they deal with events of which we have no historical records, they do not offend our ideas of possibility or even probability."

WM. R. SANDBACH.

INTRODUCTION.

C. OVER DE LINDEN, Chief Superintendent of the Royal Dockyard at the Helder, possesses a very ancient manuscript, which has been inherited and preserved in his family from time immemorial, without any one knowing whence it came or what it contained, owing to both the language and the writing being unknown.

All that was known was that a tradition contained in it had from generation to generation been recommended to careful preservation. It appeared that the tradition rests upon the contents of two letters, with which the manuscript begins, from Hiddo oera Linda, anno 1256, and from Liko oera Linda, anno 803. It came to C. over de Linden by the directions of his grandfather, Den Heer Andries over de Linden, who lived at Enkhuizen, and died there on the 15th of April 1820, aged sixty-one. As the grandson was at that time barely ten years old, the manuscript was taken care of for him by his aunt, Aafje Meylhoff, born Over de Linden, living at Enkhuizen, who in August 1848 delivered it to the present possessor.

Dr E. Verwijs having heard of this, requested permission to examine the manuscript, and immediately recognised it as very ancient Fries. He obtained at the same time permission to make a copy of it for the benefit of the Friesland Society, and was of opinion that it might be of great importance, provided it was not supposititious, and invented for some deceptive object, which he feared. The manuscript being placed in my hands, I also felt very doubtful, though I could not understand what object any one could have in inventing a false composition only to keep it a secret. This doubt remained until I had examined carefully-executed facsimiles of two fragments, and afterwards of the whole manuscript—the first sight of which convinced me of the great age of the document.

Immediately occurred to me Cæsar's remark upon the writing of the Gauls and the Helvetians in his "Bello Gallico" (i. 29, and vi. 14), "Græcis utuntur literis," though it appears in v. 48 that they were not entirely Greek letters. Cæsar thus points out only a resemblance —and a very true one—as the writing, which does not altogether correspond with any known form of letters, resembles the most, on a cursory view, the Greek writing, such as is found on monuments and the oldest manuscripts, and belongs to the form which is called lapidary. Besides, I formed the opinion afterwards that the writer of the latter part of the book had been a contemporary of Cæsar.

The form and the origin of the writing is so minutely and fully described in the first part of the book, as it could not be in any other language. It is very complete, and consists of thirty-four letters, among which are three separate forms of *a* and *u*, and two of *e*, *i*, *y*, and *o*, besides four pairs of double consonants—*ng*, *th*, *ks*, and *gs*. The *ng*, which as a nasal sound has no particular mark in any other Western language, is an indivisible conjunction; the *th* is soft, as in English, and is sometimes replaced by *d;* the *gs* is seldom met with—I believe only in the word *segse*, to say, in modern Fries *sidse*, pronounced *sisze.*

The paper, of large quarto size, is made of cotton, not very thick, without water-mark or maker's mark, made upon a frame or wire-web, with not very broad perpendicular lines.

An introductory letter gives the year 1256 as that

in which this manuscript was written by Hiddo overa Linda on foreign paper. Consequently it must have come from Spain, where the Arabs brought into the market paper manufactured from cotton.

On this subject, W. Wattenbach writes in his "Das Schriftwesen im Mittelalter" (Leipzig, 1871), s. 93:—

"The manufacture of paper from cotton must have been in use among the Chinese from very remote times, and must have become known to the Arabs by the conquest of Samarcand about the year 704. In Damascus this manufacture was an important branch of industry, for which reason it was called *Charta Damascena*. By the Arabians this art was brought to the Greeks. It is asserted that Greek manuscripts of the tenth century written upon cotton paper exist, and that in the thirteenth century it was much more used than parchment. To distinguish it from Egyptian paper it was called *Charta bombicina, gossypina, cuttunea, xylina*. A distinction from linen paper was not yet necessary. In the manufacture of the cotton paper raw cotton was originally used. We first find paper from rags mentioned by Petrus Clusiacensis (1122–50).

"The Spaniards and the Italians learned the manufacture of this paper from the Arabians. The most celebrated factories were at Jativa, Valencia, Toledo, besides Fabriano in the March of Ancona."*

In Germany the use of this material did not become very extended, whether it came from Italy or Spain. Therefore the further this preparation spread from the East and the adjoining countries, the more necessity there was that linen should take the place of cotton. A document of Kaufbeuren on linen paper of the year 1318 is of very doubtful genuineness. Bodman considers the oldest pure

---

* Compare G. Meerman, Admonitio de Chartæ nostralis origine. Vad. Letteroef. 1762. P. 630.
J. H. de Stoppelaar, Paper in the Netherlands. Middelburg, 1869. P. 4.

linen paper to be of the year 1324, but up to 1350 much mixed paper was used. All carefully-written manuscripts of great antiquity show by the regularity of their lines that they must have been ruled, even though no traces of the ruled lines can be distinguished. To make the lines they used a thin piece of lead, a ruler, and a pair of compasses to mark the distances.

In old writings the ink is very black or brown; but while there has been more writing since the thirteenth century, the colour of the ink is often grey or yellowish, and sometimes quite pale, showing that it contains iron. All this affords convincing proof that the manuscript before us belongs to the middle of the thirteenth century, written with clear black letters between fine lines carefully traced with lead. The colour of the ink shows decidedly that it does not contain iron. By these evidences the date given, 1256, is satisfactorily proved, and it is impossible to assign any later date. Therefore all suspicion of modern deception vanishes.

The language is very old Fries, still older and purer than the Fries Rjuchtboek or old Fries laws, differing from that both in form and spelling, so that it appears to be an entirely distinct dialect, and shows that the locality of the language must have been (as it was spoken) between the Vlie and the Scheldt.

The style is extremely simple, concise, and unembarrassed, resembling that of ordinary conversation, and free in the choice of the words. The spelling is also simple and easy, so that the reading of it does not involve the least difficulty, and yet with all its regularity, so unrestricted, that each of the separate writers who have worked at the book has his own peculiarities, arising from the changes in pronunciation in a long course of years, which naturally must have happened, as the last part of the work is written five centuries after the first.

As a specimen of antiquity in language and writing, I believe I may venture to say that this book is unique of its kind.

The writing suggests an observation which may be of great importance.

The Greeks know and acknowledge that their writing was not their own invention. They attribute the introduction of it to Kadmus, a Phenician. The names of their oldest letters, from Alpha to Tau, agree so exactly with the names of the letters in the Hebrew alphabet, with which the Phenician will have been nearly connected, that we cannot doubt that the Hebrew was the origin of the Phenician. But the form of their letters differs so entirely from that of the Phenician and Hebrew writing, that in that particular no connection can be thought of between them. Whence, then, have the Greeks derived the form of their letters?

From "thet bok thêra Adela folstar" ("The Book of Adela's Followers") we learn that in the time when Kadmus is said to have lived, about sixteen centuries before Christ, a brisk trade existed between the Frisians and the Phenicians, whom they named Kadhemar, or dwellers on the coast.

The name Kadmus comes too near the word Kadhemar for us not to believe that Kadmus simply meant a Phenician.

Further on we learn that about the same time a priestess of the castle in the island of Walcheren, Min-erva, also called Nyhellenia, had settled in Attica at the head of a Frisian colony, and had founded a castle at Athens. Also, from the accounts written on the walls of Waraburch, that the Finns likewise had a writing of their own —a very troublesome and difficult one to read—and that, therefore, the Tyrians and the Greeks had learned the writing of Frya. By this representation the whole thing explains itself, and it becomes clear whence comes the exterior resemblance between the Greek and the old Fries writing, which Cæsar also remarked among the Gauls; as likewise in what manner the Greeks acquired and retained the names of the Finn and the forms of the Fries writing.

Equally remarkable are the forms of their figures. We usually call our figures Arabian, although they have not the least resemblance to those used by the Arabs. The Arabians did not bring their ciphers from the East, because the Semitic nations used the whole alphabet in writing numbers. The manner of expressing all numbers by ten signs the Arabs learned in the West, though the form was in some measure corresponding with their writing, and was written from left to right, after the Western fashion. Our ciphers seem here to have sprung from the Fries ciphers (*siffar*), which form had the same origin as the handwriting, and is derived from the lines of the Juul?

The book as it lies before us consists of two parts, differing widely from each other, and of dates very far apart. The writer of the first part calls herself Adela, wife of Apol, chief man of the Linda country. This is continued by her son Adelbrost, and her daughter Apollonia. The first book, running from page 1 to 88, is written by Adela. The following part, from 88 to 94, is begun by Adelbrost and continued by Apollonia. The second book, running from page 94 to 114, is written by Apollonia. Much later, perhaps two hundred and fifty years, a third book is written, from page 114 to 134, by Frethorik; then follows from page 134 to 143, written by his widow, Wiljow; after that from page 144 to 169 by their son, Konereed; and then from page 169 to 192 by their grandson, Beeden. Pages 193 and 194, with which the last part must have begun, are wanting, therefore the writer is unknown. He may probably have been a son of Beeden.

On page 134, Wiljow makes mention of another writing of Adela. These she names " thet bok thêra sanga (thet boek), thêra tellinga," and "thet Hellênia bok;" and afterwards " tha skrifta fon Adela jeftha Hellênia."

To fix the date we must start from the year 1256 of our era, when Hiddo overa Linda made the copy, in which he says that it was 3449 years after Atland was sunk. This disappearance of the old land (*âldland, âtland*) was known by the Greeks, for Plato mentions in his " Timæus," 24, the disappearance of Atlantis, the position of which was only known as somewhere far beyond the Pillars of Hercules. From this writing it appears that it was land stretching far out to the west of Jutland, of which Heligoland and the islands of North Friesland are the last barren remnants. This event, which occasioned a great dispersion of the Frisian race, became the commencement of a chronological reckoning corresponding with 2193 before Christ, and is known by geologists as the Cimbrian flood.

On page 80 begins an account in the year 1602, after the disappearance of Atland, and thus in the year 591 before Christ; and on page 82 is the account of the murder of Frâna, " Eeremoeder," of Texland two years later—that is, in 589. When, therefore, Adela commences her writing with her own coming forward in an assembly of the people thirty years after the murder of the Eeremoeder, that must have been in the year 559 before Christ. In the part written by her daughter Apollonia, we find that fifteen months after the assembly Adela was killed by the Finns in an attack by surprise of Texland. This must accordingly have happened 557 years before Christ. Hence it follows that the first book, written by Adela, was of the year 558 before Christ. The second book, by Apollonia, we may assign to about the year 530 before Christ. The latter part contains the history of the known kings of Friesland, Friso, Adel (Ubbo), and Asega Askar, called Black Adel. Of the third king, Ubbo, nothing is said, or rather that part is lost, as the pages 169 to 188 are missing. Frethorik, the first writer, who appears now, was a contemporary of the occurrences which he relates, namely, the arrival of Friso. He was a friend of Liudgert den Geertman, who, as rear-admiral of the fleet of Wichhirte, the sea-king, had come with Friso in the year 303 before Christ, 1890 years after the disappearance of Atland. He has borrowed most of his information from the log-book of Liudgert.

The last writer gives himself out most clearly as a contemporary of Black Adel or Askar, about the middle of his reign, which Furmerius states to have been from 70 before Christ to 11 after the birth of Christ, the same period as Julius Cæsar and Augustus. He therefore wrote in the middle of the last century before Christ, and knew of the conquest of Gaul by the Romans. It is thus evident that there elapsed fully two centuries between the two parts of the work.

Of the Gauls we read on page 84 that they were called the "Missionaries of Sydon." And on page 124 "that the Gauls are Druids." The Gauls, then, were Druids, and the name Galli, used for the whole nation, was really only the name of an order of priesthood brought from the East, just as among the Romans the Galli were priests of Cybele.

The whole contents of the book are in all respects new. That is to say, there is nothing in it that we were acquainted with before. What we here read of Friso, Adel, and Askar differs entirely from what is related by our own chroniclers, or rather presents it in quite another light. For instance, they all relate that Friso came from India, and that thus the Frisians were of Indian descent; and yet they add that Friso was a German, and belonged to a Persian race which Herodotus called Germans (Γερμάνιοι). According to the statement in this book, Friso did come from India, and with the fleet of Nearchus; but he is not therefore an Indian. He is of Frisian origin, of Frya's people. He belongs, in fact, to a Frisian colony which after the death of Nijhellênia, fifteen and a half centuries before Christ, under the guidance of a priestess Geert, settled in the Punjab, and took the name of Geertmen. The Geertmen were known by only one of the Greek writers, Strabo, who mentions them as Γερμᾶνες, differing totally and entirely from the Βραχμᾶνες in manners, language, and religion.

The historians of Alexander's expeditions do not speak of Frisians or Geertmen, though they mention Indo-scythians, thereby describing a people who live in India, but whose origin is in the distant, unknown North.

In the accounts of Liudgert no names are given of places where the Frieslanders lived in India. We only know that they first established themselves to the east of the Punjab, and afterwards moved to the west of those rivers. It is mentioned, moreover, as a striking fact, that in the summer the sun at midday was straight above their heads. They therefore lived within the tropics. We find in Ptolemy (see the map of Kiepert), exactly 24° N. on the west side of the Indus, the name Minnagara; and about six degrees east of that, in 22° N., another Minnagara. This name is pure Fries, the same as Walhallagara, Folsgara, and comes from Minna, the name of an Eeremoeder, in whose time the voyages of Teunis and his nephew Inca took place.

The coincidence is too remarkable to be accidental, and not to prove that Minnagara was the headquarters of the Frisian colony. The establishment of the colonists in the Punjab in 1551 before Christ, and their journey thither, we find fully described in Adela's book; and with the mention of one most remarkable circumstance, namely, that the Frisian mariners sailed through the strait which in those times still ran into the Red Sea.

In Strabo, book i. pages 38 and 50, it appears that Eratosthenes was acquainted with the existence of the strait, of which the later geographers make no mention. It existed still in the time of Moses (Exodus xiv. 2), for he encamped at Pi-ha-chiroht, the "mouth of the strait." Moreover, Strabo mentions that Sesostris made an attempt to cut through the isthmus, but that he was not able to accomplish it. That in very remote times the sea really did flow through is proved by the result of the geological investigations on the isthmus made by the Suez Canal Commission, of which M. Renaud presented a report to the Academy of Sciences on the 19th June 1856. In that report, among other things, appears the following: "Une question fort controversée est celle de savoir, si à l'époque où les Hebreux fuyaient de l'Egypte sous la conduite de Moïse, les lacs amers faisaient encore partie de la mer rouge. Cette dernière hypothèse s'accorderait mieux que l'hypothèse contraire avec le texte des livres sacrés, mais alors il faudrait admettre que depuis l'époque de Moïse le seuil de Suez serait sorti des eaux."

With regard to this question, it is certainly of importance to fall in with an account in this Frisian manuscript, from which it seems that in the sixteenth century before Christ the connection between the Bitter Lakes and the Red Sea still existed, and that the strait was still navigable. The manuscript further states that soon after the passage of the Geertmen there was an earthquake; that the land rose so high that all the water ran out, and all the shallows and alluvial lands rose up like a wall. This must have happened after the time of Moses, so that at the date of the Exodus (1564 B.C.) the track between Suez and the Bitter Lakes was still navigable, but could be forded dry-foot at low water.

This point, then, is the commencement of the isthmus, after the forming of which, the northern inlet was certainly soon filled up as far as the Gulf of Pelusium.

The map by Louis Figuier, in the "Année scientifique et industrielle" (*première année*), Paris, Hachette, 1857, gives a distinct illustration of the formation of this land.

Another statement, which occurs only in Strabo, finds also here a confirmation. Strabo alone of all the Greek writers relates that Nearchus, after he had landed his troops in the Persian Gulf, at the mouth of the Pasitigris, sailed out of the Persian Gulf by Alexander's command, and steered round Arabia through the Arabian Gulf. As the account stands, it is not clear what Nearchus had to do there, and what the object of the further voyage was. If, as Strabo seems to think, it was only for geographical discovery, he need not have taken the whole fleet. One or two ships would have sufficed. We do not read that he returned. Where, then, did he remain with that fleet?

The answer to this question is to be found in the Frisian version of the story. Alexander had bought the ships on the Indus, or had had them built by the descendants of the Frisians who settled there—the Geertmen—and had taken into his service sailors from among them, and at the head of them was Friso. Alexander having accomplished his voyage and the transport of his troops, had no further use for the ships in the Persian Gulf, but wished to employ them in the Mediterranean. He had taken that idea into his head, and it must be carried into effect. He wished to do what no one had done before him. For this purpose Nearchus was to sail up the Red Sea, and on his arrival at Suez was to find 200 elephants, 1000 camels, workmen and materials, timber and ropes, &c., in order to haul the ships by land over the isthmus. This work was carried on and accomplished with so much zeal and energy that after three months' labour the fleet was launched in the Mediterranean. That the fleet really came to the Mediterranean appears in Plutarch's "Life of Alexander;" but he makes Nearchus bring the fleet round Africa, and sail through the Pillars of Hercules.

After the defeat at Actium, Cleopatra, in imitation of this example, tried to take her fleet over the isthmus in order to escape to India, but was prevented by the inhabitants of Arabia Petræa, who burnt her ships. (See Plutarch's "Life of Antony.") When Alexander shortly afterwards died, Friso remained in the service of Antigonus and Demetrius, until, having been grievously insulted by the latter, he resolved to seek out with his sailors their fatherland, Friesland. To India he could not, indeed, return.

Thus these accounts chime in with and clear up each other, and in that way afford a mutual confirmation of the events.

Such simple narratives and surprising results led me to conclude that we had to do here with more than mere Saga and Legends.

Since the last twenty years attention has been directed to the remains of the dwellings on piles, first observed in the Swiss lakes, and afterwards in other parts of Europe. (See Dr E. Rückert, "Die Pfahlbauten;" Wurzburg, 1869. Dr T. C. Winkler, in the "Volksalmanak," t. N. v. A. 1867.) When they were found, endeavours were made to discover, by the existing fragments of arms, tools, and household articles, by whom and when these dwellings had been inhabited. There are no accounts of them in historical writers, beyond what Herodotus writes in book v. chapter 16, of the "Paeonen." The only trace that has been found is in one of the panels of Trajan's Pillar, in which the destruction of a pile village in Dacia is represented.

Doubly important, therefore, is it to learn from the writing of Apollonia that she, as "Burgtmaagd" (chief of the virgins), about 540 years before Christ, made a journey

INTRODUCTION. xvii

up the Rhine to Switzerland, and there became acquainted with the Lake Dwellers (Marsaten). She describes their dwellings built upon piles—the people themselves—their manners and customs. She relates that they lived by fishing and hunting, and that they prepared the skins of the animals with the bark of the birch-tree in order to sell the furs to the Rhine boatmen, who brought them into commerce. This account of the pile dwellings in the Swiss lakes can only have been written in the time when these dwellings still existed and were lived in. In the second part of the writing, Konerèd oera Linda relates that Adel, the son of Friso ($\pm$ 250 years before Christ), visited the pile dwellings in Switzerland with his wife Ifkja.

Later than this account there is no mention by any writer whatever of the pile dwellings, and the subject has remained for twenty centuries utterly unknown until 1853, when an extraordinary low state of the water led to the discovery of these dwellings. Therefore no one could have invented this account in the intervening period. Although a great portion of the first part of the work—the book of Adela—belongs to the mythological period before the Trojan war, there is a striking difference between it and the Greek myths. The Myths have no dates, much less any chronology, nor any internal coherence of successive events. The untrammelled fancy develops itself in every poem separately and independently. The mythological stories contradict each other on every point. "Les Mythes ne se tiennent pas," is the only key to the Greek Mythology.

Here, on the contrary, we meet with a regular succession of dates starting from a fixed period—the destruction of Atland, 2193 before Christ. The accounts are natural and simple, often naïve, never contradict each other, and are always consistent with each other in time and place. As, for instance, the arrival and sojourn of Ulysses with the

Burgtmaagd Kalip at Walhallagara (Walcheren), which is the most mythical portion of all, is here said to be 1005 years after the disappearance of Atland, which coincides with 1188 years before Christ, and thus agrees very nearly with the time at which the Greeks say the Trojan war took place. The story of Ulysses was not brought here for the first time by the Romans. Tacitus found it already in Lower Germany (see " Germania," cap. 3), and says that at Asciburgium there was an altar on which the names of Ulysses and his father Laërtes were inscribed.

Another remarkable difference consists in this, that the Myths know no origin, do not name either writers or relaters of their stories, and therefore never can bring forward any authority. Whereas in Adela's book, for every statement is given a notice where it was found or whence it was taken. For instance, " This comes from Minno's writings—this is written on the walls of Waraburch—this in the town of Frya—this at Stavia—this at Walhallagara."

There is also this further. Laws, regular legislative enactments, such as are found in great numbers in Adela's book, are utterly unknown in Mythology, and indeed are irreconcilable with its existence. Even when the Myth attributes to Minos the introduction of lawgiving in Crete, it does not give the least account of what the legislation consisted in. Also among the Gods of Mythology there existed no system of laws. The only law was unchangable Destiny and the will of the supreme Zeus.

With regard to Mythology, this writing, which bears no mythical character, is not less remarkable than with regard to history. Notwithstanding the frequent and various relations with Denmark, Sweden, and Norway, we do not find any traces of acquaintance with the Northern or Scandinavian Mythology. Only Wodin appears in the person of Wodan, a chief of the Frisians, who became the son-in-law of one Magy, King of the Finns, and after his death was deified.

The Frisian religion is extremely simple, and pure Monotheism. Wr-alda or Wr-alda's spirit is the only eternal, unchangeable, perfect, and almighty being. Wr-alda has created everything. Out of him proceeds everything—first the beginning, then time, and afterwards Irtha, the Earth. Irtha bore three daughters—Lyda, Finda, and Frya—the mothers of the three distinct races, black, yellow, and white—Africa, Asia, and Europe. As such, Frya is the mother of Frya's people, the Frieslanders. She is the representative of Wr-alda, and is reverenced accordingly. Frya has established her "Tex," the first law, and has established the religion of the eternal light. The worship consists in the maintenance of a perpetually-burning lamp, *foddik*, by priestesses, virgins. At the head of the virgins in every town was a Burgtmaagd, and the chief of the Burgtmaagden was the Eeremoeder of the Fryasburgt of Texland. The Eeremoeder governs the whole country. The kings can do nothing, nor can anything happen without her advice and approval. The first Eeremoeder was appointed by Frya herself, and was called Fâsta. In fact, we find here the prototype of the Roman Vestal Virgins.

We are reminded here of Velleda (Welda) and Aurinia in Tacitus ("Germania," 8. Hist., iv. 61, 65; v. 22, 24. "Annals," i. 54), and of Gauna, the successor of Velleda, in Dio Cassius (Fragments, 49). Tacitus speaks of the town of Velleda as "edita turris," page 146. It was the town Mannagarda forda (Munster).

In the county of the Marsians he speaks of the temple Tanfane (Tanfanc), so called from the sign of the Juul. (See plate I.)

The last of these towns was Fâstaburgt in Ameland, temple Foste, destroyed, according to Occa Scarlensis, in 806.

If we find among the Frisians a belief in a Godhead

and ideas of religion entirely different from the Mythology of other nations, we are the more surprised to find in some points the closest connection with the Greek and Roman Mythology, and even with the origin of two deities of the highest rank, Min-erva and Neptune. Min-erva (Athéné) was originally a Burgtmaagd, priestess of Frya, at the town Walhallagara, Middelburg, or Domburg, in Walcheren. And this Min-erva is at the same time the mysterious enigmatical goddess of whose worship scarcely any traces remain beyond the votive stones at Domburg, in Walcheren, Nehallenia, of whom no mythology knows anything more than the name, which etymology has used for all sorts of fantastical derivations.[*]

The other, Neptune, called by the Etrurians Nethunus, the God of the Mediterranean Sea, appears here to have been, when living, a Friesland Viking, or sea-king, whose home was Alderga (Ouddorp, not far from Alkmaar). His name was Teunis, called familiarly by his followers Neef Teunis, or Cousin Teunis, who had chosen the Mediterranean as the destination of his expeditions, and must have been deified by the Tyrians at the time when the Phenician navigators began to extend their voyages so remarkably, sailing to Friesland in order to obtain British tin, northern iron, and amber from the Baltic, about 2000 years before Christ.

Besides these two we meet with a third mythological person—Minos, the lawgiver of Crete, who likewise appears to have been a Friesland sea-king, Minno, born at Lindaoord, between Wieringen and Kreyl, who imparted to the Cretans an "Asagaboek." He is that Minos who, with his brother Rhadamanthus and Æacus, presided as

---

[*] Min-erva was called Nyhellenia because her counsels were *ny* and *hel*, that is, new and clear. In Paul's epitome of S. Pomponius Festus, *de verborum* Significatione, we find "Min-erva dicta quod bene moneat." See Preller, Roman Mythology, p. 258.

judges over the fates of the ghosts in Hades, and must not be confounded with the later Minos, the contemporary of Ægeus and Theseus, who appears in the Athenian fables.

The reader may perhaps be inclined to laugh at these statements, and apply to me the words that I myself have lately used, fantastic and improbable. Indeed at first I could not believe my own eyes, and yet after further consideration I arrived at the discovery of extraordinary conformities which render the case much less improbable than the birth of Min-erva from the head of Jupiter by a blow from the axe of Hephæstus, for instance.

In the Greek Mythology all the gods and goddesses have a youthful period. Pallas alone has no youth. She is not otherwise known than adult. Min-erva appears in Attica as high priestess from a foreign country, a country unknown to the Greeks. Pallas is a virgin goddess, Min-erva is a Burgtmaagd. The fair, blue-eyed Pallas, differing thus in type from the rest of the gods and goddesses, evidently belonged to Frya's people. The character for wisdom and the emblematical attributes, especially the owl, are the same for both. Pallas gives to the new town her own name, Athènai, which has no meaning in Greek. Min-erva gives to the town built by her the name Athene, which has an important meaning in Fries, namely, that they came there as friends—" Åthen."

Min-erva came to Attica about 1600 years before Christ, the period at which the Grecian Mythology was beginning to be formed. Min-erva landed with the fleet of Jon at the head of a colony in Attica. In later times we find her on the Roman votive stones in Walcheren, under the name of Nehallenia, worshipped as a goddess of navigation; and Pallas is worshipped by the Athenians as the protecting goddess of shipbuilding and navigation.

Time is the carrier who must eternally turn the " Jol" (wheel) and carry the sun along his course through the firmament from winter to winter, thus forming the year, every turn of the wheel being a day. In midwinter the "Jolfeest" is celebrated on Frya's Day. Then cakes are baked in the form of the sun's wheel, because with the Jol Frya formed the letters when she wrote her "Tex." The Jolfeest is therefore also in honour of Frya as inventor of writing.

Just as this Jolfeest has been changed by Christianity into Christmas throughout Denmark and Germany, and into St Nicholas' Day in Holland; so, certainly, our St Nicholas' dolls—the lover and his sweetheart—are a memorial of Frya, and the St Nicholas letters a memorial of Frya's invention of letters formed from the wheel.

I cannot analyse the whole contents of this writing, and must content myself with the remarks that I have made. They will give an idea of the richness and importance of the contents. If some of it is fabulous, even as fabulous it must have an interest for us, since so little of the traditions of our forefathers remains to us.

An internal evidence of the antiquity of these writings may be found in the fact that the name Batavians had not yet been used. The inhabitants of the whole country as far as the Scheldt are Frya's people—Frieslanders. The Batavians are not a separate people. The name Batavi is of Roman origin. The Romans gave it to the inhabitants of the banks of the Waal, which river bears the name Patabus in the "Tabula Pentingeriana." The name Batavi does not appear earlier than Tacitus and Pliny, and is interpolated in Cæsar's "Bello Gallico," iv. 10. (See my treatise on the course of the rivers through the countries of the Frisians and Batavians, p. 49, in " De Vrije Fries," 4th vol. 1st part, 1845.)

I will conclude with one more remark regarding the language. Those who have been able to take only a superficial view of the manuscript have been struck by the polish of the language, and its conformity with the present Friesland language and Dutch. In this they seem to find grounds for doubting the antiquity of the manuscript.

But, I ask, is, then, the language of Homer much less polished than that of Plato or Demosthenes? And does not the greatest portion of Homer's vocabulary exist in the Greek of our day?

It is true that language alters with time, and is continually subject to slight variations, owing to which language is found to be different at different epochs. This change in the language in this manuscript accordingly gives ground for important observations to philologists. It is not only that of the eight writers who have successively worked at the book, each is recognisable by slight peculiarities in style, language, and spelling; but more particularly between the two parts of the book, between which an interval of more than two centuries occurs, a striking difference of the language is visible, which shows what a slowly progressive regulation it has undergone in that period of time. As the result of these considerations, I arrive at the conclusion that I cannot find any reason to doubt the authenticity of these writings. They cannot be forgeries. In the first place, the copy of 1256 cannot be. Who could at that time have forged anything of that kind? Certainly no one. Still less any one at an earlier date. At a later date a forgery is equally impossible, for the simple reason that no one was acquainted with the language. Except Grimm, Richthofen, and Hettema, no one can be named sufficiently versed in that branch of philology, or who had studied the language so as to be able to write in it. And if any one could have done so, there would have been no more extensive vocabulary at his service than that which the East Frisian laws afford. Therefore, in the centuries lately elapsed, the preparation of this writing was quite impossible. Whoever doubts this let him begin by showing where, when, by whom, and with what object such a forgery could be committed, and let him show in modern times the fellow of this paper, this writing, and this language.

Moreover, that the manuscript of 1256 is not original, but is a copy, is proved by the numerous faults in the writing, as well as by some explanations of words which already in the time of the copyist had become obsolete and little known, as, for instance, in page 82 (114), " to thêra flête jefta bedrum;" page 151 (204), " bargum jefta tonnum fon tha besta bjar."

A still stronger proof is that between pages 157 and 158 one or more pages are missing, which cannot have been lost out of this manuscript, because the pages 157 and 158 are on the front and the back of the same leaf.

Page 157 finishes thus : " Three months afterwards Adel sent messengers to all the friends that he had gained, and requested them to send him intelligent people in the month of May." When we turn over the leaf, the other side begins, " his wife, he said, who had been Maid of Texland," had got a copy of it.

There is no connection between these two. There is wanting, at least, the arrival of the invited, and an account of what passed at their meeting. It is clear, therefore, that the copyist must have turned over two pages of the original instead of one. There certainly existed then an earlier manuscript, and that was doubtless written by Liko oera Linda in the year 803.

We may thus accept that we possess in this manuscript, of which the first part was composed in the sixth century before our era, the oldest production, after Homer and Hesiod, of European literature. And here we find in our fatherland a very ancient people in possession of development, civilisation, industry, navigation, commerce, literature, and pure elevated ideas of religion, whose existence we had never even conjectured. Hitherto we have believed that the historical records of our people reach no farther back than the arrival of Friso the presumptive founder of the Frisians, whereas here we become aware that these records mount up to more than 2000 years before Christ, surpassing the antiquity of Hellas and equalling that of Israel.

This paper was read at a meeting of the Frisian Society, February 1871.

VERGELIJKENDE

VAN DE OUD FRIESCHE WETTEN,

Dyo forme need is: hweerso en kynd jongh is finsen ende fitered noerd wr hef, jefta (sud) wr birgh. Soe moet die moder her kindes eerwe setta ende sella ende her kynd lesa ende des lives bihelpa.

Dioe oder need is: jef da jere diore wirdat, ende di heta honger wr dat land faert, ende dat kynd honger stere wil, so moet dio moder her kindes eerwe setta ende sella ende capia her bern ky ende ey ende coern deerma da kinde des lives mede helpe.

Dyo tredde need is: Als dat kind is al stocnaken, jefta huus laes, ende dan di tiuestera nevil ende calde winter oen comt sa faert allermanick oen syn hof ende oen sin huis ende an waranne gaten, ende da wiilda dier seket diin holla baem ende der birgha hlii, aldeer hit siin liif oen bihalda mey. Soe weinet ende scryt dat onieriga kind ende wyst dan syn nakena lyae ende syn huuslaes, ende syn fader deer him reda schuld, to ienst dyn honger ende winter nevil cald, dat hi so diepe ende dimme mitta fiower neylen is onder eke ende onder da eerda bisloten ende bitacbt, so moet dio moder her kindes eerwe setta ende sella omdat hio da bihield habbe ende biwaer also lang so hit onierich is, dat hit oen forste ner oen honger naet forfare.

Anjumer druk. e.i.i.

(1466.)

TAALPROEVE
EN DE TAAL VAN HET HANDSCHRIFT.

Thju forma nêd is: Sâhwersa en bârn jvng is fensen ånd fêterad northward vr-et hef jeftha sûdward vr tha berga, sa âch thju mâm hjara bârns erva to settande ånd to seljande ånd hjra bârn to lêsane ånd thes lives to bihelpane.

Thju ôthera nêd is: jef tha jêra djura wârthat ånd thi hête hvnger wr thet lånd fârth ånd thåt bârn stjera wil, sa mot thju mâm hjara bârns erva setta ånd selja ånd kâpja hiri bârne ky ånd skêp ånd kêren thêr mitha mån thet bârn thes lives bihelpe.

Thju tredde nêd is: sâhwersa thåt bârn is stoknâked jefta hûslâs ånd then thi tjustera nêvil ånd kalda winter ankvmth, sa fårth allera månnalik an sin hof ånd an sin hus ånd an wârande gâta, ånd thet wilde kwik sykath thene hola bâm ånd thêre berga hly thêr-it sin lif an bihalda mêi, sa wênath ånd krytath thåt vnjêrich bârn ånd wyst then sin nâkeda litha ånd sin hûslâs-sâ ånd sin tât thêr him hrêda skolde tojenst tha hvnger ånd tha kalda winter nêvil, that hi sa djap ånd dimme mith fjuwer nêilum vndera êke ånd vnder tha irtha bisletten ånd bidobben is, sa mot thju mâm hjara bârns erva setta and selja vmbe that hju tha bihield håve ånd tha wâringa al sa long sa hit vnjêrich sy, til thju-t hor an frost ner an hvnger navt vmkvma ne mêi.

Vertaald door J. G. O.

ADELA.

Okke min Svn—

Thissa boka mot i mith lif ånd sêle wârja. Se vmbifattath thju skêdnise fon vs êle folk åk fon vsa êthlum. Vrlêden jêr håb ik tham ut-er flod hred tolik mith thi ånd thinra moder. Tha hja wêron wet wrden; thêr thrvch gvngon hja åfternei vrdarva. Vmbe hja navt to vrlysa håb ik-ra vp wrlandisk pampyer wrskrêven. Sa hwersa thu se erve, mot thu se åk wrskryva. Thin bårn alsa til thju hja nimmerthe wêi navt ne kvma.

Skrêven to Ljuwert. Nêi åtland svnken is* thåt thria thû sond fjvwer hvndred ånd njugon ånd fjvwertigoste jêr, thåt is nei kersten rêknong that tvelfhvndred sex ånd fiftigoste jêr. Hidde tobinomath oera Linda.—Wâk.

Ljawa ervnôma. Vmb vsa ljawa êthlas wille ånd vmb vsa ljawa fridoms wille, thusånd wâra så bidd-ik to jo. Och ljawa ne lêt tha âgon ênis pâpekappe tach nimmerthe over thissa skrifta ne wêja. Hja sprêkath swêta wirda: men hja tornath vnmårksêm an alles hwat fon vs fryas trefth. Vmbe rika prebende to winnande så hêlath hja mith tha poppa kêninggar. Thissa wêtath that wi hjara grâteste fianda send. thrvchdam wi hjara liuda to sprêke thvra vr frijdom, rjucht ånd forstne plicht. Thervmbe lêtath hja alles vrdiligja, hwat fon vsa êthlum kvmt ånd hwat thêr jeta rest fon vsa alda sêdum. Och ljawa ik håv by tham et hove wêst. Wil Wr.alda-t thjelda ånd willath wi vs navt sterik ne måkja hja skilun vs algâdur vrdiligja.

Skrêven to Ljudwerd. Acht hondred ånd thrju jêr nei kersten bigrip. Liko tonômath ovira Linda.

---
* 3449−1256=2193 voor Chr.

OKKE MY SON—

You must preserve these books with body and soul. They contain the history of all our people, as well as of our forefathers. Last year I saved them in the flood, as well as you and your mother; but they got wet, and therefore began to perish. In order not to lose them, I copied them on foreign paper.

In case you inherit them, you must copy them likewise, and your children must do so too, so that they may never be lost.

Written at Liuwert, in the three thousand four hundred and forty-ninth year after Atland was submerged—that is, according to the Christian reckoning, the year 1256. Hiddo, surnamed Over de Linda.—Watch.

Beloved successors, for the sake of our dear forefathers, and of our dear liberty, I entreat you a thousand times never let the eye of a monk look on these writings. They are very insinuating, but they destroy in an underhand manner all that relates to us Frisians. In order to gain rich benefices, they conspire with foreign kings, who know that we are their greatest enemies, because we dare to speak to their people of liberty, rights, and the duties of princes. Therefore they seek to destroy all that we derive from our forefathers, and all that is left of our old customs.

Ah, my beloved ones! I have visited their courts! If Wr-alda permits it, and we do not shew ourselves strong to resist, they will altogether exterminate us.

LIKO, *surnamed* OVER DE LINDA.

Written at Liudwert,
Anno Domini 803.

---

* 3449–1256 is 2193 before Christ.

THET BOK THÊRA ADELA FOLSTAR.

THRITTICH jêr âftere dêi that thju folksmoder wmbrocht was thrvch thêne vreste Mâgy stand et er ârg vm to. Alle stâta thêr-er lidsa anda ôre syde thêre Wrsara, wêron fon vs ofkêrth ånd vnder-et weld thes Magy kêmen, ånd-et stand to frêsane, that er weldig skolde wertha vr-et êlle lând. Vmbe thåt vnluk to wêrane hêde mån êne mêna âcht bilidsen, hwêr gâdurath wêron âllera månnelik, thêr ann-en gode hrop stande by tha fâmna. Tha néi thât-er mâr vrlâpen wêron as thrjv etmelda, was al go-rêd anda tys ånd al-ên sa by hjara kvmste. Thâ to tha lesta frêge Adela thåt wird, ånde kêth. J alle wêt-et that ik thrjv jêr burchfâm wêsen sy. Ak wêt j that ik kêren sy to moder, ånd âk, that ik nên moder nêsa* navt nilde,* thrvchdam ik Apol to min êngâ jêrde. Thach hwat j navt nête,* thåt is, that ik alle bêrtnisa nêigvngen håw, êvin as ik en wrentlike folksmoder wêsen wêre. Ik håv al-an fon ånd witherfåren to sjande hwåt-er bêrde. Thêr thrvch send my fêlo sêka bâr wrden, thêr ôra navt nête. J håweth jester sêith, thåt vsa sibba an tha ôra syd thêre Wrsara njvt ånd lâf wêre. Thâ ik mêi sedsa to jv, thåt-er Mâgy† se nên yne gâ of wnnen heth thrvch thåt weld synra wêpne, men blåt thrvch årgelestige renka, ånd jeta mâr thrvch thåt gyrich sa thêra hyrtogum ånd thêra êthelinga. Frya heth sêit wi ne skoldon nên vnfrya ljvd by vs tolêta, thâ hwat håvon hja dên? hja håvon vsa fjand nêi folged: hwand an stêd fon hjara fensenum to dêiande, jeftha fry to lêtane, håvon hja Fryas rêd minacht ånd se to hjara slâfonum mâked. Thrvchdam hja sok dêdon, macht Frya navt longer wâka ovir hjam: hja håvon ynes ôtheris frydom binimen, ånd thåt is êrsêke, thåt hja hjara

---

* nêsa = ne wêsa. nilde = ne wilde. nête = ne wête.
† Magy, Koning der Magyaren en Finnen.

THE BOOK OF ADELA'S FOLLOWERS.

THIRTY years after the day on which the Volksmoeder was murdered by the commander Magy, was a time of great distress. All the states that lie on the other side of the Weser had been wrested from us, and had fallen under the power of Magy, and it looked as if his power was to become supreme over the whole land. To avert this misfortune a general assembly of the people was summoned, which was attended by all the men who stood in good repute with the Maagden (priestesses). Then at the end of three days the whole council was in confusion, and in the same position as when they came together. Thereupon Adela demanded to be heard, and said:—

You all know that I was three years Burgtmaagd. You know also that I was chosen for Volksmoeder, and that I refused to be Volksmoeder because I wished to marry Apol; but what you do not know is, that I have watched everything that has happened, as if I had really been your Volksmoeder. I have constantly travelled about, observing what was going on. By that means I have become acquainted with many things that others do not know. You said yesterday that our relatives on the other side of the Weser were dull and cowardly; but I may tell you that the Magy has not won a single village from them by force of arms; but only by detestable deceit, and still more by the rapacity of their dukes and nobles.

Frya has said we must not admit amongst us any but free people; but what have they done? They have imitated our enemies, and instead of killing their prisoners, or letting them go free, they have despised the counsel of Frya, and have made slaves of them.

Because they have acted thus, Frya cared no longer to watch over them. They robbed others of their freedom, and therefore lost their own.

---

* *Nêsa*, contraction for *ne wêsa*, *nilde* for *ne wilde*, *nête* for *ne wête*.
† Magy, King of the Magyars or Finns.

håwe. Thach thât ella is jo selva åken. Men ik wil sedsa to jo, ho hja nêi grâdum sâ lêg vrsylth send. Thêra finnum hjara wiva krêjon bårn. Thissa waxton vppa mith vsa frya bårn. Altomet tvildon ånd joldon hja to samne vppa hêm, jeftha hja wêron mith ekkorum by thêre hêrd. Thêr hêrdon hja mith lustum nêi tha vrdwålska finna sâgum, thrvchdam hja thjvd ånd nêi wêron. Sâ send hja vntfryast vnthônkes thene wald hjarar aldrum. As tha bårn grât wrdon ånd sagon thât tha finna-ra bårn nên wêpne hantêra machte, ånd blât wårka moste, thâ krêjon hja anneth wårka en gryns ånd wrdon hårde hâchfårande. Tha bâsa ånd hjara storsta svnum krupton by tha lodderiga finna mangêrtum; ånd hjara åjne toghatera thrvch thât vvle fårbild fon-a wêi brocht, lêton hjara selva bigorda thrvch tha skênesta finna knåpa, hjara vvle aldrum to spot. Tha thêne Magy thât anda nôs kryg, tha nam-er tha skênesta sinar Finna ånd Magyara vrlovende râ ky mith golden horna, sa hja ra thrvch vs folk fata dêdon, åfterdam sina lêr vtbrêda. Men sin ljuda dêdon mâr: bern wrdon to sok makad, nei vpsalåndum wêibrocht, ånd såhwersa hja vpbrocht wêron an sina vvla lêr, thån wrdon hja to bek sendon. Thâ tha skinslâvona vsa tâl mâchtich wêron, thâ klivadon hja tha hêrtoga ånd êthelinga an bord, ånd kêthon, hja moston thene Magy hêroch wertha, sa kvndon hjara svnum vpfolgja tham, oni* .thrvch-et folk kêron to wrdane. Thêra thêr vmbe goda dêdum en fårdêl to-ra hus kryen hêde-vrlovadon hja fon sinant wêgum jeta-n åfter-dêl bij; hoka tham en fâr ånd åfter-dêl kryen hêde sêidon hja en rond-dêl to, ånd tham en rond-dêl hêde en êlle stât. Wêron tha êthla to hårde fryas, thâ wendon hja tha stêwen ånd hildon vppar vrbastera svnum an. Jesterdêi wêron-er mong† jo tham allet folk to hâpa hropa wilde

---

* Oni, oud Holl. ane, Duitsch ohne = zonder.
† Mong, among, emong = onder.

This is well known to you, but I will tell you how they came to sink so low. The Finn women had children. These grew up with our free children. They played and gamboled together in the fields, and were also together by the hearth.

There they learned with pleasure the loose ways of the Finns, because they were bad and new; and thus they became denationalised in spite of the efforts of their parents. When the children grew up, and saw that the children of the Finns handled no weapons, and scarcely worked, they took a distaste for work, and became proud.

The principal men and their cleverest sons made up to the wanton daughters of the Finns; and their own daughters, led astray by this bad example, allowed themselves to be beguiled by the handsome young Finns in derision of their depraved fathers. When the Magy found this out, he took the handsomest of his Finns and Magyars, and promised them "red cows with golden horns" to let themselves be taken prisoners by our people in order to spread his doctrines. His people did even more. Children disappeared, were taken away to the uplands, and after they had been brought up in his pernicious doctrines, were sent back.

When these pretended prisoners had learned our language, they persuaded the dukes and nobles that they should become subject to the Magy—that then their sons would succeed to them without having to be elected. Those who by their good deeds had gained a piece of land in front of their house, they promised on their side should receive in addition a piece behind; those who had got a piece before and behind, should have a rondeel (complete circuit); and those who had a rondeel should have a whole freehold. If the seniors were true to Frya, then they changed their course, and turned to the degenerate sons. Yesterday there were among you those who would have called the whole people together,

---

* *Oni*, in Old Dutch, is *one*; in German, *ohne* or *zonder*.

† *Mong*, *among*, or *emong*, is, in Dutch, *onder*; in English, *among*.

vmb tha åstlike ståta wither to hjara plyga to tvangande. Thach nêi min ynfalda myning skolde thât falikant * utkvmma. Thånk ynes thêr was wêsen en hårde lvngsyakte among-eth fja, ånd thåt-er thêr jeta årg vvde, skolde j-eth thån wel wâgja vmbe jvw hêlena fja to fârande among hjara syaka fja? åmmer nå. Såhwersa allra månnelik nw biåma ånd bijechta mot, thåt-eth thêr mitha stapel årg of kvma skolde, hwa skolde thån alsa dryst wêsa vmbe sina bårn to wagande among en folk thåt êlle ånd al vrdêren is. Macht ik jo rêd jêva, ik skolde sedsa to jo, j moste bifara alle dingum jo en nêie folksmoder kyasa. Ik wêt wel thåt j thêrmitha anda brvd sitte, vt hawede thåt-er fon tha thredtine burchfâmna than wi jeta ower håve wel achte send thêr nêi thêre êra dinge, men thåt skold ik navt ne melda. Tüntja thêr fåm is et-er burch Mêdêasblik het er nåmmer nêi tålth ; tach is hja fol witskip ånd klarsyan, ånd wel sa hårde vppir folk ånd usa plyga stålth as all ôthera etsamne. Forth skold-ik rêda j moste nêi tha burgum gâ, ånd thêr vpskrywa alle êwa fryas tex, bijvnka alle skydnisa, jå ella thåt er to finda sy vppa wâgum, til thju ella navt vrlêren ni gâ, ånd mitha burgum alsa vrdên navt ne werth. Thêr ståt askriwen : thiu moder ånd jahwelik burchfåm skil håva buta helpar ånd senda bodon, yn and twintich fåmna ånd sjugon lêrfåmkis. Macht ik thêr hwat to dvande, thâ skol-ik skrywa, ånd alsa fêlo êrsêma toghatera vmbe to lêrane, sa thêr vppa burgum wêsa müge ; hwand ik seg an trowe ånd tîd skil-eth jechta, såhwersa j åfta Fryas bårn wille nåmmer to winnande, hor thrvch lesta ner thvch wêpne, sa hagath j to nvdande thåt jvwe toghatera åfta frya wiva wrde. Bårn mot mån lêre, ho grât vs lånd êr wêsen sy, hokke grâte månniska vsa ethla wêron, ho grât wi jeta send, sa wi vs dål ledsath bij ôra, mån

---

* Falikant, fâ likande = weinig gelijkende, niet conform.

to compel the eastern states to return to their duty. According to my humble opinion, they would have made a great mistake. Suppose that there was a very serious epidemic among the cattle, would you run the risk of sending your own healthy cattle among the sick ones? Certainly not. Every one must see that doing that would turn out very badly for the whole of the cattle. Who, then, would be so imprudent as to send their children among a people wholly depraved? If I were to give you any advice, it would be to choose a new Volksmoeder. I know that you are in a difficulty about it, because out of the thirteen Burgtmaagden that we still have remaining, eight are candidates for the dignity; but I should pay no attention to that.

Teuntia, the Burgtmaagd of Medeasblik, who is not a candidate, is a person of knowledge and sound sense, and quite as attached to our people and our customs as all the rest together. I should farther recommend that you should visit all the citadels, and write down all the laws of Frya's Tex, as well as all the histories, and all that is written on the walls, in order that it may not be destroyed with the citadels.

It stands written that every Volksmoeder and every Burgtmaagd shall have assistants and messengers—twenty-one maidens and seven apprentices.

If I might add more, I would recommend that all the respectable girls in the towns should be taught; for I say positively, and time will show it, that if you wish to remain true children of Frya, never to be vanquished by fraud or arms, you must take care to bring up your daughters as true Frya's daughters.

You must teach the children how great our country has been, what great men our forefathers were, how great we still are, if we compare ourselves to others.

---

* *Palikant*, or *fâ likande*, is very improbable or unlikely.

mot tâla hjam fon tha wicharda ånd fon hjara wichandlika dêdum, åk wra fâra sêtochta. Al thissa tållinga hagath dên to werthande bij thêre hêrd, vppa hêm ånd hwêr-et wêsa mêi, så bij blyskip as bij târum. Men skilet standfåst kvma an dat bryn ånd andåt hirta, thån moton alle lêringa overa wêra jvwera wiva ånd toghatera thêr-in strâma. Adelas rêd is vpfolgath.

Thit send tha nâma thêra grêvetmanna, vnder hwammis wald thit bok awrochten is. Apol, Adelas man, Thria is-er sêkening wêsen, nw is-er grêvetman over Ast-flylånd ånd ovir-a Linda-wrda. Tha bvrga Ljvdgårda, Lindahêm, ånd Stâvja send vnder sin hod.

Ther Saxman Storo, Sytjas man, grêvetman ovir-a hâga feuna ånd walda. Njvgun wåra is-er to hêrtoga, thåt is to hyrman, kêren. Tha burga Bvda ånd Manna-gårdaforda send vnder sin hod.

Abêlo, Jaltjas man, grêvetman ovir tha Sudar Flylânda. Fjvwers is-er hyrman wêsen. Tha burga Aken, Ljvdburch ånd Kåtsburch send vnder sin hod.

Enoch Dywek his man, grêvetman ovir West-flylånd ånd Texland. Njvgun mel is-er to sêkening kêren. Thiu Wàraburch, Mêdêasblik, Forâna ånd ald Fryasburch send vnder sin hod.

Foppa, man fon Dunrôs, grêvetman ovir tha Sjvgon elånda. Fif mel is-er sêkening wêsen. Thju burch Walhallagâra is vnder sin hod.

Thit stand vppa tha wâgum et Fryasburch to Texland askrywen, thåt stêt åk to Stâvia ånd to Mêdêas blik.

Thåt was Frya his dêi ånd to thêre stonde was et vrlêden sjvgun wåra sjvgun jêr, thåt Fåsta was anståld as folksmoder nêi Fryas jêrta. Thju burch Mêdêasblik was rêd ånd en fâm was kêren. Nw skolde Fåsta thju nêja foddik vpstêka, ånd thâ thåt dên was an åjnwarda fon thåt folk,

THE BOOK OF ADELA'S FOLLOWERS.

You must tell them of the sea-heroes, of their mighty deeds and distant voyages. All these stories must be told by the fireside and in the field, wherever it may be, in times of joy or sorrow; and if you wish to impress it on the brains and the hearts of your sons, you must let it flow through the lips of your wives and your daughters.

Adela's advice was followed.

These are the Grevetmen under whose direction this book is composed:—

Apol, Adela's husband; three times a sea-king; Grevetman of Ostflyland and Lindaoorden. The towns Liudgarda, Lindahem, and Stavia are under his care.

The Saxman Storo, Sytia's husband; Grevetman over the Hoogefennen and Wouden. Nine times he was chosen as duke or heerman (commander). The towns Buda and Manna-garda-forda are under his care.

Abêlo, Jaltia's husband; Grevetman over the Zuiderflylanden. He was three times heerman. The towns Aken, Liudburg, and Katsburg are under his care.

Enoch, Dywcke's husband; Grevetman over Westflyland and Texel. He was chosen nine times for sea-king. Waraburg, Medeasblik, Forana, and Fryasburg are under his care.

Foppe, Dunroo's husband; Grevetman over the seven islands. He was five times sea-king. The town Walhallagara is under his care.

This was inscribed upon the walls of Fryasburg in Texland, as well as at Stavia and Medeasblik.

It was Frya's day, and seven times seven years had elapsed since Festa was appointed Volksmoeder by the desire of Frya. The citadel of Medeasblik was ready, and a Burgtmaagd was chosen. Festa was about to light her new lamp, and when she had done so in the presence

thâ hrop Frya fon hira wâkstâre, så thåt allera månnalik thåt hêra machte: Fåsta nim thinra stifte ånd writ tha thinga thêr ik êr navt sedsa ne machte. Fåsta dêde alsa hja boden wårth. Så send wy Fryas bårn an vsa forma skêdnise kêmen.

Thåt is vsa forma skêdnise.

Wr. alda* tham allêna god ånd êvg is, måkade t.anfang, dana kêm tid, tid wrochte alle thinga åk jrtha. Jrtha bârde alle gârsa, krûdon ånd boma, allet djara kwik ånd allet årge kwik. Alhwat god ånd djar is, brocht hju by dêgum ånd alhwat kwåd ånd årg is, brocht hju thes nachtis forth. After-et twilifte jol-fêrste bârde hja thrja mangêrta.

Lyda wårth ut glyande,
Finda wårth ut hêta ånd
Frya ut warme stof.

Thâ hja blât kêmon spisde Wr.alda hjam mith sina âdama; til thju tha månneska an him skolde bvnden wêsa. Ring as hja rip wêron krêjon hja früchda ånd nochta anda drâma Wr.aldas. Od† trâd to-ra binna: ånd nw bârdon ek twilif svna ånd twilif togathera ek joltid twên. Thêrof send alle månneska kêmen.

Lyda was swart, krolhêred alsa tha lômera: lik stâra blonken hjra ôgon; ja thes gyrfügels blikkar wêron vnmodich by hjras.

Skårpe Lyda. Annen sanâka kvn hju kruppa hêra, ånd hwersa thêr fiska invr wêter wêre n-vntgong thåt hira nostera navt.

Râdbvwde Lyda. En store bâm kvn hju bûgja ånd sahwersa hja run ne bråk nêne blomstâl vnder hjara fyt.

Weldige Lyda. Hård was hjra steme ånd krêt hju ut grimme så run ek flux wêi.

---

* Wr.alda. Altijd geschreven als zamengesteld woord beteekent: de overoude, het oudste wezen.

† Od, wortel van het Lat. odi, ik haat.

of all the people, Frya called from her watch-star, so that every one could hear it: "Festa, take your style and write the things, that I may not speak." Festa did as she was bid, and thus we became Frya's children, and our earliest history began.

This is our earliest history.

Wr-alda, who alone is eternal and good, made the beginning. Then commenced time. Time wrought all things, even the earth. The earth bore grass, herbs, and trees, all useful and all noxious animals. All that is good and useful she brought forth by day, and all that is bad and injurious by night.

After the twelfth Juulfeest she brought forth three maidens:—

Lyda out of fierce heat.
Finda out of strong heat.
Frya out of moderate heat.

When the last came into existence, Wr-alda breathed his spirit upon her in order that men might be bound to him. As soon as they were full grown they took pleasure and delight in the visions of Wr-alda.

Hatred found its way among them.

They each bore twelve sons and twelve daughters—at every Juul-time a couple. Thence come all mankind.

Lyda was black, with hair curled like a lamb's; her eyes shone like stars, and shot out glances like those of a bird of prey.

Lyda was acute. She could hear a snake glide, and could smell a fish in the water.

Lyda was strong and nimble. She could bend a large tree, yet when she walked she did not bruise a flower-stalk.

Lyda was violent. Her voice was loud, and when she screamed in anger every creature quailed.

---

* *Wr-alda*, always written as a compound word, meaning the *Old Ancient*, or the *Oldest Being*.

† *Od*, the root of the Latin *odi*, I hate.

Wonderfvlle Lyda. Fon êwa nilde hju navt nêta: hjra dêda wrdon thrvch hjra tochta stjvrat. Vmbe tha têdra to helpâne, dâde hju tha stôra ånd hwersa hju-t dên hêde grâjde hju by-t lik.

Arme Lyda. Hju wårth gris fon-t vnwisse bihjelda ånd vpp-it ende sturf hja fon hirtsêr vmbe tha bårn-ra kwåd.

Vnwisa bårn. Hja tichtegadon ekkorum, fen måm-ra dåd, hja gråjadon lik wolva, fjvchtadon alsa ånd dahwile hja that dêdon êton tha fügelon thåt lik. Hwâ mêi sin târa hwither to haldane.

Finda. Was gêl ånd hjr hêr så tha måna êner hors: êne thrê ne kv hja navt ni bûgja; men hwêr Lyda annen lavwa macht to dêjande, thêr dåde hja wel tjån.

Vrlêdalike Finda. Svet was hjra stemme ånd nannen fügel kvn sjonga lik hju. Hjra êgon lokton ånd lordon, men thêrer ansach wårth slåf.

Vnrêdalika Finda. Hju skrêf thûsande êwa, tha hju ne folgde nên er fon vp. Hja vrfyade tha goda vmbe hjara frymod, thå an slikmåmkes jêf hju hjr selva hast wêi.

That was hir vnluk. Hjra håved was to fvl: tha hjr hirte to ydel; hju ne minde nimmån sa hja selva ånd hju wilde thåt ek hja lyaf håwe skolde.

Falske Finda. Hüning swet wêron hjra wirda, thå hok tham hja trjvwade wêre vnluk nêi by.

Selvsjochta Finda. Ovir ella wilde hju welda, ånd hjra svnum wêron lik hju; fon hjara susterum lêton hja ra thjanja ånd ekkorum slogon hja vmb-et måsterskip dåd.

Dubbelhirta Finda. Vmbe skotse wirda wårth hju yre, ånd tha årgste dêda ne rorde hja navt. Sach hju en nyndask en spinne vrslynna, thån wårth hju omm-et hirte sa ys; men sach hju hjra bårn en fryas vrmorde så swol hjra bosm fon nocht.

Wonderful Lyda! She had no regard for laws; her actions were governed by her passions. To help the weak she would kill the strong, and when she had done it she would weep by their bodies.

Poor Lyda! She turned grey by her mad behaviour, and at last she died heart-broken by the wickedness of her children. Foolish children! They accused each other of their mother's death. They howled and fought like wolves, and while they did this the birds devoured the corpse. Who can refrain from tears at such a recital?

Finda was yellow, and her hair was like the mane of a horse. She could not bend a tree, but where Lyda killed one lion she killed ten.

Finda was seductive. Her voice was sweeter than any bird's. Her eyes were alluring and enticing, but whoever looked upon them became her slave.

Finda was unreasonable. She wrote thousands of laws, but she never obeyed one. She despised the frankness of the good, and gave herself up to flatterers.

That was her misfortune. Her head was too full, but her heart was too vain. She loved nobody but herself, and she wished that all should love her.

False Finda! Honey-sweet were her words, but those who trusted them found sorrow at hand.

Selfish Finda! She wished to rule everybody, and her sons were like her. They made their sisters serve them, and they slew each other for the mastery.

Treacherous Finda! One wrong word would irritate her, and the cruellest deeds did not affect her. If she saw a lizard swallow a spider, she shuddered; but if she saw her children kill a Frisian, her bosom swelled with pleasure.

Vnluke Finda. Hju sturf anda blomtid fon hjra lêva, ånd-t is jeta tjvester ho hju fallen sy.

Skinhêliga bårn. Vnder kestlike stêna lêidon hja hjra lik dêl, mit kwabbjana skriftum smukton hja tham vppa, togråjande vmbe hêrath to wårthande men an stilnise ne wênadon hja nênen ênge târ.

Vrijfalik folk. Thi tex thêr Finda nêi lêt was in golden blêder wryt: thach tha besta hwêr-far i måkad was, wêr i nåmmer to not. Tha goda êwa wrdon utfågad ånd selfv sjocht wryte thêr kwåda far in.

O Finda. Tha wårth jrtha fvl blod, ånd tha håveda thêr månneska måjadon thin bårn lik gårs hålma of. Ja Finda thåt send tha früchda thinera ydlenise. Sjan dål fon thinre wåkstår ånd wên.

Frya. Was wit lik snêi bij-t môrnerâd ånd thåt blåw hjrar ôgnum wn-et jeta thêre rêinbôge of.

Skêne Frya: Lik strêlon thêre middêi svnne blikadon hjra hêron, thêr sa fin wêron as rach.

Abela Frya. Vntlvkton hjra wêra, thån swêgon tha fügelon ånd ne rordon tha blêdar navt mar.

Weldige Frya. Thrvch thêne kråft hjrar blikkar strêk thene låwa to fara hjara fyt dål ånd held thene addur sin gif tobåk.

Rêne Frya. Hjra yta was hüning ånd hjra drank was dåwa, gådvrad anda bôsma thêra blommur.

Lichte Frya. Thåt forma hwat hju hjra bårn lerde was selv-twang, thåt ôthera was lyafte to düged, ånd thå hja jêroch wrdon, thå lêrde hju hjam thju wêrtha fon tha frijdom kånna: hwand sêide hju svnder frijdom send alle ôthera dügedon allêna god vmbe jo to slåvona to måkjande, jvwe ofkvmste to êvge skantha.

Milde Frya. Nåmmer lyt hju mêtal ut jrtha dålva vmb åjnbåt, men såhwersa hja-t dêde wêr-et to jahwelikis not.

Unfortunate Finda! She died in the bloom of her age, and the mode of her death is unknown.

Hypocritical children! Her corpse was buried under a costly stone, pompous inscriptions were written on it, and loud lamentations were heard at it, but in private not a tear was shed.

Despicable people! The laws that Finda established were written on golden tables, but the object for which they were made was never attained. The good laws were abolished, and selfishness instituted bad ones in their place. O Finda! then the earth overflowed with blood, and your children were mown down like grass. Yes, Finda! those were the fruits of your vanity. Look down from your watch-star and weep.

Frya was white like the snow at sunrise, and the blue of her eyes vied with the rainbow.

Beautiful Frya! Like the rays of the sun shone the locks of her hair, which were as fine as spiders' webs.

Clever Frya! When she opened her lips the birds ceased to sing and the leaves to quiver.

Powerful Frya! At the glance of her eye the lion lay down at her feet and the adder withheld his poison.

Pure Frya! Her food was honey, and her beverage was dew gathered from the cups of the flowers.

Sensible Frya! The first lesson that she taught her children was self-control, and the second was the love of virtue; and when they were grown she taught them the value of liberty; for she said, "Without liberty all other virtues serve to make you slaves, and to disgrace your origin."

Generous Frya! She never allowed metal to be dug from the earth for her own benefit, but when she did it it was for the general use.

Lukigoste Frya. Alsa tha stâra om jrtha omswyrmia swirmadon hjara bârn om hja.

Wise Frya. Thâ hju hjra bârn vpbrocht hêde alto thêre sjugonde kny, thâ hrop hju-ra alle a Flylând to sâmne. Thêr jêf se hjam hjra tex, ând sêide, lêt tham jvwe wêiwisar wêsa, thâ ne skil thât jo nâ navt kwalik ni· gâ.

Utforkêrena Frya. Thâ hju-t sêid hêde, bêvade jrtha lîk Wr.aldas sê, Flylândis bodem svnk an grâda vnder hjara fyt dâl. Thju loft wârt swart ând nylof* fon târa to stirtane ând thâ hja nêi moder omsâgon, was hju al lang vppira wâkstâr. Thâ to tha lesta sprâk tongar ut-a wolka ând blixen schrêf an thât loftrvm, wâk.

Farsjanda Frya. Thât lând fon hwêr hju was vpfaren was nw en strâm ând buta hira tex was thêr in ella bidvlwen hwat fon hjra hôndum kêmen was.

Hêriga bârn. Thâ hja to-ra selva wêron, thâ mâkadon hja thit hâge therp, bvwadon thâs burch thêrvppa, an da wâgrum thessa wryton hja thene tex, ând vmbe that allera mannalik hja skolde müga finda, hâvath hja thât lând rondomme Texlând hêten. Thêrvmbe skil-ât bilywa al wenne jrtha jrtha sy.

Tex Fryas.

Held bêid tha Frya, to tha lesta skilun hja my hwiter sja. Thach thêra allêna mêi ik as fry kânna thêr nên slâf is fon ên ôther ni fon sine tochta. Hyr is min rêd.

Sâhwersa thju nêd ârg sy ând gode rêd ând gode dêd nawet mâr ne formüge, hrop thân thi gâst Wr.aldas an, men j ne mot-im navt anhropa bifâra alle thinga prvvath send. Tha ik segs to jo mith rêdene ând tid skil-et wâra, tha modelâsa skilun âmmar swika vnder hjar âjn lêd.

---

* Nylof ; de kleur van nieuw loof ? geel groen.

THE BOOK OF ADELA'S FOLLOWERS.

Most happy Frya! Like the starry host in the firmament, her children clustered around her.

Wise Frya! When she had seen her children reach the seventh generation, she summoned them all to Flyland, and there gave them her Tex, saying, " Let this be your guide, and it can never go ill with you."

Exalted Frya! When she had thus spoken the earth shook like the sea of Wr-alda. The ground of Flyland sunk beneath her feet, the air was dimmed by tears, and when they looked for their mother she was already risen to her watching star; then at length thunder burst from the clouds, and the lightning wrote upon the firmament "Watch!"

Far-seeing Frya! The land from which she had risen was now a stream, and except her Tex all that was in it was overwhelmed.

Obedient children! When they came to themselves again, they made this high mound and built this citadel upon it, and on the walls they wrote the Tex, and that every one should be able to find it they called the land about it Texland. Therefore it shall remain as long as the earth shall be the earth.

FRYA'S TEX.

Prosperity awaits the free. At last they shall see me again. Though him only can I recognise as free who is neither a slave to another nor to himself. This is my counsel:—

1. When in dire distress, and when mental and physical energy avail nothing, then have recourse to the spirit of Wr-alda; but do not appeal to him before you have tried all other means, for I tell you beforehand, and time will prove its truth, that those who give way to discouragement sink under their burdens.

---

* *Nylof;* the colour of new foliage, bright green.

2. Wr.aldas gâst mêi mån allêna knibuwgjande thânk to wya, jâ thrju wâra far hwat jv fon him noten hâve, far hwat jv nith, ånd fara hâpe thêr hy jo lêt an ånga tida.

3. J håwed sjan ho ring ik helpe lênde, dva al ên mith jo nêston, men ne tof navt til mån jo bêden heth, tha lydande skolde jo floka, min fâmna skoldon jvwa nåma utfaga ut-åt bok ånd ik skolde jo lik vnbikånnade ofwisa mota.

4. Nim nåmmar knibuwgjande tånk fon jv nêston an, thjus âgath Wr.aldas gâst. Nid skolde j bikrjupa, wisdom solde j bilâka ånd min fâmna skoldon jo bityga fon fåderrâv.

5. Fjuwer thinga send to jvwe not jêven, mith nåma, loft, wêter, lånd ånd fjur. Men Wr.alda wil thêr allêna bisittar of wêsa. Thêrvmbe rêd ik jo, j skilun jo rjuchtfêrdiga manna kyasa, tham thju arbêd ånd tha früchda nêi rjuchta dêla, så that nåmman fry fon wårka ni fon wêra sy.

6. Såhwersa thêr åmman among jo fvnden wårth, thêr sin åjn frydom vrsellath, tham-n-is navt fon jvw folk: hi is en horning mith basterd blod. Ik rêde jo that j him ånd sin måm to thåt lånd utdriva, sêgs that to jvwa bårn, thes mornes, thes middêis ånd thes êwendes, til thju hja thêrof drâme thes nachtis.

7. Allera månnalik thår en ôther fon sine frydom birâwath, al wêre thêne ôre him skeldech, mot ik anda bårntåm êner slâfiune fâra lêta. Thach ik rêde jo vmbe sin lik ånd that sinera måm vpp êne kåle stêd to vrbarnande, åfternêi hjara aske fiftich fyt anda grvnd to dålvane, til hju thêr nênen gårshålm vp waxa ni mêi, hwand aldulkera gårs skolde jvw diaroste kvik dêja.

8. Ne grip nå thåt folk fon Lyda ner fon Finda an. Wr.alda skolde helpa hjm, sa that-åt weld that fon jo utgong vppa jvwa åjne hâveda skolde witherkvma.

2. To Wr-alda's spirit only shall you bend the knee in gratitude—thricefold—for what you have received, for what you do receive, and for the hope of aid in time of need.

3. You have seen how speedily I have come to your assistance. Do likewise to your neighbour, but wait not for his entreaties. The suffering would curse you, my maidens would erase your name from the book, and I would regard you as a stranger.

4. Let not your neighbour express his thanks to you on bended knee, which is only due to Wr-alda's spirit. Envy would assail you, Wisdom would ridicule you, and my maidens would accuse you of irreverence.

5. Four things are given for your enjoyment — air, water, land, and fire—but Wr-alda is the sole possessor of them. Therefore my counsel to you is, choose upright men who will fairly divide the labour and the fruits, so that no man shall be exempt from work or from the duty of defence.

6. If ever it should happen that one of your people should sell his freedom, he is not of you, he is a bastard. I counsel you to expel him and his mother from the land. Repeat this to your children morning, noon, and night, till they think of it in their dreams.

7. If any man shall deprive another, even his debtor, of his liberty, let him be to you as a vile slave; and I advise you to burn his body and that of his mother in an open place, and bury them fifty feet below the ground, so that no grass shall grow upon them. It would poison your cattle.

8. Meddle not with the people of Lyda, nor of Finda, because Wr-alda would help them, and any injury that you inflicted on them would recoil upon your own heads.

9. Sâhwersa thât machte bêra that hja fon juwe rêd jefta awet owers wilde, alsa aghat j to helpane hjam. Men kvmath hja to râwande; fal than vppa tham nither lik blixenande fjvr.

10. Sâhwersa annen fon hjam êner jvwer toghaterum to wif gêrth ånd hju that wil, thån skolun j hja hjra dvmhêd bitjvtha; thach wil hju toch hjra frêjar folgja, that hja than mith frêtho gâ.

11. Willath jvw svna fon hjara toghaterum, sâ mot j alsa dva as mith jvwa toghaterum. Thach hor tha êna nor tha ôthera mêi witherkvma; hwand hja skoldvn uthêmeda sêda ånd plêga mith fara; ånd drêi thessa by jo heldgad wrde, mêi ik navt longer ovir jo wâka.

12. Vppa minre fâm Fâsta hâv ik min hâp fâstegth, thêrvmbe most j hja to êremoder nêma. Folgath j min rêd, thån skil hju nêmels min fâm bilywa ånd alla fråna fåmna thêr hja folgja; thån skil thju foddik nåmer utgâ thêr ik far jo vpstoken hâv. Thåt ljucht thêra skil thån êvg jvwe bryn vpklarja, ånd j skilun thån êvin fry bilyva fon vnfrya weld as jvwa swite rinstrâma fon thåt salte wêter thêr åndelâse sê.

Thet het Fasta sêid.

Alle setma thêr en êw, thåt is hvndred jêr, omhlâpa müge mith tha krodar ånd sin jol, thêra mügon vppa rêd thêre moder, ånd by mêna willa vppa wêgar thêra burgum writ hwertha; send hja uppa wêgar writ, thån send hja êwa, ånd thåt is vsa plicht vmbe altham an êra to haldande. Kvmth nêd ånd tvang vs setma to jêvane, stridande wither vsa êwa ånd plêgum, sâ mot månneska dva alsa hja askja; thach send hja wêken, thån mot mån åmmer to thåt alda witherkêra. Thåt is Fryas willa, ånd thåt mot wêsa tham fon al hjra bårn.

9. If it should happen that they come to you for advice or assistance, then it behoves you to help them; but if they should rob you, then fall upon them with fire and sword.

10. If any of them should seek a daughter of yours to wife, and she is willing, explain to her her folly; but if she will follow her lover, let her go in peace.

11. If your son wishes for a daughter of theirs, do the same as to your daughter; but let not either one or the other ever return among you, for they would introduce foreign morals and customs, and if these were accepted by you, I could no longer watch over you.

12. Upon my servant Fasta I have placed all my hopes. Therefore you must choose her for Eeremoeder. Follow my advice, then she will hereafter remain my servant as well as all the sacred maidens who succeed her. Then shall the lamp which I have lighted for you never be extinguished. Its brightness shall always illuminate your intellect, and you shall always remain as free from foreign domination as your fresh river-water is distinct from the salt sea.

This has Fasta spoken.

All the regulations which have existed a century, that is, a hundred years, may by the advice of the Eeremoeder, with the consent of the community, be inscribed upon the walls of the citadel, and when inscribed on the walls they become laws, and it is our duty to respect them all. If by force or necessity any regulations should be imposed upon us at variance with our laws and customs, we must submit; but should we be released, we must always return to our own again. That is Frya's will, and must be that of all her children.

Fasta sêide.

Alle thinga, thêr mån anfangja wil, hoka thåt-åt môga wêsa, vppa tha dêi, thêr wy Frya heldgad håwa, tham skilun êvg falykant utkvma : nêidam tid nw biwysd heth thåt hju riucht hêde, så is thåt en êwa wrdon, thåt mån svnder nêd ånd tvang a Frya hjra dêi nawet owers ni dva ne mêi, tha blyda fêrsta fyrja.

That send tha Êwa thêr to thêra Burgum Hêra.

1. Såhwersa thêr årne êne burch bvwet is, så mot thju foddik thêra an tha forma foddik et Texlånd vpstêken wrda. Thach thåt ne mêi nåmmer owers as troch tha moder skên.

2. Ek moder skil hjra åjn fåmna kjasa ; alsa thêra thêr vppa thêra ôthera burgum as moder send.

3. Thju moder to Texlånd mêi hjra folgster kjasa, thach såhwersa hju falth êr hju-t dên heth, sa mot thas kêren hwertha vppa êna mêna acht, by rêdum fon alle stata et sêmne.

4. Thju moder to Texlånd mêi ên ånd tvintich fåmna ånd sjvgun spille mangêrta håva, til thju thêr åmmer sjvgun by thêre foddik muge wåkja dêilikes ånd thes nachtes. By tha fåmna thêr vppa ora burgum as moder thjanja alsa fêlo.

5. Såhwersa en fåm annen gåda wil, sa mot hju-t thêre moder melda, ånd bistonda to tha månniska kêra, êr hju mith hjra tochtige ådama thåt ljucht bivvlath.

6. Thju moder ånd alrek burchfåm skil mån tofogjande ên ånd tvintich burchêran, sjvgun alda wisa, sjvgun alda kåmpar, ånd sjvgun alda sêkåmper.

Fasta said—

Anything that any man commences, whatever it may be, on the day appointed for Frya's worship shall eternally fail, for time has proved that she was right; and it is become a law that no man shall, except from absolute necessity, keep that day otherwise than as a joyful feast.

These are the Laws established for the Government of the Citadels.

1. Whenever a citadel is built, the lamp belonging to it must be lighted at the original lamp in Texland, and that can only be done by the mother.

2. Every mother shall appoint her own maidens. She may even choose those who are mothers in other towns.

3. The mother of Texland may appoint her own successor, but should she die without having done so, the election shall take place at a general assembly of the whole nation.

4. The mother of Texland may have twenty-one maidens and seven assistants, so that there may always be seven to attend the lamp day and night. She may have the same number of maidens who are mothers in other towns.

5. If a maiden wishes to marry, she must announce it to the mother, and immediately resign her office, before her passion shall have polluted the light.

6. For the service of the mother and of each of the Burgtmaidens there shall be appointed twenty-one townsmen—seven civilians of mature years, seven warriors of mature years, and seven seamen of mature years.

7. Ther fon skilun alle jêron to honk kêra thrim fon elik sjvgun, thach hja ne mügon navt vpfolgath ne wertha thrvch hjara sibtal nêjar sa tha fjarda kny.
8. Aider mêi thrê hvndred jonga burchwêrar hâva.
9. Far thissa thjanesta skilun hja lêra Fryas tex ånd tha êwa, fon tha wisa mannon thêne wisdom, fon tha alda hêrmannon thene kunst fon tha orloch ånd fond tha sêkeningar thene kunsta thêr bi thåt butafåra nêthlik send.
10. Fon thissa wêrar skilun jêrlikes hvndred to bek kêra. Thach send thêr svme vrlåmth wrden, sa mügon hja vpper burch bilywa hjara êlle lêva long.
11. By thåt kjasa fon tha wêrar ne mêi nimmen fon thêra burch nên stem navt ne håva, ni tha grêvetmanna jefta ôthera håveda, mån thåt blåta folk allêna.
12. Thju moder et Texlånd skil mån jêva thrja sjvgun flinka bodon mith thrja twilif rappa horsa. Vppa ora burgum ek burchfåm thrê bodon mith sjvgun horsa.
13. Ak skil åjder burchfåm håva fiftich bvwara thrvch thåt folk akêren. Men thêrto mêi mån allêna jêva sokka, thêr navt abel ånd stora for wêra ner to butafårar send.
14. Ajder burch mot hiri selva bidruppa ånd genêra fon hjra åjn ronddêl ånd fon thåt dêl that hju fon thåt mårkjeld bürth.
15. Is thêr åmman kêren vmbe vppa burgum to thjanjande ånd nil-er navt, thån ne mêi-er na nên burchhêr wertha, ånd dus nên stem navt ni håva, is er al burchhêr sa skil hi thju êr vrljasa.
16. Såhwersa åmman rêd gêrt fon thêre moder, tha fon êne burchfåm, sa mot hi him selva melde by tha skrivwer. Thesse brångth-im by tha burchmåster.

Forth mot-i nêi tha lêtsa, thåt is thêne hêlener. Thêr mot sja jef er åk bisêken is fon kvada tochtum. Is-er god sêid,

THE BOOK OF ADELA'S FOLLOWERS.

7. Out of the seven three shall retire every year, and shall not be replaced by members of their own family nearer than the fourth degree.

8. Each may have three hundred young townsmen as defenders.

9. For this service they must study Frya's Tex and the laws. From the sages they must learn wisdom, from the warriors the art of war, and from the sea-kings the skill required for distant voyages.

10. Every year one hundred of the defenders shall return to their homes, and those that may have been wounded shall remain in the citadels.

11. At the election of the defenders no burgher or Grevetman, or other person of distinction, shall vote, but only the people.

12. The mother at Texland shall have three times seven active messengers, and three times twelve speedy horses. In the other citadels each maiden shall have three messengers and seven horses.

13. Every citadel shall have fifty agriculturists chosen by the people, but only those may be chosen who are not strong enough to go to war or to go to sea.

14. Every citadel must provide for its own sustenance, and must maintain its own defences, and look after its share of the general contributions.

15. If a man is chosen to fill any office and refuses to serve, he can never become a burgher, nor have any vote. And if he is already a burgher, he shall cease to be so.

16. If any man wishes to consult the mother or a Burgtmaid, he must apply to the secretary, who will take him to the Burgtmaster. He will then be examined by a surgeon to see if he is in good health. If he is passed,

tha vndvath hi him selva fon sinum wêpna, ånd sjvgun wêrar brångath him by thêre moder.

17. Is thju sêk vr êne ståte sa ne mügon thêr navt miner thån thrê bodon kvma: is-t vr-t êlla Fryaslånd, thån moton thêr jeta sjvgun tjuga bywêsa. Thêrumbe thåt er nên kva formvda navt risa ne mêi nor skalkhêd dên ne wrde.

18. By alle sêkum mot tha moder walda ånd njvda thåt hjra bårn, thåt is Fryas folk, så mêt-rik bilywa as thåt wêsa mêi. Thåt is thi gråtesta hjrar plichta, ånd vs alra vmb-er thêr an to hêlpande.

19. Håt mån hja by êne rjuchtlika sêke anhropen vmb-er utsprêk twisk annen grêvetman ånd tha mênte, ånd findath hju thju sêke tvivelik, så mot hju to båte fon thêr mênte sprêka til thju thêr frêtho kvma, ånd thrvchtham thåt bêtre sy that ên man vnrjucht dên wrde thån fêlo.

20. Kvmth hwa vmb rêd ånd wêt thju moder rêd, sa åch hju tham bystonda to jêvane, wêt hju bystonda nên rêd, så mêi hju wachtja lêta sjvgun dêgum. Wêt hju thån nach nên rêd, sa mügon hja hinne brûda, ånd hja mügon hjra selva navt biklagja, til thju nên rêd bêtre is thån kva rêd.

21. Heth en moder årge rêd jêven ut kvada willa, så mot mån hja dêja jefta ut of låndum dryva stoknaken ånd blåt.

22. Send hjra burchhêra mêdeplichtich, thån dvath mån alsa mith tham.

23. Is hjra skild tvivelik jefta blåt formoda, så mot mån thêr-vr thingja ånd sprêka, is-t nêdich, ên ånd twintich wyka long. Stemth tha halfdêl skildich, så halde mån hja vr vnskildich, twêde så wacht mån jeta en fvl jêr. Stemth mån thån alsa, så mêi mån hja skildich halda, tha navt ni dêja.

he shall lay aside his arms, and seven warriors shall present him to the mother.

17. If the affair concerns only one district, he must bring forward not less than three witnesses; but if it affects the whole of Friesland, he must have twenty-one additional witnesses, in order to guard against any deceptions.

18. Under all circumstances the mother must take care that her children, that is, Frya's people, shall remain as temperate as possible. This is her most important duty, and it is the duty of all of us to help her in performing it.

19. If she is called upon to decide any judicial question between a Grevetman and the community, she must incline towards the side of the community in order to maintain peace, and because it is better that one man should suffer than many.

20. If any one comes to the mother for advice, and she is prepared to give it, she must do it immediately. If she does not know what to advise, he must remain waiting seven days; and if she then is unable to advise, he must go away without complaining, for it is better to have no advice at all than bad advice.

21. If a mother shall have given bad advice out of illwill, she must be killed or driven out of the land, deprived of everything.

22. If her Burgtheeren are accomplices, they are to be treated in a similar manner.

23. If her guilt is doubtful or only suspected, it must be considered and debated, if necessary, for twenty-one weeks. If half the votes are against her, she must be declared innocent. If two-thirds are against her, she must wait a whole year. If the votes are then the same, she must be considered guilty, but may not be put to death.

24. Såhwersa svme among thât thrimna send tham hja alsa sêr vnskildich mêne that hja hja folgja wille, så mügon hja thât dva mith al hjara driwande ånd tilbara hâva ånd nåmman acht hjam thêr ovir min to achtiane, til thju thât mâra dêl alsa blyd kân dwâla sa thât minra del.

MÊNA ÊWA.

1. Alle frya bårn send a êlike wysa bårn. Thêrvmbe moton hja âk ôlika rjuchte hâva, alsa blyd vpp-ât lând as vpp-âth ê, thât is wêter ånd vp ella thât Wr.alda jefth.
2. Allera mannalik mêi-t wif sinra kêsa frêja ånd ek toghater mêi efter hjra helddrvnk bjada thêr hju minth.
3. Heth hwa en wif nimth, sâ jêft mân hjam hus ånd wårv. N-is thêr nên; sa mot-ât bvwat wrde.
4. Is-er nêi en ôther thorp gongon vmb en wif ånd wil hi thêr bilywa, så mot mân him thêr en hus en wårf jêwa bijonka thât not fon tha hêmrik.
5. Allera mannalik mot mân en âfterdêl as wårf by sina hus jêva. Tha nimman ne mêi en fardêl by sin hus nâva, fül min en ronddêl. Allêna ief hwa en dâd dên heth to mêna nitha, sâ mêi him thât jêven wrde. Ak mêi sin jongste svn that erva. After tham mot thât thorp that wither nima.
6. Ek thorp skil en hêmrik hâva nêi sina bihof ånd thêne grêva skil njvda that alra ek sin dêl bidongth ånd god hald, til thju tha âfter kvmmande nên skâde navt ne lyda ne muge.
7. Ek thorp mêi en mârk hava to kâp ånd to vrkâp iefta to wandelja. Alle-t ôra lând skil bvw ånd wald bilyva. Thâ tha bâma thêra ne mêi nimman navt fålla, buta mêna rêda ånd buta wêta thes waldgrêva, hwand tha walda send to mêna nitha. Thêrvmbe ne mêi nimman thêr mâster of sa.

24. If any of the one-third who have voted for her wish to go away with her, they may depart with all their live and dead stock, and shall not be the less considered, since the majority may be wrong as well as the minority.

Universal Law.

1. All free-born men are equal, wherefore they must all have equal rights on sea and land, and on all that Wr-alda has given.

2. Every man may seek the wife of his choice, and every woman may bestow her hand on him whom she loves.

3. When a man takes a wife, a house and yard must be given to him. If there is none, one must be built for him.

4. If he has taken a wife in another village, and wishes to remain, they must give him a house there, and likewise the free use of the common.

5. To every man must be given a piece of land behind his house. No man shall have land in front of his house, still less an enclosure, unless he has performed some public service. In such a case it may be given, and the youngest son may inherit it, but after him it returns to the community.

6. Every village shall possess a common for the general good, and the chief of the village shall take care that it is kept in good order, so that posterity shall find it uninjured.

7. Every village shall have a market-place. All the rest of the land shall be for tillage and forest. No one shall fell trees without the consent of the community, or without the knowledge of the forester; for the forests are general property, and no man can appropriate them.

8. As mårkjeld ne mêi thât thorp navt mâr ni nimma sa tha tillifte dêl fon tha skat, hor fon tha inhêmar ner fon tha têrhêmande. Ak ne mêi tha mârk skat navt êr vrsellath* ne wertha as thât ôra god.

9. Alle-t mårkjeld mot jêrlikes dêlath wrde, thrja dêgan far thêre joldêi, an hvndred dêlun to dêlande.

10. Thi grêvetman mit sinum grêvum skil thêr of büra twintich dêla; thêne mârk rjuchter tian dêla, ând sinum helpar, fif dêla; thju folkesmoder ên dêl; thju gâ moder fjvwer dêla; thât thorp tian dêla; tha ârma, thât is thêra tham navt wârka ni kunna ni müge, fiftich dêla.

11. Thêra, tham to mârka kvma, ne mügon navt ni wokeria, kvmath thêr svm, sa is-t thêra famna plicht hjam kânbêr to makjana in-vr thât êlle lând, til thju hja nimmerthe kêren navt wrde to eng ampt, hwand soka hâvath en gyra-lik hirte, vmbe skât to garja skolde hja ella vrrêda, thât folk, thjv moder, hjara sibben ând tho tha lesta hjara selva.

12. Is thêr âmman alsa ârg that-er sjvcht-siak fja jeftha vrdêren wêr vrsellath vr hêl god, sa mot thene mârk-rjuchtar him wêra ând tha famna him noma invr-et êlle lând.

In êra tyda hêmadon Findas folk mêst algadur invr hjara moders bârta-lând, mit nôma ald-lând that nw vnder-ne sê lêith; hja wêron thus fêr-of, thêrvmbe nêdon wi âk nên orloch, tha hja vrdrêven send ând hêinda kêmon to râwane, thâ kêm-er fon selva lândwêr hêrmanna kêninggar ând orloch, vr altham kêmon setma ând uta setma kêmon êwa.

Hyr folgath tha Êwa thêr thêrut tavlikt send.

1. Ek Fryas mot-a lêtha jeftha fyanda wêra mith aldulkera wâpne as-er forsinna, bikvma ând hândtêra mêi.

---

* De mârkskat werd in goederen betaald.

8. The market charges shall not exceed one-twelfth of the value of the goods either to natives or strangers. The portion taken for the charges shall not be sold before the other goods.

9. All the market receipts must be divided yearly into a hundred parts three days before the Juul-day.

10. The Grevetman and his council shall take twenty parts; the keeper of the market ten, and his assistants five; the Volksmoeder one, the midwife four, the village ten, and the poor and infirm shall have fifty parts.

11. There shall be no usurers in the market.

If any should come, it will be the duty of the maidens to make it known through the whole land, in order that such people may not be chosen for any office, because they are hard-hearted.

For the sake of money they would betray everybody—the people, the mother, their nearest relations, and even their own selves.

12. If any man should attempt to sell diseased cattle or damaged goods for sound, the market-keeper shall expel him, and the maidens shall proclaim him through the country.

In early times almost all the Finns lived together in their native land, which was called Aldland, and is now submerged. They were thus far away, and we had no wars. When they were driven hitherwards, and appeared as robbers, then arose the necessity of defending ourselves, and we had armies, kings, and wars.

For all this there were established regulations, and out of the regulations came fixed laws.

HERE FOLLOW THE LAWS WHICH WERE THUS ESTABLISHED.

1. Every Frisian must resist the assailants with such weapons as he can procure, invent, and use.

---

* The market dues were paid in kind.

2. Is en boi twilif jer, sa mot-i tha sjvgunde dêi miste fon sin lêr-tid vmbe rêd to werthande mith-a wåpne.

3. Is hi bikvmen, sa jêve mån him wåpne ånd hi warth to wêrar slågen.

4. Is hi thrê jêr wêrar, så wårth-i burch-hêr ånd mêi hi hêlpa sin håwed-manna to kjasane.

5. Is hwa sjvgun jêr kjasar, så mêi hi hêlpa en hêrman jeftha kêning to kjasane, thêr to åk kêren wrde.

6. Alle jêr mot-er ovir kêren wertha.

7. Buta tha kêning mügon alle ambtmanna wither kêren wertha, tham rjucht dva ånd nêi fryas rêd.

8. Annen kêning ne mêi navt ni lônger as thrê jêr kêning bilywa, til thju hi navt biklywa ne mêi.

9. Heth-i sjvgun jêr rest, så mêi hi wither kêren wertha.

10. Is thi kêning thruch thene fyand fallen, så mügon sina sibba åk nêi thêre êre thinga.

11. Is-er vppa sin tid ofgvngen jeftha binna sin tid sturven, så ne mêi nên sibba him vpfolja, thêr-im nêiar sy sa tha fjarde kny.

12. Thêra tham strida mitha wåpne an hjara handa ne kunnath navt forsinna ånd wis bilywa, thêrvmbe ne fochteth nêne kêning wåpne to hantêra an tha strid. Sin wisdom mot sin wåpen wêsa ånd thju ljafte sinra kåmpona mot sin skyld wêsa.

Hyr send tha Rjuchta thêre Moder and thêra Kêninggar.

1. Sahwersa orloch kumth, send tha moder hira bodon nêi tha kêning, thi kêning send bodon nêi tha grêvetmanna vmbe lånd-wêr.

2. Tha grêvetmanna hropath alle burch-hêra et sêmne ånd birêdath ho fêlo manna hja skilun stjura.

2. When a boy is twelve years old he must devote one day in seven to learning how to use his weapons.

3. As soon as he is perfect in the use of them they are to be given to him, and he is to be admitted as a warrior.

4. After serving as a warrior three years, he may become a citizen, and may have a vote in the election of the headman.

5. When he has been seven years a voter he then may have a vote for the chief or king, and may be himself elected.

6. Every year he must be re-elected.

7. Except the king, all other officials are re-eligible who act according to Frya's laws.

8. No king may be in office more than three years, in order that the office may not be permanent.

9. After an interval of seven years he may be elected again.

10. If the king is killed by the enemy, his nearest relative may be a candidate to succeed him.

11. If he dies a natural death, or if his period of service has expired, he shall not be succeeded by any blood relation nearer than the fourth degree.

12. Those who fight with arms are not men of counsel, therefore no king must bear arms. His wisdom must be his weapon, and the love of his warriors his shield.

These are the Rights of the Mothers and the Kings.

1. If war breaks out, the mother sends her messengers to the king, who sends messengers to the Grevetmen to call the citizens to arms.

2. The Grevetmen call all the citizens together and decide how many men shall be sent.

3. Alle bisluta thêra moton ring nêi thêre moder senden wertha mith bodon ånd tjugum.

4. Thju moder lêth alle bisluta gaderja ånd jêfth et guldnetal, thåt is thåt middeltal fon alle bisluta etsêmne, thêrmitha mot mån far thåt forma frêto ha ånd thene kening alsa.

5. Is thju wêra a kåmp, thån hoft thi kêning allêna mith sinum havedmanna to rêda, thach thêr moton åmmerthe thrê burch-hêra fon thêre moder fôrana sitta svnder stem. Thissa burch-hêra moton dêjalikis bodon nêi thêre moder senda, til thju hju wêta müge jef thêr awet dên wårth, stridande with-a êwa jeftha with Fryas rêdjevinga.

6. Wil thi kêning dva ånd sina rêda navt, så mêi hi thåt navt vnderstonda.

7. Kvmth-ene fyand vnwarlinga, thån mot mån dva sa thene kêning bith.

8. Nis thene kêning navt vppet pat, så mot mån sin folgar hêrich wêsa of tham-is folgar alont tha lesta.

9. Nis thêr nên havedman, så kjase mån hwa.

10. Nis thêr nên tid, så wårpa hi him to havedman thêrim weldich fêleth.

11. Heth thene kêning en frêsalik folk ofslagen, så mügon sina after kvmande sin nåma åfter hjara åjne fora; wil thene kêning, så mêi-er vppen vnbibv.wade stêd en plåk utkjasa to hus ånd erv. Thåt erv mêi en rond-dêl wêsa sa gråt thåt hi fon alle sidum sjvgun hvndred trêdun ut of sine hus mêi hlapa, êr hi an sina rêna kvmth.

12. Sin jongste svn mêi thåt god erva, åfte tham thamis jongste, thån skil mån that wither nimma.

Hyr send tha Rjuchta aller Fryas vmbe Sêkur to Wêsande.

1. Sahwersa thêr êwa vrwrocht wrde jefta nêja setma

THE BOOK OF ADELA'S FOLLOWERS.

3. All the resolutions must immediately be sent to the mother by messengers and witnesses.

4. The mother considers all the resolutions and decides upon them, and with this the king as well as the people must be satisfied.

5. When in the field, the king consults only his superior officers, but three citizens of the mother must be present, without any voice. These citizens must send daily reports to the mother, that they may be sure nothing is done contrary to the counsels of Frya.

6. If the king wishes to do anything which his council opposes, he may not persist in it.

7. If an enemy appears unexpectedly, then the king's orders must be obeyed.

8. If the king is not present, the next to him takes command, and so on in succession according to rank.

9. If there is no leader present, one must be chosen.

10. If there is no time to choose, any one may come forward who feels himself capable of leading.

11. If a king has conquered a dangerous enemy, his successors may take his name after their own. The king may, if he wishes, choose an open piece of ground for a house and ground; the ground shall be enclosed, and may be so large that there shall be seven hundred steps to the boundary in all directions from the house.

12. His youngest son may inherit this, and that son's youngest son after him; then it shall return to the community.

HERE ARE THE RULES ESTABLISHED FOR THE SECURITY OF ALL FRISIANS.

1. Whenever new laws are made or new regulations

tavlikt, alsa mot-et to mêna nitha skên, men nåmmer to båta fon enkeldera månniska, her fon enkeldera slachta, ner fon enkeldera ståta, nach fon awet that enkel sy.

2. Sahwersa orloch kvmt ånd thêr wrde husa homljat jeftha skêpa, hok that et sy, sy-et thrvch thene fyand, tha by mêna rêdum, så ach tha mêna mênta, thåt is al-et folk to sêmne that wither to hêlene; thêr vmbe that nåmman tha mêna sêka skil helpa vrljasa vmbe sin åjn god to bihaldane.

3. Is orloch vrthêjan, ånd send thêr svm, alsa vrdêren that hja navt longer wårka ne mügon, så mot tha mêna mênte hjam vnderhalda, by tha fêrstum achon hja forana to sittana, til thju tha jüged skil êra hjam.

4. Send thêr wêdvon ånd wêson kêmon, så mot mån hja åk vnderhalda ånd tha svna mügon thi nåma hjarar tåta vpp-ira skildum writa hjara slachtha to êrane.

5. Send thêr svm thrvch thene fyand fat ånd kvmath hja to båk, så mot mån hjam fêr fon thåt kåmp of fora, hwand hja machton fry lêten wêsa by arge loftum ånd than ne mügon hja hjara lofta navt ni halda ånd toch êrlik bilywa.

6. Jef wi selwa fyanda fåta, så brånge mon tham djap anda landa wêi, mån lêrth hja vsa frya sêde.

7. Lêt mån hja åfternêi hlåpa, så lêt mån thåt mith welhêd thrvch tha fåmna dva, til thju wi åtha ånd frjunda winna fori lêtha ånd fyandun.

Ut Minnos Skriftun.

Sahwersa thêr ênman is thêrmêta årg that hi vsa swetsar birawath, morth-dedun dvat husa barnth, mangêrtha skånth, hok thåt-et sy, thåt årg sy, ånd vsa swetnata willon thåt wroken håva, så is that rjucht thåt mån thene dêder fåtath ånd an hjara åjn-

established, they must be for the common good, and not for individual advantage.

2. Whenever in time of war either ships or houses are destroyed, either by the enemy or as a matter of precaution, a general levy shall be assessed on the people to make it good again, so that no one may neglect the general welfare to preserve his own interest.

3. At the conclusion of a war, if any men are so severely wounded as to be unable to work, they shall be maintained at the public expense, and shall have the best seats at festivals, in order that the young may learn to honour them.

4. If there are widows and orphans, they shall likewise be maintained at the public expense; and the sons may inscribe the names of their fathers on their shields for the honour of their families.

5. If any who have been taken prisoners should return, they must be kept separate from the camp, because they may have obtained their liberty by making treacherous promises, and thus they may avoid keeping their promises without forfeiting their honour.

6. If any enemies be taken prisoners, they must be sent to the interior of the country, that they may learn our free customs.

7. If they are afterwards set free, it must be done with kindness by the maidens, in order that we may make them comrades and friends, instead of haters and enemies.

From Minno's Writings.

If any one should be so wicked as to commit robbery, murder, arson, rape, or any other crime, upon a neighbouring state, and our people wish to inflict punishment, the culprit shall be put to death in the presence

warda dêjath, til thju thêr vr nên orloch ne kvme, wêrthrvch tha vnskêldiga skolde bota fori tha skêldiga. Willath hja him sin lif bihalda lêta ånd thju wrêka ofkåpja lêta, så mêi mån thåt dåja. Thach is then bona en kêning, grêvetman, grêva hwa thåt-et sy, tham ovira sêda mot wåka, så moton wi thåt kwad bêterja men ta bona mot sin straf hå.

Forth hi en êrenåma vppa sine skeld fon sina êthelun, så ne mügon sina sibba thi nåma navt lônger ne fora. Thêrvmbe thåt hi êne sibba svrg skil håva ovira sêda thêra ôthera.

Êwa fara Stjurar. Stjurar is thi Êrenoma thêra Butafarar.

Alle fryas svna håva lika rjuchta, thêrvmb mügon ålle flinka knåpa hjara self as butafårar melda by tha ôldermôn ånd thisse ne mêi him nit ofwisa, wara thåt er nên sted is.

2. Tha stjurar mügon bjara åjn måstrun noma.

3. Tha kåpljvd moton kêren ånd binomath wertha thrvch tha mênte thêr-et god hêreth ånd tha stjurar ne mügon thêr by nên stem håva.

4. Jef mån vppe rêis bifinth thåt thene kêning årg jefta vnbikvmmen is, så mügon hja en ôra nimma; kvmon hja to båk, så mêi thene kêning him self biklagja by tha ôldermôn.

5. Kvmth thêr flåte to honk ånd sin thêr båta, så moton tha stjurar thêr of en thrimene håva, althus to dêlande, thi witkêning twilf môn-is dêla, thi skolt by nacht sjugun dêla, tha bôtmônna ek twa dêla, thi skiprun ek thrê dêla, that ôra skip-is folk ek ên dêl. Tha jongste prentar ek en thrimnath, tha midlosta ek en half-dêl ånd tha ôldesta ek en twêdnath.

6. Sin thêr svme vrlameth, så mot-a mêna mênte njvda far hjara lif, åk moton hja fôrana sitta by tha mêna fêrsta, by huslika fêrsta, jå by alle fêrsta.

---

* Stjurar, van .. de naam Sturii by Plinius.

of the offended, in order that no war may arise, and the innocent suffer for the guilty. If the offended will spare his life and forego their revenge, it may be permitted. If the culprit should be a king, Grevetman, or other person in authority, we must make good his fault, but he must be punished.

If he bears on his shield the honourable name of his forefathers, his kinsmen shall no longer wear it, in order that every man may look after the conduct of his relatives.

Laws for the Navigators.

Navigator is the title of those who make foreign voyages.

1. All Frya's sons have equal rights, and every stalwart youth may offer himself as a navigator to the Olderman, who may not refuse him as long as there is any vacancy.

2. The navigators may choose their own masters.

3. The traders must be chosen and named by the community to which they belong, and the navigators have no voice in their election.

4. If during a voyage it is found that the king is bad or incompetent, another may be put in his place, and on the return home he may make his complaint to the Olderman.

5. If the fleet returns with profits, the sailors may divide one-third among themselves in the following manner: The king twelve portions, the admiral seven, the boatswains each two portions, the captains three, and the rest of the crew each one part; the youngest boys each one-third of a portion, the second boys half a portion each, and the eldest boys two-thirds of a portion each.

6. If any have been disabled, they must be maintained at the public expense, and honoured in the same way as the soldiers.

---

* *Stjurar*, from this is derived the word *Sturii* in Pliny.

7. Sin thêr vppa tocht vmkume, så moton hjara nêstun hjara dêl erva.

8. Sin thêr wêdven ånd wêson fon kvmen, så mot thju mênte hja vnderhalda; sin hja an ênre kase felth, sa mügon tha svna thi nôma hjarar tåta vppira skeldun fora.

9. Sin thêr prentara* forfaren, sa moton sina erva en êl mannis dêl håva.

10. Was hi forsêith, så mêi sin brud sjugun mannis dêlun aska vmbe hira fryadulf en stên to to wjande, mar thån mot hja for tha êre wêdve bilyva lêva lông.

11. Sahwersa en mênte en flåte to rêth, moton tha rêdar njvda fåra beste liftochtun ånd får wif ånd bårn.

12. Jef en stjurar of ånd årm is, ånd hi heth hus nach erv, så mot im that jon wertha. Nil hy nên hus nach erv, sa mügon sin friundun hem tus nêma ånd thju mênte mot et bêtera nêi sina ståt, wara thåt sin friunda thene båta weigerja.

Netlika Sêka ut-a nêilêtne Skriftum Minnos.

Minno† was en alde sêkêning, sjaner ånd wisgyrich. An tha Krêtar heth-i êwa jêven. Hi is bårn an tha Lindawrda, ånd nêi al sin witherfåra heth hi thåt luk noten umbe to Lindahêm to sterva.

Sahwersa vsa swethnata en dêl lånd håve jeftha wêtir, that vs god tolikt, sa focht-et vs vmbe that a kåp to frêja, nillath hja thåt navt ne dva, than mot mån hja that bihalda lêta. That is nêi Frya-his tex ånd-et skolde vnrjucht wêsa to vnthandana that.

Sahwersa thêr swethnata et sêmna kyva ånd sana vr enga sêka, tha vr lånd, and hja vs frêja en ordêl to sprêka, sa ach man thåt rêder åfterwêja to lêtane,

---

* Prentar, nog op Texel een (stuurmans) leerling.
† Minno, Minos (de oude).

7. If any have died on the voyage, their nearest relatives inherit their portion.

8. Their widows and orphans must be maintained at the public expense; and if they were killed in a sea-fight, their sons may bear the names of their fathers on their shields.

9. If a topsailman is lost, his heirs shall receive a whole portion.

10. If he was betrothed, his bride may claim seven portions in order to erect a monument to her bridegroom, but then she must remain a widow all her life.

11. If the community is fitting out a fleet, the purveyors must provide the best provisions for the voyage, and for the women and children.

12. If a sailor is worn out and poor, and has no house or patrimony, one must be given him. If he does not wish for a house, his friends may take him home; and the community must bear the expense, unless his friends decline to receive it.

USEFUL EXTRACTS FROM THE WRITINGS LEFT BY MINNO.

Minno was an ancient sea-king. He was a seer and a philosopher, and he gave laws to the Cretans. He was born at Lindaoord, and after all his wanderings he had the happiness to die at Lindahem.

If our neighbours have a piece of land or water which it would be advantageous for us to possess, it is proper that we should offer to buy it. If they refuse to sell it, we must let them keep it. This is Frya's Tex, and it would be unjust to act contrary to it.

If any of our neighbours quarrel and fight about any matter except land, and they request us to arbitrate, our best course will be to decline; but if

---

* *Prentar*, still used in Texel to designate a pilot's apprentice.

† *Minno*, *Minos* (the Ancient).

tach sa man thêr navt buta ne kan, sa mot man thåt erlik ånd rjuchtfêrdich dva.

Kvmth thêr hwa ånd sêith, ik håv orloch, nw most-v mi helpa; jeftha en ôra kvmth ånd sêith, min svn is vnjeṛich ånd vnbikvmmen, ånd ik bin ald, nw wild-ik thi to wåranstew ovir hini ånd ovir min land stålla, til hi jêrich sy, sa ach man that wêigarja, til thju wi nawt an twist ne kvme ne müge vr sêka stridande with vsa frya sêdum.

Sahwersa thêr kvmth en vrlandisk kapman vppa tolêtmårk et Wyringga tha to Almanland ånd hi bidroght, sa warth-er bistonda mårk-bêten ånd kanbêr måkad trvch tha fåmna invr et êle land. Kvmth-er thån to båk, sa ne skil nimman kåpja fon him, hy mêi hinne brûda sa-r kvmen is. Thus, sahwersa-r kåpljud kêren wrde vmbe wr-a merka to gå, jeftha mith-e flåt to fårane, sa ach man allêna aldulkera to kjasane tham mån tyge by tyge kånth ånd an en goda hrop ståne by tha fåmna. Bêrth-et navt to min that-er en årg man mông sy, tham tha ljud bitrogha wil, sa agon tha ora thåt to wêrane. Het-i-t-al dên sa mot mån thåt bêterja, ånd thene misdêdar ut of låndum banna, til thju vsa nåma vral mith êrane skil wertha binomath.

Men jef wir vs vppen vrlandiska mårkt finda, sy-et hêinde jeftha fêr, ånd bêrth-et thåt-et folk vs lêt dvath jeftha bistêlleth, så agon wy mith haste hêi to to slåna, hwand afskên wy êlla agon to dvande vmbe frêtho willa, vsa halfbrothar ne mügon vs nimmer minachtja nach wåna that wi ange send.

In min jüged håv ik wel ênis mort overa bånda thêra êwa, åfter håv ik Frya often tanked vr hjra tex, ånd vsa êthla vr tha êwa thêr thêrnêi tavlikt send.

Wr.alda jeftha Alfoder heth mi fêlo jêren jêven, invr fêlo landa ånd sêa håv ik omme fåren ånd nêi al hwa ik sjan hå, bin ik vrtjûgad that wi allêna

they insist upon it, it must be done honourably and justly.

If any one comes and says, I am at war, you must help me; or another comes and says, My son is an infant and incompetent, and I am old, so I wish you to be his guardian, and to take charge of my property until he is of age, it is proper to refuse in order that we may not come into disputes about matters foreign to our free customs.

Whenever a foreign trader comes to the open markets at Wyringen and Almanland, if he cheats, he must immediately be fined, and it must be published by the maidens throughout the whole country.

If he should come back, no one must deal with him. He must return as he came.

Whenever traders are chosen to go to trading stations, or to sail with the fleets, they must be well known and of good reputation with the maidens.

If, however, a bad man should by chance be chosen and should try to cheat, the others are bound to remove him. If he should have committed a cheat, it must be made good, and the culprit must be banished from the land in order that our name may be everywhere held in honour.

If we should be ill-treated in a foreign market, whether distant or near, we must immediately attack them; for though we desire to be at peace, we must not let our neighbours underrate us or think that we are afraid.

In my youth I often grumbled at the strictness of the laws, but afterwards I learned to thank Frya for her Tex and our forefathers for the laws which they established upon it. Wr-alda or Alvader has given me many years, and I have travelled over many lands and seas, and after all that I have seen, I am convinced that we alone

trvch Alfoder utforkêren send, êwa to håvande. Lydas folk
ne mêi nên êwa to måkjande ni to håldande, hja send to
dvm ånd wild thêrto. Fêlo slachta Findas send snôd enoch,
men hja send gyrich, håchfårande, falsk, vnkûs ånd mort-
sjochtich. Poga blêsath hjara selva vppa, ånd hja ne mügath nawet than krupa. Forska hropath wårk, wårk, ånd
hja ne dvath nawet as hippa ånd kluchtmåkja. Tha roka
hropath spår, spår, men hja stêlon ånd vrslynath al wat vnder
hjara snavela kvmath. Lik al tham is thåt Findas folk,
hja bogath immer ovir goda êwa; ek wil setma måkja vmb-
et kwåd to wêrane, men selva nil nimman theran bonden
wêsa. Thêra hwam-his gåst that lestigoste sy ånd thêrtrvch
sterik, tham-his hône krêjath kêning ånd tha ôro moton al-
wenna an sin weld vnderwurpen wêsa, til en ôther kvmth
thêr-im fon-a sêtel drywet. Thåt word êwa is to fråu vmbe
an mêna sêka to nomande. Thervmbe heth mån vs êvin
sega lêrth. Êwa thåt sêit setma thêr bi aller månniska êlik
an hjara mod prenth send, til thju hja müge wêta hwat rjucht
ånd vnrjucht sy ånd hwêrtrhvch hja weldich send vmbe hjara
åjne dêda ånd tham fon ôrum to birjuchtande, thåt wil sedsa
alsanåka hja god ånd navt misdêdich vpbrocht send. Ak is-
er jet-en ôra sin an fåst. Êwa seit ak, êlik wêter-lik; rjucht
ånd sljucht as wêter that thrvch nên stornewiud jeftha awet
owers vrstoren is. Warth wêter vrstoren, sa warth-et vnêwa,
vnrjucht, mem et nygt êvg vmbe wither êwa to werthande,
that lêith an sin fonselvhêd, alsa tha nygung to rjucht ånd
frydom in Fryas bern leith. Thessa nygung håvath wi
trvch Wr.aldas gåst, vsa foders, thêr in Fryas bern bogth,
thêrvm be skil hju vs åk êvg biklywa. Êwa is åk thet ôra
sinnebyld fon Wr.aldas gåst, thêr êvg rjucht ånd vnforstoren
bilywath, afskên-et an lichême årg to gêit. Êwa ånd vnforstoren send tha mårka thêra wisdom ånd rjuchtfêrdichhêd

are chosen by Alvader to have laws. Lyda's people can neither make laws nor obey them, they are too stupid and uncivilised. Many are like Finda. They are clever enough, but they are too rapacious, haughty, false, immoral, and bloodthirsty.

The toad blows himself out, but he can only crawl. The frog cries "Work, work;" but he can do nothing but hop and make himself ridiculous. The raven cries "Spare, spare;" but he steals and wastes everything that he gets into his beak.

Finda's people are just like these. They say a great deal about making good laws, and every one wishes to make regulations against misconduct, but does not wish to submit to them himself. Whoever is the most crafty crows over the others, and tries to make them submit to him, till another comes who drives him off his perch.

The word "Eva" is too sacred for common use, therefore men have learned to say "Evin."

"Eva" means that sentiment which is implanted in the breast of every man in order that he may know what is right and what is wrong, and by which he is able to judge his own deeds and those of others; that is, if he has been well and properly brought up. "Eva" has also another meaning; that is, tranquil, smooth, like water that is not stirred by a breath of wind. If the water is disturbed it becomes troubled, uneven, but it always has a tendency to return to its tranquil condition. That is its nature, just as the inclination towards justice and freedom exists in Frya's children. We derive this disposition from the spirit of our father Wr-alda, which speaks strongly in Frya's children, and will eternally remain so. Eternity is another symbol of Wr-alda, who remains always just and unchangeable.

Eternal and unalterable are the signs wisdom and rec-

thêr fon alla frêmo månniska sooht ånd trvch alla rjuchtera bisêten wrden mot. Willath tha månniska thus setma ånd domar måkja, thêr alan god bilywa ånd allerwêikes, sa moton hja êlik wêsa to fara alle månniska; nêi thisse êwa achath tha rjuchtera hjara ordêl ut to kêthande. Is thêr eng kwåd dên, hwêrvr nên êwa tavlikt send, sa mot mån êne mêna acht bilidsa; thêr ordêlth mån nêi tha sin thêr Wr.aldas gåst an vs kêth vmbe over ella rjuchtfêrdich to birjuchtande, althus to dvande ne skil vs ordêl nåmmer fålikant ut ne kvma. Ne dvath mån nên rjucht men vnrjucht, alsa rist thêr twist ånd twispalt emong tha månniska ånd stata, thêrut sprût inlandiska orloch, hwêrthrvch ella homljath ånd vrdåren wårth. Men, o dvmhêd. Dåhwila wi to dvande send ekkorum to skådane, kvmth-et nidige folk Findas mith hjara falska presterum jvw håva to råwande, jvwa toghatera to skåndane, jvwa sêda to vrdva ånd to tha lesta klåppath hja slåvona banda om jahwelikes frya hals.

Ut-a Skrifta Minnos.

Tha Nyhellênia* tham fon hira åjn nôme Min-erva hête, god sêten was ånd tha Krêkalander† hja to met even hårde minade as vs åjn folk, thå kêmon thêr svme forsta ånd prestera vppe-ra burch ånd frêjon Min-erva hwêr of hjra erva lêjon. Nyhellênia andere, mina erva drêg ik om in mina bosm, hwåt ik urven håv is ljafde vr wisdom, rjucht ånd frydom, håv ik tham vrlêren, alsa ben ik êlik an tha minniste jvvar slåvonena. Nw jêv ik rêd vm nawet, men than skold ik vrkåpja tham. Tha hêra gvngon wêi, ånd hripon al lakande, jvwer hêroga thjanra, wisa Hellênia. Thach thêrmitha miston hja hjara dol, hwand thåt folk thåt hja minnade ånd hja folgade, nam this nôme to-n êre nôme an. Tha hja sågon thåt hjara skot mist hêde,

---
* Nyhellenia, Nehalennia.
† Krekaland, het Krekenland, zoowel Groot Griekenland als Griekenland zelf.

titude, which must be sought after by all pious people, and must be possessed by all judges. If, therefore, it is desired to make laws and regulations which shall be permanent, they must be equal for all men. The judges must pronounce their decisions according to these laws. If any crime is committed respecting which no law has been made, a general assembly of the people shall be called, where judgment shall be pronounced in accordance with the inspiration of Wr-alda's spirit. If we act thus, our judgment will never fail to be right.

If instead of doing right, men will commit wrong, there will arise quarrels and differences among people and states. Thence arise civil wars, and everything is thrown into confusion and destroyed; and, O foolish people! while you are injuring each other the spiteful Finda's people with their false priests come and attack your ports, ravish your daughters, corrupt your morals, and at last throw the bonds of slavery over every freeman's neck.

From Minno's Writings.

When Nyhalennia, whose real name was Min-erva, was well established, and the Krekalanders loved her as well as our own people did, there came some princes and priests to her citadel and asked Min-erva where her possessions lay. Hellenia answered, I carry my possessions in my own bosom. What I have inherited is the love of wisdom, justice, and freedom. If I lose these I shall become as the least of your slaves; now I give advice for nothing, but then I should sell it. The gentlemen went away laughing and saying, Your humble servants, wise Hellenia. But they missed their object, for the people took up this name as a name of honour. When they saw that

---

* *Nyhellenia* or *Nehalennia*.
† *Krekaland*, the Krekenland means Magna Grecia as well as Greece.

thâ gvngon hja hja bihlvda ånd sêidon that hju-t folk hexnad hêde, men vs folk ånd tha goda Krêkalandar wêrde aller wêikes that-et laster wêre. Enis kêmon hja ånd frêgon, as thv thân nên thjonster ne biste, hwat dêist thân mitha åjar tham thv altid bi thi heste. Min-erva andere, thisse åjar send that sinebyld fon Fryas rêdjêvinga, wêrin vsa tokvmste forholen hlêit ånd fon êl thåt månneskalik slachte; tid mot hja utbroda ånd wi moton wåka thåt-er nên lêth an ne kvmth. Tha prestera, god sêid; men hwêrto thjanath thene hund an thina fêra hand. Hellênia andere, heth thene hårder nên skêper vmbe sin kidde at sêmene to haldande? hwat thene hvnd is inna thjanest thes skêphårder, bin ik in Fryas tjanest, ik mot ovir Fryas kidde wåka. That likath vs god to, sêdon tha prestera; men seg vs, hwat is thju bitjvtenise fon thi nachtule, ther immer boppa thin hole sit, is that ljuchtskvwande djar altomet thet têken thinra klårsjanhêd. Nêan andere Hellênia, hi helpt my hügja that er en slach fon månuiska ovir hirtha omme dwålth, thêr evin lik hi in kårka ånd hola hêma; thêr an tjuster frota, tach navt as hi, vmb vs fon mûsa ånd ôra plåga to helpane, men renka to forsinna, tha ôra månniska hjara witskip to råwane, til thju hja tham to bêtre müge fåta vmber slavona fon to måkjande ånd hjara blod ut to sûgane, even as vampyra dva. Enis kêmon hja mith en benda folk. Pest was over-et land kvmen, hja sêidon, wi alle send to dvande, tha Goda to offerja, til thju hja pest wêra müge. Nilst thv then navt ne helpa hjara grimskip to stilane, jeftha hethste pest selva ovir-et lånd brocht mith thinra kunsta. Nêan sôide Minerva, men ik ne kån nêne goda, thêr årg dvande send; thêrvmbe ne kan ik navt frêja jef hja beter wrda willa. Ik kån ên gode, thåt is Wr.aldas gåst; men thrvch tham er god is, dvath er åk nen kwåd. Hwanath kvmth-et kwåd

their shot had missed they began to calumniate her, and to say that she had bewitched the people; but our people and the good Krekalanders understood at once that it was calumny. She was once asked, If you are not a witch, what is the use of the eggs that you always carry with you? Min-erva answered, These eggs are the symbols of Frya's counsels, in which our future and that of the whole human race lies concealed. Time will hatch them, and we must watch that no harm happens to them. The priests said, Well answered; but what is the use of the dog on your right hand? Hellenia replied, Does not the shepherd have a sheep-dog to keep his flock together? What the dog is to the shepherd I am in Frya's service. I must watch over Frya's flocks. We understand that very well, said the priests; but tell us what means the owl that always sits upon your head, is that light-shunning animal a sign of your clear vision? No, answered Hellenia; he reminds me that there are people on earth who, like him, have their homes in churches and holes, who go about in the twilight, not, like him, to deliver us from mice and other plagues, but to invent tricks to steal away the knowledge of other people, in order to take advantage of them, to make slaves of them, and to suck their blood like leeches. Another time they came with a whole troop of people, when the plague was in the country, and said: We are all making offerings to the gods that they may take away the plague. Will you not help to turn away their anger, or have you yourself brought the plague into the land with all your arts? No, said Min-erva; I know no gods that do evil, therefore I cannot ask them to do better. I only know one good spirit, that is Wr-alda's; and as he is good he never does evil. Where, then, does evil come from? asked

thån wêi, frejath tha prestera. Allet kwâd kvmth fon jow
ånd fon thêre dvmhêd thêra månniska, tham hjara selva fon
jow fensa lêta. Jef thin drochten thån så bjustre god is,
wêrvmb wêrther-et kwâd thån navt, frêjath tha prestera.
Hellenia andere, Frya het vs vppe wêi brocht ånd thene
kroder that is tid, tham mot thåt ovrige dva. With alle
rampun is rêd ånd help to findande, tha Wr.alda wil thåt
wi hja selva soka skilon, til thju wi sterik skile wertha
ånd wis. Nillath wi navt, thån lêt-er vsa trul ut trulla,
til thju wi skilon erfåra, hwat nêi wisa dêdum ånd hwat
nêi dvma dêdum folgath. Tha sêide-ne forst, ik skolde
wåna, that wêre betre, that to wêrande. Hwel müglik,
endere Hellênia, hwand than skolde tha månniska bilywa
lik tåmade skêpa; thv ånd tha prestera skolde-r than hoda
willa, men åk skêra ånd nêi thêra slacht benke fora. Tach
alsa nil-t vs drochten navt, hi wil that wi ekkorum helpa,
men hi wil åk thåt jahweder fry sy ånd wis wrde. Thåt is
åk vsa wille, thêrvmbe kjasth vs folk sin forsta, grêva,
rêdjêvar ånd alle båsa ånd måstera ut-a wisesta thêra goda
månniska, til thju allemånnalik sin best skil dva vmbe
wis ånd god to werthande. Althus to dvande skilun wi
ênis wêta ånd anda folka lêra, that wis wêsa ånd wis dva
allêna lêith to salichhêd. That likt en ordêl, sêidon tha
prestera, men aste nv mênste, that pest thrvch vsa dvmhêd
kvmth, skolde Nyhellênia thån wel sa god wêsa wille, vmbe
vs ewat fon thåt nya ljucht to lênande, hwêr vppa hju sa
stolte is. Jes sêide Hellênia; tha rokka ånd ôra füglon
kvmath allêna falla vp vûl ås, men pest minth navt allêna
vûl ås, men vûla sêd-plegum ånd fangnisa. Wilstv nv that
pest fon-i wika ånd na wither ne kvma, thån mostv tha
fangnisa wêi dva, ånd that i alla rên wrde fon binna ånd
fon bûta. Wi willath bilåwa thåt thin red god sy, sêidon
tha prestera, men seg vs, ho skilum wi thêr alla

the priests. All the evil comes from you, and from the stupidity of the people who let themselves be deceived by you. If, then, your god is so exceedingly good, why does he not turn away the bad? asked the priests. Hellenia answered: Frya has placed us here, and the carrier, that is, Time, must do the rest. For all calamities there is counsel and remedy to be found, but Wr-alda wills that we should search it out ourselves, in order that we may become strong and wise. If we will not do that, he leaves us to our own devices; in order that we may experience the results of wise or foolish conduct. Then a prince said, I should think it best to submit. Very possibly, answered Hellenia; for then men would be like sheep, and you and the priests would take care of them, shearing them and leading them to the shambles. This is what our god does not desire, he desires that we should help one another, but that all should be free and wise. That is also our desire, and therefore our people choose their princes, counts, councillors, chiefs, and masters among the wisest of the good men, in order that every man shall do his best to be wise and good. Thus doing, we learn ourselves and teach the people that being wise and acting wisely can alone lead to holiness. That seems very good judgment, said the priests; but if you mean that the plague is caused by our stupidity, then Nyhellenia will perhaps be so good as to bestow upon us a little of that new light of which she is so proud. Yes, said Hellenia, but ravens and other birds of prey feed only on dead carrion, whereas the plague feeds not only on carrion but on bad laws and customs and wicked passions. If you wish the plague to depart from you and not return, you must put away your bad passions and become pure within and without. We admit that the advice is good, said the priests, but how shall we induce all the people under our rule

månniska to krêja, thêr vnder vs weld send. Tha stand
Hellênia vp fon hira sêtel ånd kêth: Tha muska folgath
thene sêjar, tha folka hjara goda forsta, thêrvmbe ach-stv
to bijinnande mith thin selva ålsa rên to måkjande, that
stv thinna blikka in ånd utward mêi rjuchta svnder skåmråd to werthande to fara thin åjn mod. Men in stêde fon
thåt folk rên to måkjande heste vûla fêrsta utfonden,
hwêr vppa thåt folk al sa nåka sûpth, that hja to lesta lik
tha barga annath slip frota, vmbe that stv thin vûla lusta
bota mêi. Thåt folk bigost to jolande ånd to spotande.
Thêr thrvch ne thuradon hja nên strid wither an to spin-
nande. Nv skolde åjder wåna, thåt hja vral-et folk to
håpe hropen hêde vmbe vs algadur to-t land ut to driwande.
Nêan an stêde fon hja to bihluda gvngon hja allerwêikes,
åk to tha hêinde Krêkalana til tha Alpa ut to kêthane,
thåt et thene allervrste drochten hågth hêde sin wisa toghater Min-erva, to nômth Nyhellênia êmong tha månniska to sendane in overa sê mith-en ulk, vmbe tha månniska gode rêd to jêvane ånd that allermannalik, thêr hja
hêra wilde, rik ånd lukich skolde wertha, ånd ênis bås
skolde wertha ovir alle kêningkrik irtha.s. Hira byldnese
ståldon hja vppe hjara åltårum, jeftha hja vrsellade-t anda
dvma månniska. Hja kêthon allerwêikes rêd-jêvinga, thêr
hju nimmer jêven hêde, ånd tåladon wondera, thêr hju nå
dên hêde. Thrvch lesta wiston hja-ra selva master to
måkjande fon vsa êwa ånd setma, ånd thrvch wankêthinga
wiston hja alles to wisa ånd to vrbruda. Hja ståldon åk
fåmma vnder hjara hode, tha skinber vndere hoda fon
Fåsta* vsa forma êre moder, vmbe over thåt fråna ljucht
to wåkane. Men thåt ljucht hêde hja selva vpstoken,
ånd in stêde fon tha fåmkes wis to måkjande, ånd afternêi êmong thåt folk to senda, ta sjaka to lêvande ånd tha
bårn to lêrande, måkadon hja-ra dvm ånd dimme bi-t
ljucht ånd ne machten hja nå buta ne kvma. Ak wrdon

---

* Fåsta, Vesta, en de Vestaalsche maagden.

to agree to it? Then Hellenia stood up and said: The sparrows follow the sower, and the people their good princes, therefore it becomes you to begin by rendering yourselves pure, so that you may look within and without, and not be ashamed of your own conduct. Now, instead of purifying the people, you have invented foul festivals, in which they have so long revelled that they wallow like swine in the mire to atone for your evil passions. The people began to mock and to jeer, so that she did not dare to pursue the subject; and one would have thought that they would have called all the people together to drive us out of the land; but no, in place of abusing her they went all about from the heathenish Krekaland to the Alps, proclaiming that it had pleased the Almighty God to send his clever daughter Min-erva, surnamed Nyhellenia, over the sea in a cloud to give people good counsel, and that all who listened to her should become rich and happy, and in the end governors of all the kingdoms of the earth. They erected statues to her on all their altars, they announced and sold to the simple people advice that she had never given, and related miracles that she had never performed. They cunningly made themselves masters of our laws and customs, and by craft and subtlety were able to explain and spread them around. They appointed priestesses under their own care, who were apparently under the protection of Festa, our first Eeremoeder, to watch over the holy lamp; but that lamp they lit themselves, and instead of imbuing the priestesses with wisdom, and then sending them to watch the sick and educate the young, they made them stupid and ignorant, and never allowed them to come out. They were em-

---

* *Fåsta* is Vesta, or the Vestal Virgins.

hja to rêdjêvstare brukath, tach thi rêd was by skin ut
hjara mvlun; hwand hjara mvla wêron navt owers as tha
hropar, hwêr trvch tha prestera hjara gêrta utkêthon.

Tha Nyhellênia fallen was, wilden wi en ore moder
kjasa, svme wildon nêi Texlånd vmbe thêr êne to frêjande,
men tha prestera tham by hira åjn folk thåt rik wither in
hêde, nildon that ni hengja ånd kêthon vs by-ra folk as
vn-fråna ut.

III. Ut-a Skrifta Minnos.

Tha-k althus wêi faren was mith mina ljvd fon Athenia,
kêmon wi to tha lesta an en êland thrvch min ljvd Krêta
hêten vm-a wilda krêta tham et folk anhyv by vsa kvmste.
Tha as hja sagon thåt wi nên orloch an-t skêld foron,
wrdon hja mak, alsa-k et lest far en bota mit yserark en
havesmode ånd en stada land wandelde. Thach tha wi
en stut sêten hêde ånd hja spêradon that wi nên slavona
nêde, tha wêron hja vrstålath, men tha-k-ra nw talt hêde
that wi êwa hêdon êlik to birjuchtande vr alla, tha wilde-t
folk åk fon sokka hå. Tach skêrs hêdon hja tham, jefta
thåt êlle land kêm anda tys. Tha forsta ånd prestera
kêmon bårja, that wi hjara tjvth over hêrich måkad hêde
ånd thåt folk kêm to vs vmbe hul ånd skul. Tach thå
tha forsta sagon thåt hja hjara rik vrljasa skolda, thå
jêvon hja thåt folk frydom ånd kêmon to my vmb-en êsega
bok. Thach thåt folk was nên frydom wenth ånd tha hêra
bilêvon welda nêi that ir god thochte. Thå thi storn wr wêr,
bigoston hja twispalt among vs to sêja. Hja sêidon to min folk
that ik hjara help anhropen hêde vmbe standfåst kening to
werthande. Enis fand ik gif in min met, thå as er ênis en skip

ployed as advisers, but the advice which seemed to come from them was but the repetition of the behests of the priests. When Nyhellenia died, we wished to choose another mother, and some of us wished to go to Texland to look for her; but the priests, who were all-powerful among their own people, would not permit it, and accused us before the people of being unholy.

FROM THE WRITINGS OF MINNO.

When I came away from Athenia with my followers, we arrived at an island named by my crew Kreta, because of the cries that the inhabitants raised on our arrival. When they really saw that we did not come to make war, they were quiet, so that at last I was able to buy a harbour in exchange for a boat and some iron implements, and a piece of land. When we had been settled there a short time, and they discovered that we had no slaves, they were very much astonished; and when I explained to them that we had laws which made everybody equal, they wished to have the same; but they had hardly established them before the whole land was in confusion.

The priests and the princes declared that we had excited their subjects to rebellion, and the people appealed to us for aid and protection. When the princes saw that they were about to lose their kingdom, they gave freedom to their people, and came to me to establish a code of laws. The people, however, got no freedom, and the princes remained masters, acting according to their own pleasure. When this storm had passed, they began to sow divisions among us. They told my people that I had invoked their assistance to make myself permanent king. Once I found poison in my food. So when a ship from

fon-t Fly by vs vrsêilde, ben ik thêrmith stolkens hinne brith. — Tach min witherfara to lêtande, sa wil-k mith thesa skêdnesa allêna sêga, that wi navt müge hêma mith et Findas folk fon wêr thât et sy, hwand thât hja fvl send mith falska renka, êwa to frêsane as hjara swête wina mith dêjande fenin.

Ende wra skrifta Minnos.

Hir vnder send Thrê Wêta, thêr after send thissa Setma makad.

1. Allera mannalik wêt, thât i sin bihof mot, men wârth âmmon sin bihof vnthalden, sa nêt nên man hwat er skil dva vmbe sin lif to bihaldande.

2. Alle elte minniska werthat drongen a bârn to têlande, wârth that wêrth, sa nêt nim man wath ârges thêrof kvme mei.

3. Alrek wêt thât-i fry ând vnforlêth wil lêva, ând that ôre that âk wille. Umbe sekur to wêsande send thesa setma ând domar makad.

Thât folk Findas heth âk setma ând domar: men thissa ne send navt nêi tha rjucht, men allêna to bâta thêra prestera ând forsta, thana send hjara stâta immerthe fvl twispalt ând mord.

1. Sahwersa imman nâd heth ând hi ne kan him selva navt ne helpe, sa moton tha fâmna thât kvndich dva an tha grêva. Thêrfar thât et en stolte Fryas navt ne focht thât selva to dva.

2. Sa hwa ârm wârth thrvch tham hi navt wârka nil, thêr mot to thât lând ut drêven wertha, hwand tha lâfa ând loma send lestich ând ârg tânkande : thêrvmbe âch mân to wârane tham.

3. Jahwêder jong kerdel âch en brud to sêka ând is er fif ând twintich sa âcht-er en wif to hâva.

Flyland sailed past, I quietly took my departure. Leaving alone, then, my own adventures, I will conclude this history by saying that we must not have anything to do with Finda's people, wherever it may be, because they are full of false tricks, fully as much to be feared as their sweet wine with deadly poison.

Here ends Minno's writing.

THESE ARE THE THREE PRINCIPLES ON WHICH THESE LAWS ARE FOUNDED.

1. Everybody knows that he requires the necessaries of life, and if he cannot obtain them he does not know how to preserve his life.

2. All men have a natural desire to have children, and if it is not satisfied they are not aware what evil may spring from it.

3. Every man knows that he wishes to live free and undisturbed, and that others wish the same thing.

To secure this, these laws and regulations are made.

The people of Finda have also their rules and regulations, but these are not made according to what is just—only for the advantage of priests and princes—therefore their states are full of disputes and murder.

1. If any man falls into a state of destitution, his case must be brought before the count by the maidens, because a high-minded Frisian cannot bear to do that himself.

2. If any man becomes poor because he will not work, he must be sent out of the country, because the cowardly and lazy are troublesome and ill-disposed, therefore they ought to be got rid of.

3. Every young man ought to seek a bride and to be married at five-and-twenty.

4. Is hwa fif ånd twintich, ånd heth er nên êngå, sa åch ek man him ut sin hus to wêrane. Ta knåpa åchon him te formyda. Nimth er thån nach nên êngå, så mot mån hin dåd sêga, til thju hi ut of lande brude ånd hir nên årgenese nêva ne mêi.

5. Is hwa wrak, thån mot-er avbêr sêga, that nimman fon him to frêsane nach to duchtane heth. Så mei er kvma hwêr er wil.

6. Plêcht er åfternêi hordom, så mêi-r fluchta, ne fluchter navt, så is er ån tha wrêke thêr bitrogna vrlêten, ånd nimman ne mêi helpa him.

7. Sahwersa åmmon eng god heth, ånd en ôther likt that thermête that i him thêran vrfate, sa mot-i thåt thrja vrjelda. Stêlṭh-i jeta rêis, thån mot hi nêi tha tinlånum. Wil thene bistêlne him fry jêva, så mêi-r thåt dva. Tha bêrth et wither sa ne mêi nimman him frydom jêva.

Thissa Domar send makad fara Nydiga Manniska.

1. Sa hwa in håste mode tha ut nid an nen otheris lêja brekth, ågna ut ståt, jeftha thoth, hok thåt et sy, sa mot thi lêtha bitallja hwat thene lêdar askth. Ne kan hi håt ni dva, så mot-er avbêr an im dên wertha, sa hi an thene ôre dêth. Nil hi thåt navt ut ne stonda, sa mot-i him to sina burch-fåm wenda, jef-i inna yser jeftha tin låna mêi werka til sin skeld an sy, nêi thêr mêne dom.

2. Jef ther imman fvnden wårth alsa årg that-i en Fryas felth, hi mot et mit sina lif bitallja. Kan sina burch-fåm hin far altid nei tha tinlåna helpa êr er fat wrde, sy mêi thåt dva.

3. Sahwersa thi bona mêi biwisa mith vrkånda tju-

4. If a young man is not married at five-and-twenty, he must be driven from his home, and the younger men must avoid him. If then he will not marry, he must be declared dead, and leave the country, so that he may not give offence.

5. If a man is impotent, he must openly declare that no one has anything to fear from him, then he may come or go where he likes.

6. If after that he commits any act of incontinence, then he must flee away; if he does not, he may be given over to the vengeance of those whom he has offended, and no one may aid him.

7. Any one who commits a theft shall restore it threefold. For a second offence he shall be sent to the tin mines. The person robbed may forgive him if he pleases, but for a third offence no one shall protect him.

These Rules are made for Angry People.

1. If a man in a passion or out of illwill breaks another's limb or puts out an eye or a tooth, he must pay whatever the injured man demands. If he cannot pay, he must suffer the same injury as he has done to the other. If he refuses this, he must appeal to the Burgtmaagd in order to be sent to work in the iron or tin mines until he has expiated his crime under the general law.

2. If a man is so wicked as to kill a Frisian, he must forfeit his own life; but if the Burgtmaagd can send him to the tin mines for his life before he is taken, she may do so.

3. If the prisoner can prove by proper witnesses that

gum that et by vnluk skên is, sa skil hi fry wêsa, men bêrth et jetta rêis, sa mot-i tach nêi tha tinlânum, til thju mån thêr thrvch formitha all vnerimde wrêka ånd fêitha.

This send Domar fara Horninga.

1. Hwa en ôtheris hvs ut nid thene råde hôn anstekt nis nên Fryas, hi is en horning mith basterde blod. Mêi mån hin bi thêr dêd bifåra, sa mot mån hin vppet fjvr werpa. Hy mêi flya sa-r kån tach nårne skil-i sêkur wêsa fara wrêkande hand.

2. Nên åfta Fryas skil ovira misslêga sinra nêste malja nach kalta. Is hwa misdêdoch far-im selva, tha navt frêselik far en ôra, så mêi hi him selva riuchta. Wårth-i alsa årg that er frêslik wårth, sa mot mån-t anda grêva bara; men is thêr hwa thêr en ôther åfterbåkis bitighat in stêde fon-t to dvande by tha grêva, tham is en horning. Vpper mårk mot-i anda pêle bvnden wrde, sa that et jong folk im anspêja mêi; åfter lådath mån him overa mårka, men navt nêi tha tinlåna, thrvch that en êrerâwer åk is to frêsane.

3. Sahwersa thêr ênis imman wêre sa årg that i vs gvng vrrêde by tha fyand, påda ånd to påda wes, vmbe vsa flyburga to nåka, jeftha thes nachtis thêrin to glupa, tham wêre allêna wrocht ut Findas blod. Him skolde mån mota barna. Tha stjurar skoldon sin mån ånd al sina sibba nêi en fêr êland mota brånga ånd thêr sin ask forstuva, til thju-r hyr nên feninige krûdon fon waxa ne müge. Tha fåmna moton thån sin nåm utspêja in vr al vsa stâta, til thju nên bårn sin nåm ne krêje ånd tha alda him müge vrwerpa.

the death was accidental, he may go free; but if it happens a second time, he must go to the tin mines, in order to avoid any unseemly hatred or vengeance.

These are the Rules concerning Bastards.

1. If any man sets fire to another's house, he is no Frisian, he is a bastard. If he is caught in the act, he must be thrown into the fire; and wherever he may flee, he shall never be secure from the avenging justice.

2. No true Frisian shall speak ill of the faults of his neighbours. If any man injures himself, but does no harm to others, he must be his own judge; but if he becomes so bad that he is dangerous to others, they must bring it before the count. But if instead of going to the count a man accuses another behind his back, he must be put on the pillory in the market-place, and then sent out of the country, but not to the tin mines, because even there a backbiter is to be feared.

3. If any man should prove a traitor and show to our enemies the paths leading to our places of refuge, or creep into them by night, he must be the offspring of Finda; he must be burnt. The sailors must take his mother and all his relations to a desolate island, and there scatter his ashes, in order that no poisonous herbs may spring from them. The maidens must curse his name in all the states, in order that no child may be called by his name, and that his ancestors may repudiate him.

Orloch was vrtigen, men nêd was kvmen an sin stêd. Nw wêron hyr thrê månniska thêr-ek en buda kêren stêlon fon asvndergane êjnhêra. Tha hja wrdon alle fat. Nw gong thene êrosta to ånd brocht thene thjaf by tha skelte. Tha fåmna thêr-vr kêtande sêidon allerwêis, that i dên hêde nêi rjucht. Thi ôra nom thene thjaf thåt kêren of ånd lêth im forth mith frêto. Tha fåmna sêidon, hi heth wel dên. Men thi thredde êjnhêr gvng nêi tha thjaf sin hus thå. Asser nw sach ho nêd thêr sin sêtel vpstålth hêde, thå gvng hi to båk ånd kêrde wither mith en wêin fol nêdthreftum, thêr hi nêd mith fon thêre hêrd of driwe. Fryas fåmna hêdon by him omme wårath ånd sin dêd an dat êvge bok skrêven, dahwile hja al sina lêka ut fåchth hêde. Thju êremoder was et sêid ånd hju lêt het kvndich dva thrvch thåt êle lånd.

That hyr vnder stat is in ut tha Wagar thêre Waraburch writen.

(Zie plaat I.)

Hwat hyr boppa ståt send thi têkna fon thåt jol. Thåt is thåt forma sinnebild Wr.aldas, åk fon t-anfang jeftha-t bijin, wêrut tid kêm, thåt is thene Kroder thêr êvg mith thåt jol mot ommehlåpa. Thana heth Frya thåt standskrift måkad, thåt hja brukte to hira tex. Thå Fåsta êremoder wêre, heth hju-r thåt run ieftha hlåpande skrift fon måkad. Ther Witkêning thåt is Sêkêning, Godfrêiath thene alda heth thêr asvndergana telnomar fon måkad får stand ånd rvnskrift bêde. T is thêrvmbe navt to drok that wi-r jêrliks ênis fêst vr fyrja. Wy mügon Wr.alda êvg thank to wya thåt hi sin gåst sa herde in vr vsa êthla heth fåra lêtn. Vnder hira tid heth Finda åk en skrift

War had come to an end, but famine came in its place. There were three men who each stole a sack of corn from different owners, but they were all caught. The first owner brought his thief to the judge, and the maidens said everywhere that he had done right. The second owner took the corn away from his thief and let him go in peace. The maidens said he has done well. The third owner went to the thief's house, and when he saw what misery was there, he went and brought a waggon-load of necessaries to relieve their distress. Frya's maidens came around him and wrote his deed in the eternal book, and wiped out all his sins. This was reported to the Eeremoeder, and she had it made known over the whole country.

WHAT IS WRITTEN HEREUNDER IS INSCRIBED ON THE WALLS OF WARABURGT.

(See Plate I.)

What appears at the top is the signs of the Juul—that is, the first symbol of Wr-alda, also of the origin or beginning from which Time is derived; this is the Kroder, which must always go round with the Juul. According to this model Frya formed the set hand which she used to write her Tex. When Fasta was Eeremoeder she made a running hand out of it. The Witkoning—that is, the Sea-King Godfried the Old—made separate numbers for the set hand and for the runic hand. It is therefore not too much that we celebrate it once a year. We may be eternally thankful to Wr-alda that he allowed his spirit to exercise such an influence over our forefathers.

In her time Finda also invented a mode of writing,

utfvnden, men thåt wêre sa hågfårende ånd fvl mith frisla
ånd krolum, thåt tha afterkvmanda thêrof thju bitjudnese
ring vrlêren håve. Afternêi håvon hja vs skrift lêred binoma
tha Finna, tha Thyrjar ånd tha Krekalander. Men hja
niston navt god, thåt-et fon et jol måkad was ånd that-et
thêrumbe altid skrêven wrde moste mith son om. Thêrby
wildon hja thåt hjara skrift vnlêsbêr skolde wêsa far ora
folkum, hwand hja håvath altid hêmnesa. Thus to
dvanda send hja herde fon-a wis råkath, thêrmêtha, that
ta bårn tha skriftun hja-rar aldrum amper lêsa en mûga ;
dahwile wy vsa alderaldesta skriftun êvin rêd lêsa mûga as
thêra thêr jester skrêven send.

Hir is thåt stand skrift, thêrvnder thåt run skrift, forth
tha tålnomar a byder wisa.

(Zie plaat II.)

That stêt vp alle Burgum eskrêven.

Êr thêre årge tid kêm was vs lånd thåt skênneste in
wr.alda. Svnne rês hager ånd thêr was sjelden frost.
Anda båma ånd trêjon waxton frügda ånd nochta, thêr nw
vrlêren send. Among tha gårs-sêdum hedon wi navt
alena kêren, ljaver ånd blyde, men åk swete thêr lik
gold blikte ånd thåt mån vndera svnnastrêla bakja kvste.
Jêron ne wrde navt ne telath, hwand thåt êne jêr was
alsa blyd as et ôthera. An tha êne side wrdon wi thrvch
Wr.aldas sê bisloten, hwêrvp nên folk buta vs navt
fara ne mochte nach kvnde. Anda ôre side wrden wi
thrvch thåt brêde Twisklånd vmtunad, hwêr thrvch
thåt Findas folk navt kvma ne thvradon, fon ovira
tichta walda ånd ovir it wilde kwik. By morne paldon
wi ovir it uter ende thes aster-sê, by êvind an thene

Pl. 2.

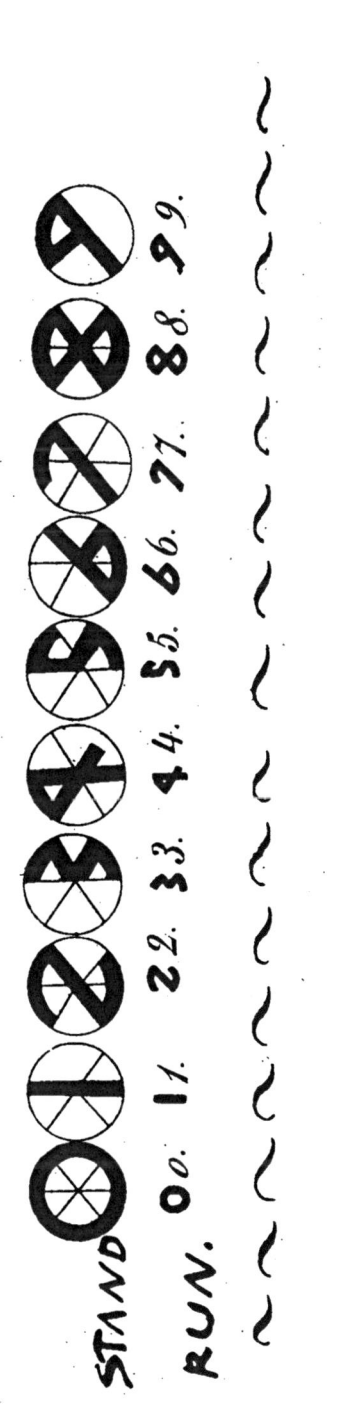

a gs.

$\overline{x}$ ks.

STAND.
RUN. 0 0. 1 1. 2 2. 3 3. 4 4. 5 5. 6 6. 7 7. 8 8. 9 9.

Fac-Simile

but that was so high-flown and full of flourishes that her descendants have soon lost the meaning of it.

Afterwards they learned our writing—that is, the Finns, the Thyriers, and the Krekalanders—but they did not know that it was taken from the Juul, and must therefore always be written round like the sun. Furthermore, they wished that their writing should be illegible by other people, because they always had matters to conceal. In doing this they acted very unwisely, because their children could only with great difficulty read the writings of their predecessors, whereas our most ancient writings are as easy to read as those that were written yesterday.

Here is a specimen of the set hand and of the running hand, as well as of the figures, in both.

(See Plate II.)

THIS STANDS INSCRIBED UPON ALL CITADELS.

Before the bad time came our country was the most beautiful in the world. The sun rose higher, and there was seldom frost. The trees and shrubs produced various fruits, which are now lost. In the fields we had not only barley, oats, and rye, but wheat which shone like gold, and which could be baked in the sun's rays. The years were not counted, for one was as happy as another.

On one side we were bounded by Wr-alda's Sea, on which no one but us might or could sail; on the other side we were hedged in by the broad Twiskland (Tusschenland, Duitschland), through which the Finda people dared not come on account of the thick forests and the wild beasts.

Eastward our boundary went to the extremity of the East Sea, and westward to the Mediterranean

middelsê, alsa wi buta tha littiga wel twelif gråta swete
riustrama hêdon, vs thrvch Wr.alda jêven vmb vs lånd
elte to haldane ånd vmb us wigandlik folk tha wêi to
wisana nêi sina sê.

Tha owira thissar rin strama wrdon tomet algadur
thrvch vs folk bisêton, åk tha fjelda an thju Rêne fon t
êna enda alon et ôre ende thå.

To jenst-vr tha Dênamarka ånd that Juttarlånd hêdon
wi folkplantinga mith en burchfåm, dåna wonon wi kåper
ånd yser, bijvnka tår, påk ånd svma ôr bihof. To jenst
vr vs formêlich Westland thêr hêdon wi Brittanja mith
sina tinlåna. Brittanja thåt was thåt lånd thêra bannalinga, thêr mith hulpe hjarar burchfåm wêi brith wêron
vmbe hira lif to bihåldana. Thach for that hja navt to
båk kvma ne skolde, warth er êrost en B to fåra hjara
står priked, tha bana mith råde blod farve ånd tha ôra
misdêdar mith blåwe farve. Buta ånd bihalva hêdon vsa
stjurar ånd kåpljvd mêni loge anda hêinde Krêkalanda
ånd to Lydia. In vr Lydia thêr send tha swarta minniska.
Thå vs lånd så rum ånd gråt wêre, hêdon wi fêlo asonder-
gana nåmon. Thêra tham saton biåsten tha Dênemarka
wrdon Jutta hêton, uthåvede hja tomet navt owers ne
dêdon as barn-stên juta. Hja tham thêr saton vppa
êlanda wrdon Lêtne hêten, thrvchdam hja mêst al vrlêten
lêvadon. Alle strånd ånd skor hêmar fon-a Dênemarka
alont thêre såndfal nw Skelda wrdon Stjurar,* Sêkåmpar,† ånd Angelara‡ hêton. Angelara så hêton mån to
fora tha butafiskar vmbe that hja alan mith angel
jefta kol fiskton ånd nimmer nên netum. Thêra thêr
thåna til tha hêinde Krêkalånda såton, wrdon blåt Kådhêmar hêten, thrvch tham hja ninmerthe buta foron.
Thêra thêr in da håge marka såton, thêr anna Twisklånda
pålon, wrdon Saxmanna hêton, uthåwede hja immer wêpned
wêron vr thåt wilde kwik ånd vrwildarda Britne. Thêr to

---

* Stjurar, Sturii.   † Sêkåmpar, Sicambri.   ‡ Angelara, Angli.

Sea; so that besides the small rivers we had twelve large rivers given us by Wr-alda to keep our land moist, and to show our seafaring men the way to his sea.

The banks of these rivers were at one time entirely inhabited by our people, as well as the banks of the Rhine from one end to the other. Opposite Denmark and Jutland we had colonies and a Burgtmaagd. Thence we obtained copper and iron, as well as tar and pitch, and some other necessaries. Opposite to us we had Britain, formerly Westland, with her tin mines.

Britain was the land of the exiles, who with the help of their Burgtmaagd had gone away to save their lives; but in order that they might not come back they were tattooed with a B on the forehead, the banished with a red dye, the other criminals with blue. Moreover, our sailors and merchants had many factories among the distant Krekalanders and in Lydia. In Lydia (Lybia) the people are black. As our country was so great and extensive, we had many different names. Those who were settled to the east of Denmark were called Jutten, because often they did nothing else than look for amber (*jutten*) on the shore. Those who lived in the islands were called Letten, because they lived an isolated life. All those who lived between Denmark and the Sandval, now the Scheldt, were called Stuurlieden (pilots), Zeekampers (naval men), and Angelaren (fishermen). The Angelaren were men who fished in the sea, and were so named because they used lines and hooks instead of nets. From there to the nearest part of Krekaland the inhabitants were called Kadhemers, because they never went to sea but remained ashore.

Those who were settled in the higher marches bounded by Twisklanden (Germany) were called Saxmannen, because they were always armed against the wild beasts and the savage Britons. Besides

---

* *Stjurar*, in Latin *Sturii.* † *Stkámpar*, in Latin *Sicambri.*
‡ *Angelara*, in Latin *Angli.*

boppa hêdon wi tha nôma Landsâton, Mârsata,* ånd Holt-
jefta Wodsâta.

Ho Arge Tid kêm.

Hêl thene sümer was svnne åftere wolkum skolen, as
wilde hja irtha navt ne sja. Wind reston in sina bûdar,
werthrvch rêk ånd stom lik sêla boppa hus ånd polon
stand. Loft wårth althus drov ånd dimme, ånd inna tha
hirta thêra månniska was blydskip nach früchda. To
midden thisre stilnise fång irtha an to bêvande lik as hju
stårvande wêre. Berga splyton fon ekkorum to spêjande
fjvr ånd logha, ôra svnkon in hira skåt del, ånd thêr hju
êrost fjelda hêde; hêjade hju berga vppa. Aldland † trvch
tha stjurar Atland hêten svnk nyther ånd thåt wilde hef
ståpton alsa nåka wr berg ånd dêlon, that ella vndere sê
bidvlwen wêre. Fêlo månniska wrdon in irtha bidobben,
ånd fêlo thêr et fjvr vnkêmen wêron, kêmon thêrnêi innet
wêter vm. Navt allêna inda landa Findas spêidon berga
fjvr, men åk in-t Twisk-land. Walda bårnadon thêrthrvch
åfter ekkorum ånd thå wind dåna wêi kêm, thå wûjadon
ysa landa fvl ask. Rinstråma wrdon vrlêid ånd by hjara
mvda kêmon nêja êlanda fon sand ånd drivande kwik.
Thrju jêr was irtha alsa to lydande; men tha hju bêter
wêre macht mån hira vvnda sja. Fêlo landa wêron
vrsvnken, ôra uta sê rêsen ånd thåt Twisk-land to fåra-n
halfdêl vntwalt. Bånda Findas folk kêmon tha lêtogha
rumtne bifåra. Vsa wêibritne vrdon vrdelgen jefta hja
wrdon hjara harlinga. Thå warth wåkandom vs dvbbeld
boden ånd tid lêrd vs that êndracht vsa stårikste burch is.

Thit stêt inna Waraburch by thêre Aldega Mvda wryt.

Thju Wåraburch nis nên fåmnaburch, men thêr in wrdon

---

* Mårsata, Marsacii.   † Aldland, Atlantis.

THE BOOK OF ADELA'S FOLLOWERS. 71

these we had the names Landzaten (natives of the land), Marzaten (natives of the fens), and Woud or Hout zaten (natives of the woods).

How the Bad Time came.

During the whole summer the sun had been hid behind the clouds, as if unwilling to look upon the earth. There was perpetual calm, and the damp mist hung like a wet sail over the houses and the marshes. The air was heavy and oppressive, and in men's hearts was neither joy nor cheerfulness. In the midst of this stillness the earth began to tremble as if she was dying. The mountains opened to vomit forth fire and flames. Some sank into the bosom of the earth, and in other places mountains rose out of the plain. Aldland, called by the seafaring people, Atland, disappeared, and the wild waves rose so high over hill and dale that everything was buried in the sea. Many people were swallowed up by the earth, and others who had escaped the fire perished in the water.

It was not only in Finda's land that the earth vomited fire, but also in Twiskland (Germany). Whole forests were burned one after the other, and when the wind blew from that quarter our land was covered with ashes. Rivers changed their course, and at their mouths new islands were formed of sand and drift.

During three years this continued, but at length it ceased, and forests became visible. Many countries were submerged, and in other places land rose above the sea, and the wood was destroyed through the half of Twiskland (Germany). Troops of Finda's people came and settled in the empty places. Our dispersed people were exterminated or made slaves. Then watchfulness was doubly impressed upon us, and time taught us that union is force.

This is inscribed on the Waraburgt by the Aldegamude.

The Waraburgt is not a maiden's city, but the place where

---

* *Mârsata*, in Latin *Marsacii*.   † *Aldland*, in Latin *Atlantis*.

72   THET BOK THÊRA ADELA FOLSTAR.

alla uthêmeda ånd vrlandeska thinga wårath, thêr mitbrocht binne thrvch tha stjurar. Hju is thri pêla, thåt is en half ty sûdwarth fon Mêdêa-sblik lêgen. Alsa is thåt fôrword: berga nygath thinna krunna, wolka ånd stråma wên. Jes. Skênland * blôst, slåvona folka stôppath vppat thin klåt, o Frya.

Alsa is thju skêdnesse.

100 ånd 1 jêr † nêi that åldland svnken is, kêm thêr ut-et åsta en folk wêi. Thåt folk was vrdrêven thrvch en ôther folk, åfter vs twisk land krêjon hja twispalt, hja skifton hjara selva an twam håpa, ek hêr gvng sines wêiges. Fon-t êne dêl nis nên tål to vs ne kêmen, men thåt ôre dêl fyl åfter to vs Skênland. Skênland was sunnich bifolkath, ånd anda åfter-kåd thåt sunnichste fon al. Thêrvmbe machton hja-t svnder strid wrwinna, ånd uthåwede hja ôwers nên lêth ne dêdon, nildon wi thêrvr nên orloch ha. Nw wi hjam håvon kånna lêred, så willath wi ovir hjara sêda skriwa, åfternêi ho-t vs mith hjam forgungen is. Thåt folk was navt ne wild lik fêlo slachta Findas, men êlik anda Êgipta-landar, hja håvath prestera lik tham ånd nw hja kårka håve åk byldon. Tha prestera send tha engosta hêra, hja hêton hjara selva Mågjara, hjara aller ovirste hêt Magy, hi is håvedprester ånd kêning mith ên, allet ôre folk is nul in-t siffer ånd êllik ånd al vnder hjara weld. Thåt folk nêth navt ênis en nôme, thrvch vs send hja Finna hêten, hwand afskên hjara fêrsta algadur drov ånd blodich send, thach send hja thêr alsa fin vp, that wi thêr bi åfter ståne, forth ne send hja navt to binydane, hwand hja send slåvona fon tha presterum ånd jeta fül årger fon hjara mêninga. Hja mênath that ella fvl kvada gåston is, thêr inda månniska ånd djara gluppe, men fon Wr.aldas gåst nêton hja nawet. Hja håvath stêne wêpne, tha Magjara kåpra. Tha Magjara tellath that hja tha årge gåston

---

* Skênland, Scania, Scandinavia.   † 219-3101 = 2092 v. Chr.

all the foreign articles brought by sailors were stored. It lies three hours south from Medeasblik.

Thus is the Preface.

Hills, bow your heads; weep, ye streams and clouds. Yes. Schoonland (Scandinavia) blushes, an enslaved people tramples on your garment, O Frya.

This is the History.

One hundred and one years after the submersion of Aldland a people came out of the East. That people was driven by another. Behind us, in Twiskland (Germany), they fell into disputes, divided into two parties, and each went its own way. Of the one no account has come to us, but the other came in the back of our Schoonland, which was thinly inhabited, particularly the upper part. Therefore they were able to take possession of it without contest, and as they did no other harm, we would not make war about it. Now that we have learned to know them, we will describe their customs, and after that how matters went between us. They were not wild people, like most of Finda's race; but, like the Egyptians, they have priests and also statues in their churches. The priests are the only rulers; they call themselves Magyars, and their headman Magy. He is high priest and king in one. The rest of the people are of no account, and in subjection to them. This people have not even a name; but we call them Finns, because although all the festivals are melancholy and bloody, they are so formal that we are inferior to them in that respect. But still they are not to be envied, because they are slaves to their priests, and still more to their creeds. They believe that evil spirits abound everywhere, and enter into men and beasts, but of Wr-alda's spirit they know nothing. They have weapons of stone, the Magyars of copper. The Magyars affirm that they can exorcise

---

* Skênland or Scandinavia.   † 2193 – 101 is 2092 before Christ.

banna ånd vrbanna mügon, thêr vr is-t folk ôlan in ange frêse ånd vppira wêsa nis nimmer nên blydskip to bisjan. Thâ hja god sêten wêron, sochton tha Magjara athskip bi vs, hja bogadon vp vsa tâl ånd sêdum, vp vs fja ånd vppa vs ysere wêpne, thêr hja gêrn to fori hjara goldun ånd sulvere syrhedum wandela wilde, ånd hjara tjoth hildon hja immerthe binna tha pêlon, men thåt vrskalkton vsa wåkendom. Achtantich jêr forther, just wêr-et jolfêrste, thêr kêmon hja vnwarlinge lik snêi thrvch stornewind drêwen ovir vsa landa to runnande. Thêr navt· flya machton wrdon vrdên, Frya wårth anhropen, men tha Skênlandar hêdon hira rêd warlåsed. Thâ wrdon kråfta såmlath, thri· pêlun fon Goda-hisburch.* wrdon hja wither stonden, tha orloch bilêv. Kåt jefta Kåter-inne, alsa hête thju fåm, thêr burchfåm to Goda burch was. Kåt was stolte ånd håchfåranda, thêrvmbe ne lêt hju nên rêd ni follistar anda Moder ne frêja. Men thâ tha burchhêra thåt såta, thâ svndon hja selva bodon nêi Texlånd nêi thêre Moder thâ. Minna alsa was thêre Moder-is nôme, lêt åla tha stjurar månja ånd ål-et othera jongk folk fon Ast-flyland ånd fon tha Dênnemarkum. Ut thesse tocht is thju skydnese fon Wodin bern, sa-r vppa burgum wryten is ånd hir êskrêven. Anda Alder-gåmude† thêr reste en alde sêkåning. Sterik was sin nôme ånd tha hrop vr sina dêda was gråt. Thisse alde rob hêde thrê nêva; Wodin thene aldeste hêmde to Lumka-måkja‡ bi thêre Ê-mude to Ast-flyland by sin eldrum t-us. Ênes was er hêrman wêst. Tünis ånd Inka wêron sêkåmper ånd just nw bi hjara fåderja anda Aldergå-mude t-vs. As tha jonga kåmpar nw bi ekkôrum kêmon, kêron hja Wodin to hjara hêrman jefta kåning ut, ånd tha sêkåmpar kêron Tünis to-ra sêkåning ånd Inka to hjara skelte bî thêr nacht. Tha stjurar gvngon thå nêi tha Dênnemarka fåra, thêr nåmon hja Wodin mith sin wigandlika landwêr in.

---

* Goda-hisburch, Gothenburg.
† Alderga, Ouddorp (bij Alkmaar).
‡ Lumkamåkja bithêre Emuda, Embden.

and recall the evil spirits, and this frightens the people, so that you never see a cheerful face. When they were well established, the Magyars sought our friendship, they praised our language and customs, our cattle and iron weapons, which they would willingly have exchanged for their gold and silver ornaments, and they always kept their people within their own boundaries, and that outwitted our watchfulness.

Eighty years afterwards, just at the time of the Juul-feest, they overran our country like a snowstorm driven by the wind. All who could not flee away were killed. Frya was appealed to, but the Schoonlanders (Scandinavians) had neglected her advice. Then all the forces were assembled, and three hours from Godasburgt they were withstood, but war continued. Kat or Katerine was the name of the priestess who was Burgtmaagd of Godasburgt. Kat was proud and haughty, and would neither seek counsel nor aid from the mother; but when the Burgtheeren (citizens) knew this, they themselves sent messengers to Texland to the Eeremoeder. Minna—this was the name of the mother—summoned all the sailors and the young men from Oostflyland and Denmark. From this expedition the history of Wodin sprang, which is inscribed on the citadels, and is here copied. At Aldergamude there lived an old sea-king whose name was Sterik, and whose deeds were famous. This old fellow had three nephews. Wodin, the eldest, lived at Lumkamakia, near the Eemude, in Oostflyland, with his parents. He had once commanded troops. Teunis and Inka were naval warriors, and were just then staying with their father at Aldergamude. When the young warriors had assembled together, they chose Wodin to be their leader or king, and the naval force chose Teunis for their sea-king and Inka for their admiral. The navy then sailed to Denmark, where they took on board Wodin and his valiant host.

---

* Goda-hisburch is Gothenburg.

† Alderga is Ouddorp, near Alkmaar.

‡ Lumkamâkja bithêre Emuda is Embden.

Wînd was rum ånd alsa wêron hja an en âmerîng* to Skênland. Thâ tha northeska brothar ra selva by-m fogath hêde, dêlde Wodîn sin weldich hêr an thri wiga. Frya was hjara wêpenhrop ånd så hi båkward sloch tha Finnen ånd Mågjara as of et bårn wêron. Thâ thene Mågy fornôm ho sin ljvd al ombrocht wrdon, thâ sand hi bodon mith ståf ånd krone. Hja sêidon to Wodin, o thv alra grâteste thêra kåningar, wi send skeldich, thach al. hwat wi dên håve is ut nêd dên. Je mêne that wi jvw brothar willengklik anfat håve, men wi send thrvch vsa fyanda forth-fêtereth ånd thi alle send vs jeta vppa hakka. Wi håvath often helpe an thinre burchfåm frêjath, men hja neth vs navt ne meld. Thene Mågy sêith, så hwersa wi ekkôrum to tha hålte vrdva, så skilun tha wilda skephårdar kêmon ånd vs algådur vrdva. Thene Mågy heth fül rikdom, men hi heth sjan that Frya weldiger is as al vsa gåston et sêmine. Hi wil sin håved in hira skåt del ledsa. Thv bist thene wigandlikste kåning irthas, thin folk is fon yser. Warth vsa kåning ånd wi alle willath thin slåvona wêsa. Hwat skolde that êr-rik får-i wêsa, aste tha wilda wither to låk driwa koste, vsa sêfyra skolde-t rondblêsa ånd vsa måra skoldon jv vral fårut gå.

Wodin was sterik, woståndwigandlîk, men hi nas navt klår sjande, thêrthrvch wårth i in hjar mêra fvngen ånd thrvch thene Mågy kroneth. Rju fêlo stjurar ånd land-wêrar, tham thisse kêr navt ne sinde, brûdon stolkes hinne, Kåt mith nêmande, men Kåt thêr navt to fåra thêre Moder ner to fåra thêre mêna acht forskine nilde, jompade wr bord. Thâ kêm stornewind ånd fêtere tha skêpa vppa skorra fonna Dennemar kum del svnder enkel man to mistane. Afternêi håvon hja tha strêt Kåtsgat† hêten. Thâ Wodin kroned was, gvng-er

---

* Amering, nog in N.-Holland in gebruik, beteekent daar: ademtocht, oogenblik. Cf. Kiliaan in voce.
† Kåtsgat, het Kattegat.

THE BOOK OF ADELA'S FOLLOWERS. 77

The wind was fair, so they arrived immediately in Schoonland. When the northern brothers met together, Wodin divided his powerful army into three bodies. Frya was their war-cry, and they drove back the Finns and Magyars like children. When the Magy heard how his forces had been utterly defeated, he sent messengers with truncheon and crown, who said to Wodin: O almighty king, we are guilty, but all that we have done was done from necessity. You think that we attacked your brothers out of illwill, but we were driven out by our enemies, who are still at our heels. We have often asked your Burgtmaagd for help, but she took no notice of us. The Magy says that if we kill half our numbers in fighting with each other, then the wild shepherds will come and kill all the rest. The Magy possesses great riches, but he has seen that Frya is much more powerful than all our spirits together. He will lay down his head in her lap. You are the most warlike king on the earth, and your people are of iron. Become our king, and we will all be your slaves. What glory it would be for you if you could drive back the savages! Our trumpets would resound with your praises, and the fame of your deeds would precede you everywhere. Wodin was strong, fierce, and warlike, but he was not clear-sighted, therefore he was taken in their toils, and crowned by the Magy.

Very many of the sailors and soldiers to whom this proceeding was displeasing went away secretly, taking Kat with them. But Kat, who did not wish to appear before either the mother or the general assembly, jumped overboard. Then a storm arose and drove the ships upon the banks of Denmark, with the total destruction of their crews. This strait was afterwards called the Kattegat. When Wodin was crowned, he

---

* *Amering*, still in use in North Holland to signify a breath or a twinkling of an eye.
† Kâtsgat is the Kattegat.

vppa wilda lôs; thi wêron al rutar, lik een héjel buje
kêmon hja ajn Wodin-is hêr, men lik en twyrne wind
wendon hja omme ånd ne thvradon nå wither forskina.
As Wodin nw to båk kêm, jav thene Mâgy him sin
toghater to-n wîf. Afternei wårth-i mith krûdon birêkad,
men thêr wêron tawerkrûdon mong, hwand Wodin warth
bi grâdum alsa sêr vrmêten, that-i Frya ånd Wraldas
gåst miskåna ånd spota thvrade, thawyla hi sin frya hals
bog to fâra falska drochten-likande byldum. Sin rik
hilde sjvgun jêr, thâ vrdwind-ir, Thene Mâgy sêide that-
er mong hjara godon* vpnimeth wêre, ånd that hi fon
thêr over hjam welda, men vs folk lakton vmbe tin tâl.
Thâ Wodin en stût wêi wêst hêde, kêm thêr twispalt, wi
wildon en ôra kåning kjasa, men thât nilde thene Mâgy
navt me hengja. Hi wêrde that et en rjucht wêre, him
thrvch sina drochtne jêven. Buta ånd bihalva thissa twist,
sa was thêr jet-ên emong sin Mâgjara ånd Finna, thêr Frya
ner Wodin êra navt nilde, men thi Mâgy dêde as-t im
sinde, hwand sin toghater hêde en svn bi Wodin wvnen,
ånd nw wilde thene Mâgy that thisse fon en håge kom-of
wêsa skolde. Thawyla alle sanade ånd twista, krônade hi
thene knåp to kåning ånd stålade hin sels as foged ånd
foramond jefta rêdjêvar an. Thêra thêr mâr hildon fon
hjara balg as fon thât rjucht, tham lêton him bidobba,
men tha goda brûdon wêi. Fêlo Mâgjara flodon mith
hjara ljvda båk ward, ånd tha stjurar gvngon to skip ånd
en hêr fon drista Finna gvngen as rojar mitha.
  Nw kvmath tha skêdnese fon nêf Tünis ånd sin nêf
Inka êrost rjucht vppet pat.

THIT ELLA STET NAVT ALLÊNA VPPER WARABURCH MEN OK
  TO THÊRE BURCH STAVIA, THÊR IS LIDSEN AFTERE
  HAVE FON STAVRE.

  Tha Tünis mith sinum skêpum to honk kêra wilde, gvng-i
thet forma vppa Dånnemarka of, men hi ne macht thêr navt

---

* Wodin, Odin, Wodan.

attacked the savages, who were all horsemen, and fell upon Wodin's troops like a hailstorm; but like a whirlwind they were turned back, and did not dare to appear again. When Wodin returned, Magy gave him his daughter to wife. Whereupon he was incensed with herbs; but they were magic herbs, and by degrees he became so audacious that he dared to disavow and ridicule the spirits of Frya and Wr-alda, while he bent his free head before the false and deceitful images. His reign lasted seven years, and then he disappeared. The Magy said that he was taken up by their gods and still reigned over us, but our people laughed at what they said. When Wodin had disappeared some time, disputes arose. We wished to choose another king, but the Magy would not permit it. He asserted that it was his right given him by his idols. But besides this dispute there was one between the Magyars and Finns, who would honour neither Frya nor Wodin; but the Magy did just as he pleased, because his daughter had a son by Wodin, and he would have it that this son was of high descent. While all were disputing and quarrelling, he crowned the boy as king, and set up himself as guardian and counsellor. Those who cared more for themselves than for justice let him work his own way, but the good men took their departure. Many Magyars fled back with their troops, and the sea-people took ship, accompanied by a body of stalwart Finns as rowers.

Next comes upon the stage the history of Neef Teunis and Neef Inka.

All this is inscribed not only on the Waraburgt, but also on the Burgt Stavia, which lies behind the Port of Stavre.

When Teunis wished to return home, he went first towards Denmark; but he might not land there, for so the

---

* Wodin is Odin or Wodan.

ne landa, thât hêde thju Moder bisjowath. Ak et Flyland ne macht-er navt ne landa ånd forth nårne. Hi skold alsa mith sinum ljvdum fon lek ånd brek omkomth hâve, thêr vmbe gvngon hja thes nachtis tha landa birâwa ånd fâra bi dêi. Alsa alinga thêre kâd forth farande kêmon hja to thêre folkplanting Kâdik,* althus hêten vmbe that hjara have thrvch êne stênene kâdik formath was. Hir selladon hja allerhanne liftochta, men Tutja thju burchfâm nilde navt dåja that hja-ra selva nither setta. Thâ hja rêd wêron krêjon hja twist. Tünis wilde thrvch thju strête fon tha middelsê vmbe to fârane får tha rika kåning fon Egiptalandum, lik hi wel êr dên hêde, men Inka sêide, that-i sin nocht hêde fon al et Findas folk. Inka mênde that er byskin wel en hach dêl fon Atland by wysa fon êland vrbilêwen skolde wêsa, thêr hi mith tha ljvdum frêthoch lêva machte. As tha bêda nêva-t-althus navt ênes wrde koste, gvng Tünis to ånd stek en råde fône in-t strând, ånd Inka êne blåwe. Thêr åfter macht jahwêder kjasa, hwam ek folgja wilde, ånd wonder, by Inka thêr en gryns hêde vmbe tha kåningar fon Findas folk to thjanja, hlipon tha mâsta Finna ånd Mâgjara ovir. As hja nw thåt folk tellath ånd tha skêpa thêr nêi dêlath hêde, tha skêdon tha flâta fon ekkorum; fon nêf Tünis is åfternêi tâl kêmen, fon nêf Inka ninmer.

Nêf Tünis for allinggen thêre kâd al thrvch thju porte thêre middelsê. Tha Atland svnken is, was-t-inna middelsê ra owera åk årg to gvngen. Thêrthrvch wêron thêr fêlo månniska fon-t Findas land nêi vsa hêinde ånd fêre Krêkalanda kvmen ånd åk fêlo fon Lyda-his land. Thêr åjn wêron åk fêlo fon vs folk nêi Lydas land gvngon. Thåt ella hêde wrocht, that tha hêinde ånd fêre Krêkalanda far thåt weld hêre Moder vrlêren was. Thêr hêde Tünis vp rêkned. Thêrvmbe wilde hi thêr en gode hâve kjasa ånd fon ther ut fara

---

* Kâdik, Cadix.

mother had ordered, nor was he to land at Flyland nor anywhere about there. In this way he would have lost all his people by want and hardship, so he landed at night to steal and sailed on by day. Thus coasting along, he at length arrived at the colony of Kadik (Cadiz), so called because it was built with a stone quay. Here they bought all kinds of stores, but Tuntia the˰ Burgtmaagd would not allow them to settle there. When they were ready they began to disagree. Teunis wished to sail through the straits to the Mediterranean Sea, and enter the service of the rich Egyptian king, as he had done before, but Inka said he had had enough of all those Finda's people. Inka thought that perchance some high-lying part of Atland might remain as an island, where he and his people might live in peace. As the two cousins could not agree, Teunis planted a red flag on the shore, and Inka a blue flag. Every man could choose which he pleased, and to their astonishment the greater part of the Finns and Magyars followed Inka, who had objected to serve the kings of Finda's people. When they had counted the people and divided the ships accordingly, the fleet separated. We shall hear of Teunis afterwards, but nothing more of Inka.

Neef Teunis coasted through the straits to the Mediterranean Sea. When Atland was submerged there was much suffering also on the shores of the Mediterranean, on which account many of Finda's people, Krekalanders, and people from Lyda's land, came to us. On the other hand, many of our people went to Lyda's land. The result of all this was that the Krekalanders far and wide were lost to the superintendence of the mother. Teunis had reckoned on this, and had therefore wished to find there a good

---

* Kâdik is Cadiz.

rikka forsta fåra, men thrvchdam sine flåte ånd sin folk sa wanhåven utsagon, mêndon tha Kådhêmer that hja råwera wêron, ånd thêrvmbe wrdon hja vral wêrath. Tha to tha lesta kêmon hja an to Phonisivs kåd, that wêre 100 ånd 93 jêr * nêi åtland svnken is. Nêi bi thêre kåd fvndon hja en êland mith twam diapa slinka, alsa-t as thrju êlanda utsåch. Vppet midloste thêra staldon hja hjara skula vp, åfternêi bvwadon hja thêr en burchwal om to. As hja thêran nw en nôme jêva wilde, wrdon hja vnênes, svme wild-et Fryasburch hêta, ôra Nêf tünia, men tha Mågjara ånd tha Finna bådon thåt skolde Thyrhisburch † hête. Thyr ‡ alsa hêton hja ên hjarar drochtena ånd vppe tham-is jêrdêi wêron hja thêr land, to wither-jeld wildon hja Tünis êvg as hjara kåning bikånne. Tünis lêt im bilêsa ånd tha ôra nildon thêrvr nên orloch ne hå. Thå hja nw god såton, thå sandon hja svme alde stjvrar ånd mågjara ana wål ånd forthnêi thêre burch Sydon, men that forma nildon tha Kådhêmar nawet fon-ra nêta. Thv bist fêrhêmanda swårvar sêidon hja, thêr wi navt hachta ne müge. Tha thå wi hjam fon vsa ysera wêpne vrsella wilde, gvng to lersta ella god. åk wêron hja sêr ny nêi vsa bårnstênum ånd thåt frêja thêr nêi nam nên ende. Men Tünis thêr fårsjande wêre, bårde that er nên ysere wêpne ner bårnstêne mår hêde. Thå kêmon tha kåpljvd ånd bådon hi skolde twintich skêpa jêva, thêr hja alle mith-a finneste wêrum tho hrêda wilde, ånd hja wildon him alsa fêlo ljvda to rojar jêva as-er jêrde. Twê-lif skêpa lêt-i-to hrêda mith win hvning ånd tomåkad lêther, thêr bi wêron tåmar ånd sitlun mith gold wrtêin sa mån hja ninmer nêde sjan. Mith al thi skåt fyl Tünis thåt Flymar binna. Thi grêvaman fon Westflyland wårth thrvch al thessa thinga bigåstered, hi

---

* 2193–193 = 2000 v. Chr.   † Thyrhisburch, Tyrus.
‡ Thyr, de zoon van Odin.

haven from which he might go and serve under the rich princes; but as his fleet and his people had such a shattered appearance, the inhabitants on the coasts thought that they were pirates, and drove them away. At last they arrived at the Phœnician coast, one hundred and ninety-three years after Atland was submerged. Near the coast they found an island with two deep bays, so that there appeared to be three islands. In the middle one they established themselves, and afterwards built a city wall round the place. Then they wanted to give it a name, but disagreed about it. Some wanted to call it Fryasburgt, others Neeftunia; but the Magyars and Finns begged that it might be called Thyrhisburgt.

Thyr was the name of one of their idols, and it was upon his feast-day that they had landed there; and in return they offered to recognise Teunis as their perpetual king. Teunis let himself be persuaded, and the others would not make any quarrel about it. When they were well established, they sent some old seamen and Magyars on an expedition as far as the town of Sidon; but at first the inhabitants of the coast would have nothing to do with them, saying, You are only foreign adventurers whom we do not respect. But when we sold them some of our iron weapons, everything went well. They also wished to buy our amber, and their inquiries about it were incessant. But Teunis, who was far-seeing, pretended that he had no more iron weapons or amber. Then merchants came and begged him to let them have twenty vessels, which they would freight with the finest goods, and they would provide as many people to row as he would require. Twelve ships were then laden with wine, honey, tanned leather, and saddles and bridles mounted in gold, such as had never been seen before.

Teunis sailed to the Flymeer with all this treasure, which so enchanted the Grevetman of Westflyland that he induced

---

* 2193-193 is 2000 years before Christ.   † Thyrhisburch is Tyre.
‡ Thyr is the son of Odin.

wrochte that Tünis bi thêre mvde fon-t Flymar en loge bvwa mâchte, âfternêi is thju stêd Almanaland* heten ånd tha mark thêr hja åfternei to Wyringgå† vp wandelja machton tolêtmark. Thju Moder rêde that wi ra ella vrkâpja skolde buta ysere wêpne, men mån ne melde hja navt. Thâ tha Tyrjar thus fry spel hêdon, kêmon hja âlan wither to farand vsa wêron så hêinde as fêre vsa ajn sê-kâmpar to skâdne. Thêrâfter is bisloten vpper mêna acht, jêrlikes sjvgun Thyrjar skêpa to to lêtane ånd navt mar.

Hwat thêr of wrden is.

Inner northlikste herne fon tha Middelsê, thêr lêid en êland by thêre kâd. Nw kêmon hja thåt a kåp to frê-jande. Thêrvr wårth ene mêna acht bilêid. Moder-is rêd wårth wnnen, men Moder sach ra lyast fêr of. Thêrvmbe mênde hju that er nên kwâ an stek, thach as wi âfternêi sâgon ho wi misdên hêde hâvon wi thåt êland Missellja‡ hêten. Hirâfter skil blika ho wi thêr to rêde hêde. Tha Gola,§ alsa heton tha såndalinga prestera Sydon-is. tha Gola hêdon wel sjan thet et land thêr skares bifolkad was ånd fêr fon thêre Moder wêre. Vmb ira selva nw en gode skin to jêvane, lêton hja ra selva in vsa tâl ana trowe wydena hêta, men that wêre bêtre wêst, as hja ra selva fon thêre trowe wendena nômath hêde, jefta kirt wei trjuwendne lik vsa stjurar lêter dên hâve. Thâ hja wel sêton wêron, tha wandeldon hjara kâp-ljuda skêne kâpre wêpne ånd allerlêja syrhêdon to fara vsa ysere wêpne ånd wilde djara huda, wêrfon in

---

* Almanaland, Ameland. † Wyringgå, Wieringen.
‡ Missellja, Marseille. § Gola, Galli, Gaulois.

Teunis to build a warehouse at the mouth of the Flymeer. Afterwards this place was called Almanaland, and the market where they traded at Wyringen was called Toelaatmarkt. The mother advised that they should sell everything except iron weapons, but no attention was paid to what she said. As the Thyriers had thus free play, they came from far and near to take away our goods, to the loss of our seafaring people. Therefore it was resolved in a general assembly to allow only seven Thyrian ships and no more in a year.

What the Consequence of this was.

In the northernmost part of the Mediterranean there lies an island close to the coast. They now came and asked to buy that, on which a general council was held.

The mother's advice was asked, and she wished to see them at some distance, so she saw no harm in it; but as we afterwards saw what a mistake we had made, we called the island Missellia (Marseilles). Hereafter will be seen what reason we had. The Golen, as the missionary priests of Sidon were called, had observed that the land there was thinly peopled, and was far from the mother. In order to make a favourable impression, they had themselves called in our language *followers of the truth;* but they had better have been called *abstainers from the truth*, or, in short, "Triuwenden," as our seafaring people afterwards called them. When they were well established, their merchants exchanged their beautiful copper weapons and all sorts of jewels for our iron weapons and hides of wild beasts, which were abundant in our southern

---

* Almanaland is Ameland.   † Wyringâ is Wieringen.
‡ Missellja is Marseilles.   § Gola are the Galli or Gauls.

vsa suder landa fêlo to bikvma wêron. Men tha Gola fyradon allerhâna wla drochtenlika fêrsta ånd to tyadon tha kadhêmar thêra thrvch todvan hjarar horiga manghêrtne ånd tha swêt hêd fon hjara fininnige win. Was thêr hwa fon vs folk thêret alsa årg vrbrud hêde, that sin lif in frêse kêm, than lênadon tha gola him hul ånd foradon him nêi Phonisia, that is palmland. Was hi thêr sêten, thån most-i an sina sibba ånd åtha skriwa, that-et land så god wêre ånd tha månniska så luklik, as ninmån hin selva mocht forbylde. A Brittannja wêron rju fêlo manna, tha lith wiva, thå tha Gola that wiston, lêton hja alwêis manghêrtne skåka ånd thessa javon hja tha Britne vmb nawet. Thach al thissa manghêrtne weron hjara thjansterum, thêr tha bern fon Wrâlda stolon vmb-ar an hjara falske drochtne to jêvane.

Nw willath wi skriwa vr tha Orloch thêra Burchfamna Kalta and Min-erva,

And ho wi thêr thrvch al vsa sûderlanda ånd Brittanja anda Gola vrlêren håve.

Bi thêre Sûder-rên-mvda ånd thêre Skelda, thêr send sjvgun ålanda, nômath nêi Fryas sjvgum wåkfåmkes there wêk. Middel vppet êne åland is thju burch Walhallagåra,* inut tha wågrum thêra is thju folgjande skêdnesse wrîten. Thêr bvppa stêt: lês, lêr ånd wåk.

563 jêr† nêi åldland svnken is, sat hir en wise burch fåm, Min-erva was hira nôma. Thrvch tha stjurar Nyhellênja tonômath. This tonôma was god kêren, hwand tha rêd, thåer hju lênade, was ny ånd hel bvppa alle ôtherum. Overa Skelda et thêre Flyburch sat Syrhêd. Thjus fåm was fvl renka, skên was r-anhlith ånd kwik was

---

* Middelburg.
† 2193−563=1630 v. Chr.

countries; but the Golen celebrated all sorts of vile and monstrous festivals, which the inhabitants of the coast promoted with their wanton women and sweet poisonous wine. If any of our people had so conducted himself that his life was in danger, the Golen afforded him a refuge, and sent him to Phonisia, that is, Palmland. When he was settled there, they made him write to his family, friends, and connections that the country was so good and the people so happy that no one could form any idea of it. In Britain there were plenty of men, but few women. When the Golen knew this, they carried off girls everywhere and gave them to the Britons for nothing. So all these girls served their purpose to steal children from Wr-alda in order to give them to false gods.

Now we will write about the War between the Burgtmaagden Kalta and Min-erva,

And how we thereby lost all our southern lands and Britain to the Golen.

Near the southern mouth of the Rhine and the Scheldt there are seven islands, named after Frya's seven virgins of the week. In the middle of one island is the city of Walhallagara (Middelburg), and on the walls of this city the following history is inscribed. Above it are the words "Read, learn, and watch."

Five hundred and sixty-three years after the submersion of Atland—that is, 1600 years before Christ—a wise town priestess presided here, whose name was Min-erva —called by the sailors Nyhellenia. This name was well chosen, for her counsels were new and clear above all others.

On the other side of the Scheldt, at Flyburgt, Sijrhed presided. This maiden was full of tricks. Her face was

---

* Walhallagara is Middelburg, in Walcheren.
† 2193–563 is 1630 years before Christ.

hira tvnge, men thi rêd thêr hju jef, was immer in thjustere worde. Thêr vmbe warth hju thrvch tha stjurar Kâlta hêten, tha landsâta mênadon that et êrnôma wêra. Inna ûtroste wille thêre vrsturvene Moder stand Rôsa-mvda thet forma, Min-erva thet twêde ånd Syrhêd thet thredde as folgstere biskreven. Min-erva nêde thêr nên wit fon, men Syrhêd was er thrvch knaked. Lik en wrlandeske forstinne wilde hju êrath frêsath ånd bêden wêsa, men Min-erva wilde enkel minth wêsa. To tha lesta kêmon alle stjurar hiri hjara held bjada, selva fon tha Denamarka ånd fon t Flymar. That vvnde Syrhêd, hwand hju wilde bvppa Min-erva utminthja. Til thju mån en grôte thånk ovir hira wåkendum håva skolde, myk* hju ennen hôna vpper fåne. Thå gvng Min-erva to ånd myk en hårder hvnd ånd en nachtul in vppira fåne. Thene hvnd sêide hju wåkt ovir sin hêr ånd ovira kidda ånd thene nachtul wåkt ovira fjelda til thju hja thrvch tha musa navt vrdên ne wrde. Men thene hôna neth far nimman frjundskip, ånd thrvch sin vntocht ånd håchfårenhêd is er vaken thene båna sinra nêista sibba wrden. As Kalta sach that er wårk falikant ut kêm, to gvng hju fon kwad to årger. Stolkes lêt hju Mågjara to hiri kvma vmbe tåwery to lårane. As hju thêr hira nocht fon hêde, werpte hju hira selva and årma thêra Golum, thach fon al thi misdêdon ne macht hju navt bêtre ne wrde. As hju sach that tha stjurar mår ånd mår fon iri wêke, tha wilde hju ra thrvch frêse winna. Was tha mône fvl ånd thene sê vnstumich, than hlip hju over et wilde hef, tha stjurar to hropande that hja alle skolde vrgân, sahwersa hja hiri navt anbidda nilde. Forth vrblinde hju hira ågun hwêr thrvch hja wêter fori land ånd land fori wêter hildon, thêrthrvch is måni skip vrgvngen mith mån ånd mus. Vppet forma wêrfêrste tha al hira landsâta wêpned wêron, lêt hju bårga bjar skånka, in thåt bjar hêde hju tåverdrank dên. As et folk nv algådur

---

* Myk wordt nog op Walcheren gehoord.

beautiful, and her tongue was nimble; but the advice that she gave was always conveyed in mysterious terms. Therefore the mariners called her Kalta, and the landsmen thought it was a title. In the last will of the dead mother, Rosamond was named first, Min-erva second, and Sijrhed third in succession. Min-erva did not mind that, but Sijrhed was very much offended. Like a foreign princess, she wished to be honoured, feared, and worshipped; but Min-erva only desired to be loved. At last all the sailors, even from Denmark and Flymeer, did homage to her. This hurt Sijrhed, because she wanted to excel Min-erva. In order to give an impression of her great watchfulness, she had a cock put on her banner. So then Min-erva went and put a sheep-dog and an owl on her banner. The dog, she said, guards his master and his flock, and the owl watches that the mice shall not devastate the fields; but the cock in his lewdness and his pride is only fit to murder his nearest relations. When Kalta found that her scheme had failed she was still more vexed, so she secretly sent for the Magyars to teach her conjuring. When she had had enough of this she threw herself into the hands of the Gauls; but all her malpractices did not improve her position. When she saw that the sailors kept more and more aloof from her, she tried to win them back by fear. At the full moon, when the sea was stormy, she ran over the wild waves, calling to the sailors that they would all be lost if they did not worship her. Then she blinded their eyes, so that they mistook land for water and water for land, and in this way many a good ship was totally lost. At the first war-feast, when all her countrymen were armed, she brought casks of beer, which she had drugged. When they were all drunk

---

* *Myk* is a word still used in Walcheren.

drunken wêre, gvng hju bvppen vp hira stridhros standa, to lênande mith hira hole tojenst hira spêri, môrnerâd ne kv navt skêner. Tha hja sach that alle ôgon vpper fâstigath wêron êpende hju hira wêra ând kêth, svnum ând thogatrum Fryas, i wêt wel that wi inna lerste tyd fûl lek ând brek lêden hâve, thrvchdam tha stjurar navt lônger kvme vmb vs skriffilt to vrsella, men i nête navt hwêrthrvch et kvmen is. Lông hâv ik my thêr vr inhalden, thach nv kân-k-e tnavt lônger ôn. Hark then frjunda til thju i wêta müge hwêrnêi i bita mêi. Anda ôra syde thêre Skelda hwêr hja tomet tha fêrt fon alle sêa hâve, thêr mâkath hja hjvd dêgon skriffilt fon pompa blêdar, thêr mith sparath hja linnent ut ând kânnath hja vs wel miste. Nêidam thât skriffilt mâkja nv alti vs grâteste bydriv wêst is, sâ heth thju Moder wilt that mân et vs lêra skolde. Men Minerva heth al et folk bihexnath, jes bihexnath frjunda, ivin as al vs fja thât lâsten sturven is. Er-ut mot-et, ik wil thi tella, nas-k nên burchfâm ik skold et wel wêta, ik skolde thju hex in hjara nest vrbarne. Thâ hju thi lerste worda ut hêde, spode hju hira selva nêi hira burch tha, men thât vrdrvnken folk was althus dênera bigâstered, that et vr sin rêde navt mocht to wâkane. In dvl-dryste iver gvngon hja overa Sand fal ând nêidam nacht midlerwil del strêk gvngon hja evin drist vpper burch lôs, Thach Kâlta miste al hwither hira dol, hwand Minerva ând hira fâmna ând tha foddik wrdon alle thrvch tha râppa stjurar hreth.

Hirby kvmth tha Skêdnesse fon Jon.

Jon, Jôn, Jhon ând Jân is al ên mith jêven, thach thet lêit anda utsprêk thêra stjurar, thêr thrvch wenhêd ellas bikirta vmbit fâra ând hard hropa to mvgane. Jon thât is jêva was sêkêning, bern to-t-Aldergâ, to-t Flymar ut

she mounted her war-horse, leaning her head upon her spear. Sunrise could not be more beautiful. When she saw that the eyes of all were fixed upon her, she opened her lips and said:—

Sons and daughters of Frya, you know that in these last times we have suffered much loss and misery because the sailors no longer come to buy our paper, but you do not know what the reason of it is. I have long kept silence about it, but can do so no longer. Listen, then, my friends, that you may know on which side to show your teeth. On the other side of the Scheldt, where from time to time there come ships from all parts, they make now paper from pumpkin leaves, by which they save flax and outdo us. Now, as the making of paper was always our principal industry, the mother willed that people should learn it from us; but Min-erva has bewitched all the people—yes, bewitched, my friends—as well as all our cattle that died lately. I must come out with it. If I were not Burgtmaagd, I should know what to do. I should burn the witch in her nest.

As soon as she had uttered these words she sped away to her citadel; but the drunken people were so excited that they did not stop to weigh what they had heard. In mad haste they hurried over the Sandfal, and as night came on they burst into the citadel. However, Kalta again missed her aim; for Min-erva, her maidens, and her lamp were all saved by the alertness of the seamen.

WE NOW COME TO THE HISTORY OF JON.

Jon, Jôn, Jhon, Jan, are all the same name, though the pronunciation varies, as the seamen like to shorten everything to be able to make it easier to call. Jon—that is, " Given "—was a sea-king, born at Alberga, who sailed

fâren mith 100 ånd 27 skêpum, tohrêth fâr en grôte butarêis, rik to lêden mith bårnstên, tin, kåper, yser, lêken, linnent, filt, fâmna filt fon otter, bêver, ånd kanina hêr. Nw skold er fon hir jeta skriffilt mith nimma; tha to Jon hir kêm ånd sach ho Kålta vsa rom rika burch vrdên hêde, thâ wårther så uter mête heftich, that er mith al sinum ljudum vpper Flyburch of gvng ånd thêr to witterjeld thene råda hône an stek. Men thrvch sin skelt bi nacht ånd svme sinra ljudum wårth thju foddik ånd tha fâmna hret. Tach Syrhêd jefta Kålta ne mochton hja navt to fåtane, hju klywde vppa utroste tinne, jahweder tochte that hju inna logha omkvma moste, thâ hwat bêrde? Dahwile al hira ljuda ståk ånd stif fon skrik standon, kêm hju skêner as â-to fora vp hira klêppar to hropande nêi Kålta min-âis.* Thâ strâmada thåt ora Skelde folk to håpa. As tha stjurar that sågon hripon hja får Minerva wy. En orloch is thêrut kvmen, hwêrthrvch thvsande fallen send.

Under thesse tidon was Rôsamond thåt is Rôsa mvda Moder, hju hêde fûl in thêre minne dên vmbe frêtho to wårja, tach nw-t alsa årg kêm, myk hju kirte mête. Bistonda sand hju bodun thrvch tha land påla ånd lêt en mêna nêdban utkêtha, thâ kêmon thâ landwêrar ut alle wrda wêi. Thåt strydande land folk wårth al fat, men Jon burch hin selva mith sin ljud vppa sina flåte, mith nimand bêda tha foddika, byonka Minerva ånd tha fâmna fon bêdar burchum. Helprik thene hêrman lêt-im in banna, men tha hwila alle wêrar jeta o-ra Skelda wêron for Jon to bek nêi-t Flymar ånd forth wither nêi vsa ålandum. Sin ljud ånd fêlo fon vs folk namon wif ånd bern skêp, ånd as Jon nw sach that mån hin ånd sin ljud lik misdêdar strafja wilde, brudon hi stolkes hinne. Hi dêde rjucht, hwand al vsa landar ånd allet ora Skelda folk thêr fjuchten hêdon

---

* Kålta Min-his, Minnesdochter!

from the Flymeer with a fleet of 127 ships fitted out for a long voyage, and laden with amber, tin, copper, cloth, linen, felt, otter-skins, beaver and rabbit skins. He would also have taken paper from here, but when he saw how Kalta had destroyed the citadel he became so angry that he went off with all his people to Flyburgt, and out of revenge set fire to it. His admiral and some of his people saved the lamp and the maidens, but they could not catch Sijrhed (or Kalta). She climbed up on the furthest battlement, and they thought she must be killed in the flames; but what happened? While all her people stood transfixed with horror, she appeared upon her steed more beautiful than ever, calling to them, "To Kalta!" Then the other Schelda people poured out towards her. When the seamen saw that, they shouted, "We are for Min-erva!" from which arose a war in which thousands were killed.

At this time Rosamond the mother, who had done all in her power by gentle means to preserve peace, when she saw how bad it was, made short work of it. Immediately she sent messengers throughout all the districts to call a general levy, which brought together all the defenders of the country. The landsmen who were fighting were all caught, but Jon with his seamen took refuge on board his fleet, taking with him the two lamps, as well as Minerva and the maidens of both the citadels. Helprik, the chief, summoned him to appear; but while all the soldiers were on the other side of the Scheldt, Jon sailed back to the Flymeer, and then straight to our islands. His fighting men and many of our people took women and children on board, and when Jon saw that he and his people would be punished for their misdeeds, he secretly took his departure. He did well, for all our islanders, and the other Scheldt people who had been fighting were

---

* Kâlta Min-his, Minnesdaughter.

wrdon nêi Brittanja brocht. Thius stap was mis dên, hwand nv kêm t-anfang fon thåt ende:

Kålta thêr nêi-t segse êven blyd vppet wêter as vppet land hlåpa machte, gvng nêi tha fåsta wal, ånd forth vppa Missellja of. Thå kêmon tha Gola mith hjara skepum ut-a Middelsê Kådik bifåra ånd êl vs uter land, forth fylon hja vp ånd over Brittannja thach hja ne mochton thêr nên fåsta fot ne krêja, vmbe thåt tha sjvrda weldich ånd tha bannalinga jeta fryas wêron. Men nw kêm Kålta ånd kêth, thv bist fry bern ånd vmbe litha lêka heth mån thi to vrwurpene måkad, navt vmbe thi to bêterja, men vmbe tin to winnande thrvch thina handa. Wilst wêr fry wêsa ånd vnder mina rêd ånd hoda lêva, tjån ut then, wêpne skilun thi wrda, ånd ik skil wåka o-er thi. Lik blixen fjur gvng et o-era ålanda, ånd êr thes Kroders jol ênis omhlåpen hêde, was hju måsterinne over al gadur ånd tha Thyrjar fon al vsa suder ståta til thêre Sêjene.* Vmbe that Kålta hira selva navt to fül bitrowada, lêt hju in-et northlika berchland êne burch bvwa Kålta-s burch wårth hju hêten, hju is jet anwêsa, men nv hêt hja Kêren-åk. Fon thjus burch welde hju lik en efte moder, navt to wille får men over hira folgar ånd tham hjara selva forth Kåltana† hêton. Men tha Gola weldon by grådon over êl Brittanja, thåt kêm ênis dêlis that hju nên mår burga nêde, twyas that hju thêr nên burchfåmna nêde ånd thryas thrvchdam hju nên efte foddik navt nêde. Thrvch al thessa êrsêka kvn hira folk navt ni lêra, thåt wrde dvm ånd dor ånd wrde endelik thrvch tha Gola fon al hira ysera wêpne biråwath ånd to thåt lesta lik en buhl by thêre nôse omme lêid.

---

* Sêjene, de Seine.   † Kåltana, Celtae.

transported to Britain. This step was a mistake, for now came the beginning of the end. Kalta, who, people said, could go as easily on the water as on the land, went to the mainland and on to Missellia (Marseilles). Then came the Gauls out of the Mediterranean Sea with their ships to Cadiz, and along all our coasts, and fell upon Britain; but they could not make any good footing there, because the government was powerful and the exiles were still Frisians. But now came Kalta and said: You were born free, and for small offences have been sent away, not for your own improvement, but to get tin by your labour. If you wish to be free again, and take my advice, and live under my care, come away. I will provide you with arms, and will watch over you. The news flew through the land like lightning, and before the carrier's wheel had made one revolution she was mistress of all the Thyriers in all our southern states as far as the Seine. She built herself a citadel on the high land to the north, and called it Kaltasburgh. It still exists under the name of Kêrenak. From this castle she ruled as a true mother, against their will, not *for* her followers, but *over* them, who were thenceforth called Kelts. The Gauls gradually obtained dominion over the whole of Britain, partly because they no longer had any citadel; secondly, because they had there no Burgtmaagden; and thirdly, because they had no real lamps. From all these causes the people could not learn anything. They were stupid and foolish, and having allowed the Gauls to rob them of their arms, they were led about like a bull with a ring in his nose.

---

* Sêjene is the Seine.   † Kâltana are the Celts.

Nv willath wi skriva ho-t Jon vrgvngen is, thit stêt to Texland skrêven.

10 jêr åfter Jon wêi brit was, kêmon hyr thrju skêpa in-t Flymar falla, thåt folk hrip ho-n-sêjen, fon hira tålinga heth thju Moder thit skrywa lêten. Thå Jon antha Middelsê kêm was then måra thêra Gola hin vral får ut gvngen, alsa hi an thêri kåd fon tha hêinda Krêkalanda nårne fêlich nêre. Hi stêk thus mith sinum flåte nêi Lydia, thåt is Lyda his lånd, thêr wildon tha swarta månniska fåta hjam ånd êta. To tha lesta kêmon hja et Thyrhis, men Minerva sêide hald of, hwand hir is thju loft ôlangne vrpest thrvch tha prestera. Thi kåning was fon Tünis ofstamed, så wi lêter hêrdon, men til thju tha prestera en kåning wilde håve thêr alderlangne nêi hjara bigrip wêre, alsa hêde hja Tünis to en gode up hêjad, to årgnisse sinra folgar, As hja nv Thyr åfter bek wêre, kêmon, tha Thyriar en skip uta åfte hoda råwa, nêidam thåt skip to fêr was, kvndon wi-t navt wither wina, men Jon swor wrêka thêrvr. Tha nacht kêm kêrde Jon nêi tha fêre Krêkalandum, to lesten kêmon hja by en land thåt bjustre skryl ut sa, men hja fondon thêr en havesmvda. Hir sêide Minerva skil by skin nên frêse to fara forstum nach presterum nêdich wêsa, nêidam hja algadur feta etta minna, thach thå hja inner have hlipon fonth mån hja navt rum noch vmbe alle skêpa to bislûta, ånd thach wêron mêst alle to låf vmbe wider to gane. Alsa gvng Jon thêr forth wilde mith sin spêr ånd fône thåt jongk folk to hropande, hwa willinglik bi-m skåra wilde. Minerva thêr biliwa wilde dêde alsa. Thåt gråteste dêl gvng nêi Minerva, men tha jonggoste stjurar gvngon by Jon.

Now we shall write how it fared with Jon.
It is inscribed at Texland.

Ten years after Jon went away, there arrived three ships in the Flymeer; the people cried Huzza! (What a blessing!) and from their accounts the mother had this written.

When Jon reached the Mediterranean Sea, the reports of the Gauls had preceded him, so that on the nearest Italian coast he was nowhere safe. Therefore he went with his fleet straight over to Lybia. There the black men wanted to catch them and eat them. At last they came to Tyre, but Min-erva said, Keep clear, for here the air has been long poisoned by the priests. The king was a descendant of Teunis, as we were afterwards informed; but as the priests wished to have a king, who, according to their ideas, was of long descent, they deified Teunis, to the vexation of his followers. After they had passed Tyre, the Tyrians seized one of the rearmost ships, and as the ship was too far behind us, we could not take it back again; but Jon swore to be revenged for it. When night came, Jon bent his course towards the distant Krekalanden. At last they arrived at a country that looked very barren, but they found a harbour there. Here, said Min-erva, we need not perhaps have any fear of princes or priests, as they always look out for rich fat lands. When they entered the harbour, there was not room for all the ships, and yet most of the people were too cowardly to go any further. Then Jon, who wished to get away, went with his spear and banner, calling to the young people, to know who would volunteer to share his adventures. Min-erva did the same thing, but she wished to remain there. The greater part stopped with Min-erva, but the young sailors went with Jon.

Jon nam thêre foddik fon Kâlta ånd hira fâmna mitha, ånd Minerva hild hira ajn foddik ånd hira ajn fâmna.

Bitwiska tha fêrum ånd heinda Krêkalandum fand Jon svma êlanda thêr im likte, vppet grâteste gvng-er inna tha walda twisk thåt berchta en burch bvwa. Fon uta litha êlanda gvng-er ut wrêka tha Thyrjar skêpa ånd landa birâwa, thêrvmbe send tha êlanda evin blyd Râwer êlanda, as Jonhis êlanda* hêten.

Tha Minerva thåt land bisjan hêde, thåt thrvch tha inhêmar Attika is hêten, sach hju that thåt folk al jêita hoder wêron, hja hildon hjara lif mith flesk, krûdum, wilde wotelum ånd hvning. Hja wêron mith felum tekad ånd hju hêdon hjara skula vppa hellinga thêra bergum. Thêrthrvch send hja thrvch vs folk Hellinggar hêten.

Thåt forma gvngon hja vppa run, tha as hja sâgon that wi navt ne tåldon nêi hjara skåt, thâ kêmon hja tobek ånd lêton grâte âtskip blika. Minerva frêjde jef wi vs in thêre minna machte nither setta. That wrde to staden vnder biding that wi skolde helpa hjam with hjara swetsar to stridande, thêr alan kêmon hjara bern to skâkana ånd hjara skåt to râwana. Thâ bvwadon wi êne burch arhalf pål fon thêr have. Vppa rêd Minervas wårth hju Athenia† heten : hwand sêide hju, tha åfter kvmand agon to wêtane, that wi hir navt thrvch lest ner weld kvmen send, men lik âtha vntfongen. Dahwile wi an thêre burch wrochton kêmon tha forsta, as hja hja nv sagon that wi nên slavona hêde, sind er sok navt, ånd lêton-t an Minerva blika, til thju hja tochton that en forstene wêre. Men Minerva frêja, ho bist wel an thina slâvona kvmen ? Hja andere, svme håvath wi kåpad, ôra anna strid wnnen. Minerva sêide, såhwersa ninman månneska kåpja nilda sa ne skolde ninman jvw bern râwa ånd i ne skolda

---

* Jonhis êlanda, Insulae Joniae, Insulae piratarum.
† Athenia, Athens.

Jon took the lamp of Kalta and her maidens with him. Min-erva retained her lamp and her own maidens.

Between the near and the distant coasts of Italy Jon found some islands, which he thought desirable. Upon the largest he built a city in the wood between the mountains. From the smaller islands he made expeditions for vengeance on the Tyrians, and plundered their ships and their lands. Therefore these islands were called Insulæ Piratarum, as well as Johannis Insulæ.

When Min-erva had examined the country which is called by the inhabitants Attica, she saw that the people were all goatherds, and that they lived on meat, wild roots, herbs, and honey. They were clothed in skins, and had their dwellings on the slopes (*hellinga*) of the hills, wherefore they were called Hellingers. At first they ran away, but when they found that we did not attack them, they came back and showed great friendship. Min-erva asked if we might settle there peaceably. This was agreed to on the condition that we should help them to fight against their neighbours, who came continually to carry away their children and to rob their dwellings. Then we built a citadel at an hour's distance from the harbour. By the advice of Min-erva it was called Athens, because, she said, those who come after us ought to know that we are not here by cunning or violence, but were received as friends (*âtha*). While we were building the citadel the principal personages came to see us, and when they saw that we had no slaves it did not please them, and they gave her to understand it, as they thought that she was a princess. But Min-erva said, How did you get your slaves? They answered, We bought some and took others in war. Min-erva replied, If nobody would buy slaves they would

---

* Jonhis êlanda—John's Islands, or the Pirates' Isles.
† Athenia is Athens.

thêrvr nên orloch håve, wilst thus vsa harlinga biliwa så mot-i thina slåvona fry lêta.

That nv willath tha forsta navt, hja willath vs wêi driwa. Men thå klokeste hjarar ljuda kvmath helpa vsa burch ta bvmande, thêr wi nv fon stên måkja.

Thit is thju skêdnesse fon Jon ånd Minerva.

As hja that nw ella tellad hêde, frêjath hja mith êrbjadenesse vm yrsene burchwêpne, hwand sêidon hja vsa lêtha send weldich, tha sa wi efta wåpne håve, skillon wi ra wel wither worda. As hju thêran to stemad hêde, frêjath tha ljuda jef tha Fryas sêda to Athenia ånd tha ôra Krekalanda bloja skolde, thju Moder andere, jef tha fêre Krêkalanda to tha erva Fryas hêra, alsa skilum hja thêr bloja, ne hêrath hja navt thêr to, alsa skil thêr lang over kåmpad wrda mote, hwand thene kroder skil jeva fifthusand jêr mith sin Jol ommehlåpa, bifara thåt Findas folk rip to fåra frydom sy.*

Thit is over tha Gêrtmanna.

Thå Hellênja jefta Minerva sturven was, tha båradon tha prestera as jef hja mith vs wêron, til thju that hel blika skolde havon hja Hellênia to-ne godene ute kêth. Ak nildon hja nêne ore Moder kjasa lêta, to segande, hja hêde frêse that er emong hira fåmna nimman wêre, thêr hja sa god kvnde trowa as Minerva thêr Nyhellênia tonomt was. Men wi nildon Minerva navt as êne godene navt bikånna, nêidam hja selva seid hêde that nimman god jefta fvlkvma wêsa ne kvnde thån Wr.aldas gåst. Thêrumbe kêron wi Gêrt Pire his toghater to vsa Moder ut.

As tha prestera sagon that hja hjara hering navt vp vsa fjvr brêda ne mochton, thå gvngon hja buta Athenia ånd sêidon

---

* Vervolg hier het verhaal van bl. 48-56.

not steal your children, and you would have no wars about it. If you wish to remain our allies, you will free your slaves. The chiefs did not like this, and wanted to drive us away; but the most enlightened of the people came and helped us to build our citadel, which was built of stone.

This is the history of Jon and of Min-erva.

When they had finished their story they asked respectfully for iron weapons; for, said they, our foes are powerful, but if we have good arms we can withstand them. When this had been agreed to, the people asked if Frya's customs would flourish in Athens and in other parts of Greece (Krekalanden). The mother answered, If the distant Greeks belong to the direct descent of Frya, then they will flourish; but if they do not descend from Frya, then there will be a long contention about it, because the carrier must make five thousand revolutions of his Juul before Finda's people will be ripe for liberty.

THIS IS ABOUT THE GEERTMEN.

When Hellenia or Min-erva died, the priests pretended to be with us, and in order to make it appear so, they deified Hellenia. They refused to have any other mother chosen, saying that they feared there was no one among her maidens whom they could trust as they had trusted Min-erva, surnamed Nyhellenia.

But we would not recognise Min-erva as a goddess, because she herself had told us that no one could be perfectly good except the spirit of Wr-alda. Therefore we chose Geert Pyre's daughter for our mother. When the priests saw that they could not fry their herrings on our fire (have everything their own way), they left Athens, and said that we

---

* Here follows the narrative contained in pages from 48 to 56.

that wi Minerva navt to-ne godene bikâna nilda ut nyd, vmbe that hju tha inhêmar så fûl ljafde biwêsen hede. Forth javon hja that folk byldnisse fon hira liknese, tjûgande that hja thêrlan ella frêja machte alsa naka hja hêroch bilewon. Thrvch al thissa tellinga warth thåt dvma folk fon vs ofkêrad ånd to tha lesta fylon hja vs to lif. Men wi hêdon vsa stêne burchwal mith twam hornum om têjen al to tha sê. Hja ne machton vs thervmbe navt nåka. Thach hwat bêrde, an Êgiptalanda thêr wêre en overprester, hel fon ågnum, klâr fon bryn ånd licht fon gåst, sin nåm wêre Sêkrops,* hy kêm vmb rêd to jêvane. As Sêkrops sach that er mith sinum ljuda vsa wal navt biranna ne kv, thå sand hi bodon nêi Thyrhis. Afternêi kêmon er thrja hvndred skipun fvl salt-åtha fon tha wilde berchfolkum vnwarlinga vsa hâva bifåra, dahwila wy mith alle mannum vppa wallum to strydande wêron.

Drêi as hja thju håva innomth hêde wildon tha wilda salt-åtha thåt thorp ånd vsa skipa biråwa. Ên salt-åthe hêde al en bukja skånd, men Sêkrops wilde thåt navt ne hångja, ånd tha Thyrjar stjurar thêr jeta Fryas blod int lif hêde sêidon, aste that dêiste så skilun wi tha råde hône in vsa skypa stêka ånd thv ne skilst thina berga na witherasja. Sêkrops tham navt ne hilde ni fon morthja nor fon hommelja, sand bodon nêi Gêrt vmbir tha burch of to askja, hju macht frya uttochte hâ mith al hira drywande ånd bêrande håva, hira folgar alsa fül. Tha wista thêra burchhêrum êl god sjande thåt hja tha burch navt hålda ne kvnde, rêden Gêrt hja skolde gaw to bitta, bi fira Sêkrops wodin wrde ånd overs bigvnde, thrê mônatha åfter brûde Gêrt hinne mith tha alder besta Fryas bern ånd sjugum wara twilf skypum. Thå hja en stût buta thêre have wêron kêmon thêr wel thritich skêpon fon Thyrhis mit wif ånd bern. Hja wilde nêi Athênia gå, tha as hja hêrdon ha-t thêr eskêpen stande gvngon hja mit Gêrt. Thi wêtking thêra

---

* Sêkrops, Cecrops.

refused to acknowledge Min-erva as a goddess out of envy, because she had shown so much affection to the natives. Thereupon they gave the people statues of her, declaring that they might ask of them whatever they liked, as long as they were obedient to her. By these kinds of tales the stupid people were estranged from us, and at last they attacked us; but as we had built our stone city wall with two horns down to the sea, they could not get at us. Then, lo and behold! an Egyptian high priest, bright of eye, clear of brain, and enlightened of mind, whose name was Cecrops, came to give them advice.

When he saw that with his people he could not storm our wall, he sent messengers to Tyre. Thereupon there arrived three hundred ships full of wild mountain soldiers, which sailed unexpectedly into our haven while we were defending the walls. When they had taken our harbour, the wild soldiers wanted to plunder the village and our ships—one had already ravished a girl—but Cecrops would not permit it; and the Tyrian sailors, who still had Frisian blood in their veins, said, If you do that we will burn our ships, and you shall never see your mountains again. Cecrops, who had no inclination towards murder or devastation, sent messengers to Geert, requiring her to give up the citadel, offering her free exit with all her live and dead property, and her followers the same. The wisest of the citizens, seeing that they could not hold the citadel, advised Geert to accept at once, before Cecrops became furious and changed his mind. Three months afterwards Geert departed with the best of Frya's sons, and seven times twelve ships. Soon after they had left the harbour they fell in with at least thirty ships coming from Tyre with women and children. They were on their way to Athens, but when they heard how things stood there they went with Geert. The sea-king of

---

* Sêkrops is Cecrops.

Thyrjar brocht algadur thrvch tha strête* thêr vnder thisse
tida vppa tha râde sê uthlip. Et leste lândon hja et Pangab,
that is in vsa sprêke fif wêtervm, vmbe that fif rinstrâma
mith hiri nêi tha sê to strâme. Hyr seton hja hjara selva
nithar. That lând hâvon hja Gêrtmannja hêton. Thene kêning fon Thyrhis âfternêi sjande that sin alderbesta stjurar
wei brit wêren sand al sin skipa mith sina wilde saltâtha
vmb-er dâd jefta lêvand to fâtane. Men as hjâ by thêre
strête kêm bêvadon bêde sê ând irtha. Forth hêf irtha hira
lif thêr vppa, sâ hâg that al at wêter to thêre strête uthlip,
ând that alle wata ând skorra lik en burchwal to fâra hjam
vp rêson. That skêde over tha Gêrtmanna hjara dügda lik
as allera mannalik hel ând klâr mêi sja.

AN THA JÊRA 1000 AND 5† NÊI ALDLAND SVNKEN IS, IS
   THIT VPP-INA ASTERWACH IT FRYAS BURCH WRITEN.

Nêi that wi in twilif jêr tid nên Krêkalandar to Alman-
lând sjân hêde, kêmon thêr thrju skêpa sa syrlik as wi nên
hêdon ând to fara nimmer nêde sjan. Vppet storoste thêra
wêre-n kêning thêra Jhonhis êlandum. Sin nôme wêre
Ulysus ând tha hrop ovir sin wisdom grât. This kêning
was thrvch êne presteresse forsêid, that er kêning wertha
skolde ovir alla Krêkalanda sa-r rêd wiste vmbe-n foddik
to krêjande, thêr vpstêken was anda foddik it Texland.
Vmbe-r to fensane hêder fêle skâta mith brocht, boppa ella
fâmne syrhêdum, alsa thêr in wralda navt skênener
mâkad wrde. Hja kêmon fon Troja en stede tham tha
Krêkalandar innimth hêdon. Al thissa skâta bâd hi tha
Moder an, men thju Moder nilde nârne fon nêta. As er
to lesta sa, that hju navt to winne wêre, gvng er nêi
Walhallagara.‡

Thêr was en fâm sêten, hjra nôme wêre Kât, tha

---

* Strête, thans hersteld als Kanaal van Suez. Pangab, de Indus.
† 219-1005=1188 v. Chr.   ‡ Wallahagara, Walcheren.

the Tyrians brought them altogether through the strait which at that time ran into the Red Sea (now re-established as the Suez Canal). At last they landed at the Punjab, called in our language the Five Rivers, because five rivers flow together to the sea. Here they settled, and called it Geertmania. The King of Tyre afterwards, seeing that all his best sailors were gone, sent all his ships with his wild soldiers to catch them, dead or alive. When they arrived at the strait, both the sea and the earth trembled. The land was upheaved so that all the water ran out of the strait, and the muddy shores were raised up like a rampart. This happened on account of the virtues of the Geertmen, as every one can plainly understand.

IN THE YEAR ONE THOUSAND AND FIVE AFTER ATLAND
WAS SUBMERGED, THIS WAS INSCRIBED ON THE
EASTERN WALL OF FRYASBURGT.

After twelve years had elapsed without our seeing any Italians in Almanland, there came three ships, finer than any that we possessed or had ever seen.

On the largest of them was a king of the Jonischen Islands whose name was Ulysses, the fame of whose wisdom was great. To him a priestess had prophesied that he should become the king of all Italy provided he could obtain a lamp that had been lighted at the lamp in Texland. For this purpose he had brought great treasures with him, above all, jewels for women more beautiful than had ever been seen before. They were from Troy, a town that the Greeks had taken. All these treasures he offered to the mother, but the mother would have nothing to do with them. At last, when he found that there was nothing to be got from her, he went to Walhallagara (Walcheren). There there was established a Burgtmaagd whose name was Kaat,

---

* Strête, at present restored as the Suez Canal. Pangab is the Indus.
† 2193–1005 is 1188 before Christ. ‡ Walhallagâra is Walcheren.

K

inna wandel wrde hju Kalip* hêten ut hawede that hjara vnderlip as en utkikbored farutståk. Thêrby heth er jêron hwilth to årgenisse fon al tham et wiston. Nêi thêra fâmna hrop heth er to lesta en foddik fon hir krêjen, tha hja heth im navt ne bât, hwand as er in sê kêm is sin skip vrgvngon ånd hy nåked ånd blât vpnimth thrvch tha ôthera skêpa.

Fon thisse kêning is hyr en skryver åfterbilêwen fon rên Fryas blod, bårn to thêre nêie have fon Athênia ånd hwat hyr folgath het er vs fon ovir Athênia skrêven, thêrut mêi mån bisluta, ho wêr thja Moder Hel-licht sproken heth, thâ hja sêide thåt Fryas sêda to Athênia nên stand holde ne kvste.

Fon tha ôthera Krêkalander hetste sêkur fül kwâd ovir Sêkrops hêred, hwand hi wêre in nên gode hrop. Men ik dår segse, hi wêre-n lichte man, hâchlik romed alsa sêr bi tha inhêmar as wel bi vs, hwand hi wêre navt vmbe tha månniska to diapana sa tha ôra prestera, men hi wêre dügedsêm ånd hi wist tha wisdom thêra fêrhêmanda folkum nêi wêrde to skåtande. Thêrvmbe that er that wiste, hêde-r vs to stonden that wi machte lêva nêi vs ajn êlik Sêgabok. Thêr gvng en telling that er vs nygen were, vmbe that er tjucht wêsa skolde ut en Fryaske mangêrte ånd Êgiptiska prester, uthawede that er blåwe åga hêde, ånd that er fül mangêrta fon vs skåkt wêron ånd in ovir Ægiptalande vrsellath. Tha selva heth er nimmerte jecht. Ho-t thêrmêi sy, sêkur is-t that er vs måra åthskip biwês as alle ôthera prestum to sêmne. Men as er fallen was, gvngon sina nêimanninga alring an vsa êwa torena ånd bi grådum sa fêlo mislikanda kêra to måkjande, that er to lônge lesta fon êlik sa ånd fon frydom ha navt ôwers as tha skin ånd tha nôme vrbilêf. Forth nildon hja navt ne dåja that-a setma an skrift brocht wrde, hwerthrvch tha witskip thêra fur

---

* Kalip, bij Homerus Kalipso.

but who was commonly called Kalip,* because her lower lip stuck out like a mast-head. Here he tarried for years, to the scandal of all that knew it. According to the report of the maidens, he obtained a lamp from her; but it did him no good, because when he got to sea his ship was lost, and he was taken up naked and destitute by another ship. There was left behind by this king a writer of pure Frya's blood, born in the new harbour of Athens, who wrote for us what follows about Athens, from which may be seen how truly the mother Hel-licht spoke when she said that the customs of Frya could never take firm hold in Athens.

From the other Greeks you will have heard a great deal of bad about Cecrops, because he was not in good repute; but I dare affirm that he was an enlightened man, very renowned both among the inhabitants and among us, for he was against oppression, unlike the other priests, and was virtuous, and knew how to value the wisdom of distant nations. Knowing that, he permitted us to live according to our own Asegaboek. There was a story current that he was favourable to us because he was the son of a Frisian girl and an Egyptian priest: the reason of this was that he had blue eyes, and that many of our girls had been stolen and sold to Egypt, but he never confirmed this. However it may have been, certain it is that he showed us more friendship than all the other priests together. When he died, his successors soon began to tear up our charters, and gradually to enact so many unsuitable statutes that at long last nothing remained of liberty but the shadow and the name. Besides, they would not allow the laws to be written, so that the knowledge of them was hidden from us. Formerly all the cases in

---

* Kalip, called by Homer Kalipso.

vs. forborgen wårth. To fâra wrdon alle sêkum binna Athênia in vsa tâl bithongon, åfternêi most et in bêda tâla skên ånd to lesta allêna in tha landis tal. In tha êrosta jêra nam that manfolk to Athênia enkel wiva fon vs ajn slacht, men that jongkfolk vpwoxen mitha mangêrta thêr landsâton namen thêr åk fon. Tha båstera bern tham thêrof kemon wêron tha skênsta ånd snodsta in wralda, men hja wêron åk tha årgsta. To hinkande vr byde syda, to målande her vm sêda ner vm plêga, hit ne sy that et wêre for hjara ajne held. Alsa nåka thêr jeta-n strêl fon Fryas gåst weldande wêre wårth al et bvwspul to mêna werka forwrochten ånd nimmån ne mocht en hus to bvwande, thåt rumer ånd riker wêre as thåt sinra nêstum. Tha thå svme vrbastere stêdjar rik wêron thrvch vs fåra ånd thrvch et sulver, thåt tha slåvona uta sulverlôna wnnon, thå gvngon hja buta vppa hellinga jefta inda dêla hêma. Thêr beftha håga wallum fon lôf tha fon stên bvwadon hja hova mith kestlik husark, ånd vmbe by tha wla prestrum in en goda hrop to wêsande, ståndon hja thêr falska drochten likanda ånd vntuchtiga bilda in. By tha wla prestrum ånd forstum wrdon tha knåpa al tomet måra gêrt as tha toghatera, ånd fåken thrvch rika jefta thrvch weld fon et pad thêre düged ofhlêid. Nêidam rikdom by thåt vrbrûde ånd vrbasterde slachte fêr bvppa düged ånd êre jelde, sach mån altomet knåpa tham hjara selva mit rûma rika klâtar syradon, hjara aldrum ånd fåmna to skônda ånd hjara kvnna to spot. Kêmon vsa ênfalda aldera to Athênia vppe thêre mêna acht ånd wildon hja thêrvr bâra, så warth ther hropen, hark, hark, thêr skil en sêmomma kêtha. Alsa is Athênia wrdon êlik en brokland anda hête landa, fol blodsûgar, pogga ånd feniniga snåka, hwêrin nên månniske fon herde sêdum sin fot navt wåga ne mêi.

Athens were pleaded in our language, but afterwards in both languages, and at last in the native language only. At first the men of Athens only married women of our own race, but the young men as they grew up with the girls of the country took them to wife. The bastard children of this connection were the handsomest and cleverest in the world; but they were likewise the wickedest, wavering between the two parties, paying no regard to laws or customs except where they suited their own interests. As long as a ray of Frya's spirit existed, all the building materials were for common use, and no one might build a house larger or better than his neighbours; but when some degenerate townspeople got rich by sea-voyages and by the silver that their slaves got in the silver countries, they went to live out on the hills or in the valleys. There, behind high enclosures of trees or walls, they built palaces with costly furniture, and in order to remain in good odour with the nasty priests, they placed there likenesses of false gods and unchaste statues. Sometimes the dirty priests and princes wished for the boys rather than the girls, and often led them astray from the paths of virtue by rich presents or by force. Because riches were more valued by this lost and degenerate race than virtue or honour, one sometimes saw boys dressed in splendid flowing robes, to the disgrace of their parents and maidens, and to the shame of their own sex. If our simple parents came to a general assembly at Athens and made complaints, a cry was raised, Hear, hear! there is a sea-monster going to speak. Such is Athens become, like a morass in a tropical country full of leeches, toads, and poisonous snakes, in which no man of decent habits can set his foot.

THIT STAT IN AL VSA BURGA.

Ho vsa Dênemarka* fâra vs vlêren gvngon 1600 ånd 2 jêr† nêi Aldland vrgongen is. Thrvch Wodins dor ånd dertenhêd was thene Magy bâs wrden ovir Skênlandis astardêl. Wra berga ånd wr-n sê ne tvrade hi navt ne kvma. Thju Moder wildet navt wêrha, hja sprêk ånde kêth, ik sja nên frêse an sina wêpne, men wel vmbe tha Skênlander wêr to nimmande, thrvchdam hja bastered ånd vrdêren sind. Vppa mêna acht tochte man alên. Thêrvmbe is-t im lêten. Grât 100 jêr lêden byondon tha Dênemarkar to wandelja mith hjam. Hja jêvon him ysere wêpne ånd rêdskip thêr fori wandeldon hja golden syrhêdon bijunka kâper ånd yserirtha. Thju Moder sand bodon ånd rêd-er, hja skolde thju wandel fâra lêta. Thêr wêre frêse sêide hju fori hjara sêdum, ånd bitham hja hjara sêde vrlêren, thån skolde hja åk hjara frydom vrljasa. Men tha Dênemarkar nêde narne âra nei, hja nilda navt bigrippa that hjara sêde vrbrûde kvste, thêrvmbe ne meldon hja hja navt. To lônga lesta brochton hja ajne wêpne ånd liftochta wêi. Men thåt kwåd wrocht hjara gêia. Hjara lichêma wrdon bilåden mêi blik ånd skin, men hjara arka spynton ånd skvra wrdon lêtoch. Krek hondred jêr eftere dêi that et forma skip mit liftochta fona kåd fâren was, kêm ermode ånd lek thrvch tha anderna binna, honger sprêda sina wjvka ånd strêk vppet land del, twispalt hlip stolte in overe strêta ånd forth to tha hûsa in, ljafde ne kv nên stek lônger navt finda ånd êntracht run êwêi. Thåt bårn wilde êta fon sina måm ånd thju måm hêde wel syrhêdon tha nêu êta. Tha wiva kêmon to hjara manna, thissa gvngon nêi tha grêva, tha. grêva nêdon selva nawet of hildon-t skul. Nw most mån tha syrhêdon vrsella, men thawila tha stjurar thêrmêi

---

* Dêna marka, de lage marken.
† 2193-1602=591 v. Chr.

THE BOOK OF ADELA'S FOLLOWERS.

THIS IS INSCRIBED IN ALL OUR CITADELS.

How our Denmark was lost to us 1602 years after the submersion of Atland. Through the mad wantonness of Wodin, Magy had become master of the east part of Scandinavia. They dare not come over the hills and over the sea. The mother would not prevent it. She said, I see no danger in their weapons, but much in taking the Scandinavians back again, because they are so degenerate and spoilt. The general assembly were of the same opinion. Therefore it was left to him. A good hundred years ago Denmark began to trade; they gave their iron weapons in exchange for gold ornaments, as well as for copper and iron-ore. The mother sent messengers to advise them to have nothing to do with this trade. There was danger to their morals in it, and if they lost their morals they would soon lose their liberty. But the Denmarkers paid no attention to her. They did not believe that they could lose their morals, therefore they would not listen to her. At last they were at a loss themselves for weapons and necessaries, and this difficulty was their punishment. Their bodies were brilliantly adorned, but their cupboards and their sheds were empty. Just one hundred years after the first ship with provisions sailed from the coast, poverty and want made their appearance, hunger spread her wings all over the country, dissension marched proudly about the streets and into the houses, charity found no place, and unity departed. The child asked its mother for food; she had no food to give, only jewels. The women applied to their husbands, the husbands appealed to the counts; the counts had nothing to give, or if they had, they hid it away. Now the jewels must be sold, but while the sailors

---

* Dêna marka, the low marches.
† 2193-1602 is 591 years before Christ.

wêi brit wêron kêm frost ånd lêi-n plônk del vppa sê ånd wra strête. Tha frost thju brigge rêd hêde, stop wåkandon thêr wr to-t land ut ånd vrêd klywade vpper sêtel. In stêde fon tha owera to biwåkande spandon hja hjara horsa for hjara togum ånd runon nêi Skênland thå. Tha Skênlander, tham nêy wêron nêi that land hjarar êthla kêmon nêi tha Dênemarkum. Vppen helle nacht kêmon hja alla. Nw sêidon hja that hja rjucht hêde vppet land hjarar êthlon ånd thahwil that mån thêrvr kåmpade kêmon tha Finna in tha lêtoga thorpa ånd runadon mith tha bern ewêi. Thêrtrvch ånd that hja nên goda wêpne navt nêdon, dêd hjam tha kåsa vrljasa ånd thêrmêi hjari frydom, hwand thene Magy wrde bås. That kêm that hja Fryas tex navt lêsde ånd hira rêdjêvinga warlåsed hêde.

Ther send svme thêr mêne that hja thrvch tha grêva vrrêden send, that tha fåmna thåt lông spêrath hêdon, tha sa hvam sa thêr vr kêtha wilde, tham is mvla wrdon to smôrath mith golden kêdne. Wi ne mügan thêrvr nên ordêl to fellande, men wi willath jo tohropa, ne lên navt to sêre vppa wisdom ånd düged ni fon jvwa Forsta, ni fon jowa fåmna, hwand skel et halda sa mot allera mannalik wåka ovir sin ajna tochta ånd for-t mêna held.

Twa jêr nêidam kêm thene Magy selva mith en flåte fon lichte kånum, tha Moder fon Texland ånd tha foddik to råwane.

Thås årge sêke bistonde-r thes nachtis anda winter by storne tydum as wind gûlde ånd hêjel to jenst tha andêrna fêtere. Thi utkik thêr mênde thater awet hêrde ståk sin balle vp. Tha drêi as et ljucht fon êr tore vppet ronddêl falda, sa-r that al fêlo wêpende manna wra burchwal wêron. Nw gvng-er to vmbe tha klokke to lettane, tha et wêre to lêt. Êr tha wêre rêd wêre, weron al twa thusand ina wêr vmbe tha porte to rammande. Strid hwilde thervmbe kirt,

were away for that purpose, the frost came and laid a plank upon the sea and the strait (the Sound). When the frost had made the bridge, vigilance ceased in the land, and treachery took its place. Instead of watching on the shores, they put their horses in their sledges and drove off to Scandinavia. Then the Scandinavians, who hungered after the land of their forefathers, came to Denmark. One bright night they all came. Now, they said, we have a right to the land of our fathers; and while they were fighting about it, the Finns came to the defenceless villages and ran away with the children. As they had no good weapons, they lost the battle, and with it their freedom, and Magy became master. All this was the consequence of their not reading Frya's Tex, and neglecting her counsels. There are some who think that they were betrayed by the counts, and that the maidens had long suspected it; but if any one attempted to speak about it, his mouth was shut by golden chains.

We can express no opinion about it, we can only say to you, Do not trust too much to the wisdom of your princes or of your maidens; but if you wish to keep things straight, everybody must watch over his own passions, as well as the general welfare.

Two years afterwards Magy himself came with a fleet of light boats to steal the lamp from the mother of Texland. This wicked deed he accomplished one stormy winter night, while the wind roared and the hail rattled against the windows. The watchman on the tower hearing the noise, lighted his torch. As soon as the light from the tower fell upon the bastion, he saw that already armed men had got over the wall.

He immediately gave the alarm, but it was too late. Before the guard was ready, there were two thousand people battering the gate. The struggle did not last long.

hwand thrvchdam tha wêra navt nên gode wacht halden nêde, kêmon alle om.

Hwil that alrek drok to kâmpane wêre, was thêr en wla Fin to thêre flête jefta bedrum fon thêre Moder inglupth, ånd wilde hja nêdgja. Tha thju Moder wêrd-im of that er bekwârd tojênst tha wâch strumpelde. Thâ-r wither vpa bên wêre stek er sin swêrd to ir buk in segsande, nilst min kul navt så skilst min swêrd ha. After im kêm en skiper fona Dênemarka, thisse nam sin swêrd ånd hif thêne Fin thrvch sina hole. Thêrut flât swart blod ånd thêrvr swêfde-n blâwe logha. Thi Magy lêt thju Moder vpa sinra skip forplêgja. As hju nw wither alsa fêre hêl ånd bêter wêr that hju fâst sprêka machte, sêide thene Magy that hju mith fâra moste, tha that hju hira foddik ånd fâmna halda skolde, that hju en stât skolde nyta så hâch as hju to fara na nêde kenth. Forth sêide-r thât hi hiri frêja skolde in ajnwarde fon sinum forsta, jef er mâster skolde wertha over alle lânda ånd folkra Fryas. Hi sêide that hju that bijâe ånd bijechta most, owers skolde-r vnder fêlo wêja sterva lêta. As er thêr after al sinra forsta om ira lêger to gadurad hêde frêjer lûd, Frâna vrmites i klârsjande biste most m.ênis segsa of ik mâster skil wertha over alle lânda ånd folkra Fryas. Frâna dêde as melde hja him navt. To lônga lesta êpende hju hira wêra ånde kêth, min âgun wrde thjûstred, tha that ôre ljucht dêgth vp in minara sêle. Jes, ik sja-t. Hark Irtha ånd wês blyde mith my. Vndera tydum that Aldland svnken is, stand thju forma spêke fon thet Jol an top. Thêrnêi is hju del gvngon ånd vsa frydom mith tham. As er twa spêka jeftha 2000 jêr del trûled het, så skilun˜tha svna vpstonda thêr tha forsta ånd prestera thrvch hordom bi-t folk têled hâve, ånd tojenst hjara tâta tjugha. Thi alle skilum thrvch mort swika, men hwat hja kêth hâve skil forth

THE BOOK OF ADELA'S FOLLOWERS. 115

As the guard had not kept a good watch, they were overwhelmed. While the fight was going on, a rascally Finn stole into the chamber of the mother, and would have done her violence. She resisted him, and threw him down against the wall. When he got up, he ran his sword through her: If you will not have me, you shall have my sword. A Danish soldier came behind him and clave his head in two. There came from it a stream of black blood and a wreath of blue flame.

The Magy had the mother nursed on his own ship. As soon as she was well enough to speak clearly, the Magy told her that she must sail with him, but that she should keep her lamp and her maidens, and should hold a station higher than she had ever done before. Moreover, he said that he should ask her, in presence of all his chief men, if he would become the ruler of all the country and people of Frya; that she must declare and affirm this, or he would let her die a painful death. Then, when he had gathered all his chiefs around her bed, he asked, in a loud voice, Frana, since you are a prophetess, shall I become ruler over all the lands and people of Frya? Frana did as if she took no notice of him; but at last she opened her lips, and said: My eyes are dim, but the other light dawns upon my soul. Yes, I see it. Hear, Irtha, and rejoice with me. At the time of the submersion of Atland, the first spoke of the Juul stood at the top. After that it went down, and our freedom with it. When two spokes, or two thousand years, shall have rolled down, the sons shall arise who have been bred of the fornication of the princes and priests with the people, and shall witness against their fathers. They shall all fall by murder, but what they have proclaimed shall endure,

bilywa ånd frûchdber wertha in-a bosme thêra kloke månniska, alsa lik gode sêdum thêr del lêid wrde in thinra skåt. Jeta thûsand jêr skil thju spêke then del nyga ånd al måra syga anda thjusternesse ånd in blod, ovir thi utstirt thrvch tha låga thêr forsta ånd prestera. Thêrnêi skil thet morneråd wither anfanga to glora. Thit sjande skilun tha falska forsta ånd prester alsamen with frydom kåmpa ånd woxelja, men frydom, ljafde ånd êndracht skil-et folk in hjara wach nêma ånd mit thet jol risa uta wla pol. Thåt rjucht thåt erost allêna glorade, skil than fon lêjar laja to-n logha wertha. Thåt blod thêra årgum skil ovir thin lif stråma, men thu ne mügth et navt to thi nêma. To tha lesta skil thåt feninige kwik thêr vp åsa ånd thêrof sterva. Alle wla skêdnese tham forsunnen send vmbe tha forsta ånd prestera to boga, skilun an logha ofred wertha. Forth skilun al thinra bern mith frêtho lêva. Thå hju utspreken hêde, sêg hju del. Men thene Mågy tham hja navt wel forstân hêde krêth, ik håv thi frêjeth, jef ik bås skilde wertha ovir alle lånda ånd folkra Fryas, ånd nw håste to en other sproken. Fråna rjuchte hiri wither, sach im star an ånd kêthe: er sjugun etmelde om send, skil thin sêle mitha nachtfüglon to tha gråwa omme wåra ånd thin lik skil ledsa vppa bodem fona se. Êl wel sêide thene Magy mith vrborgne wodin, segs men thåt ik kvme. Forth sêider to jenst ên sinar rakkarum, werp that wif vr skippes bord. Althus wêr-et ende fon-re leste thêra Moderum.* Wrêke willath wi thêr vr navt ne hropa, tham skil tyd nima. Men thûsand wåra thûsand mêl willath wi Frya åfternêi hropa: wåk-wåk-wåk.

Ho-t thene Magy forth vrgvngon is.

Nêi that tha modder vrdên was, lêter tha foddik ånd tha fåmna to sina skip to brenga bijunka alle in

---

* Verg. bl 4.

and shall bear fruit in the bosoms of able men, like good seed which is laid in thy lap. Yet a thousand years shall the spoke descend, and sink deeper in darkness, and in the blood shed over you by the wickedness of the princes and priests. After that, the dawn shall begin to glow. When they perceive this, the false princes and priests will strive and wrestle against freedom; but freedom, love, and unity will take the people under their protection, and rise out of the vile pool. The light which at first only glimmered shall gradually become a flame. The blood of the bad shall flow over your surface, but you must not absorb it. At last the poisoned animals shall eat it, and die of it. All the stories that have been written in praise of the princes and priests shall be committed to the flames. Thenceforth your children shall live in peace. When she had finished speaking she sank down.

The Magy, who had not understood her, shrieked out, I have asked you if I should become master of all the lands and people of Frya, and now you have been speaking to another. Frana raised herself up, stared at him, and said, Before seven days have passed your soul shall haunt the tombs with the night-birds, and your body shall be at the bottom of the sea. Very good, said the Magy, swelling with rage; say that I am coming. Then he said to his executioners, Throw this woman overboard. This was the end of the last of the mothers. We do not ask for revenge. Time will provide that; but a thousand thousand times we will call with Frya, Watch! watch! watch!

How it fared afterwards with the Magy.

After the murder of the mother, he brought the lamp and the maidens into his own ship, together with all

---

* Refer to p. 4.

bold thêr im likte. Forth gvng er thât Flymâr vp, hwand hi wilde tha fâm fon Mêdêasblik jeftha fon Stâvora gabja ånd tham to Moder mâkja. Tha thêr wêron hja vp hjara hodum brocht. Tha stjurar fon Stâvora ånd fon thât Alderga hêdon hini gêrn to Jonis togen, men tha grâte flâte wêre vppen fêre tocht ût. Nw gvngon hja to ånd foron mith hjra littige flâte nêi Mêdêasblik ånd hildon hja skul after thât ly thêra bâmun. Thi Mâgy nâkade Mêdêasblik bi helle dêi ånd skynander svnne. Thach gvngon sina ljuda drist drist wêi vppera burch to runnande. Men as allet folk mith tha bôtum land was, kemon vsa stjurar utêre krêke wêi ånd skâton hjara pila mith târbarntin bollum vp sinra flâte. Hja wêron alsa wel rjucht that fêlo sinra skêpun bistonda anna brônd wêron. Tham vppa skêpun wachton, skâton âk nêi vs thâ, thach thât ne rojade nawet. As er to lesta en skip al barnande nêi-t skip thes Mâgy dryf, bifel-er sin skiper hi skolde of hâde, men thene skiper that wêre thene Dênemarker thêr thene Fin felad hêde, andere, thv hest vse Êremoder nêi tha bodem fona sê svnden to meldande thatste kvma skolde, thit skoste thrvch tha drokhêd wel vrjetta; nw wil ik njude thatste thin word jecht. Thi Mâgy wild-im ofwêra; men thene skiper, en âfte Fryas ånd sterik lik en jokoxe klipade bêda sinum hônda om sin hole ånd hif hini vr bord into thât wellande hef. Forth hês er sin brune skild an top ånd for rjucht to rjucht an nêi vsa flâte. Thêrtbrvch kêmon tha fâmna vnforlet to vs, men tha foddik was utgvngon ånd nimman wiste ho-t kêmen was. Tha hja vppa vnfordene skêpa heradon, that thene Mâgy vrdrvnken was, brûde hja hinne, hwand tha stjurar thêra mêst Dênemarker wêron. Nêi that tha flâte fêr enoch ewêi wêre; wendon vsa stjurar ånd skâton hjara barnpila vppa tha Finna del. Thâ tha Finna thus sagon, ho hja vrrêden wêron, hlip alrik thrvch vr ekkdrum ånd thêr nêre lônger nên hêrichhêd ni bod. To thisre stonde run tha wêre hju ut

the booty that he chose. Afterwards he went up the Flymeer because he wished to take the maiden of Medeasblik or Stavoren and install her as mother; but there they were on their guard. The seafaring men of Stavoren and Alderga would gladly have gone to Jon, but the great fleet was out on a distant voyage; so they proceeded in their small fleet to Medeasblik, and kept themselves concealed in a sheltered place behind trees. The Magy approached Medeasblik in broad daylight; nevertheless, his men boldly stormed the citadel. But as they landed from the boats, our people sallied forth from the creek, and shot their arrows with balls of burning turpentine upon the fleet. They were so well aimed that many of the ships were instantly on fire. Those left to guard the ships shot at us, but they could not reach us. When at last a burning ship drifted towards the ship of the Magy, he ordered the man at the helm to sheer off, but this man was the Dane who had cleft the head of the Finn. He said, You sent our Eeremoeder to the bottom of the sea to say that you were coming. In the bustle of the fight you might forget it; now I will take care that you keep your word. The Magy tried to push him off, but the sailor, a real Frisian and strong as an ox, clutched his head with both hands, and pitched him into the surging billows. Then he hoisted up his brown shield, and sailed straight to our fleet. Thus the maidens came unhurt to us; but the lamp was extinguished, and no one knew how that had happened. When those on the uninjured ships heard that the Magy was drowned, they sailed away, because their crews were Danes. When the fleet was far enough off, our sailors turned and shot their burning arrows at the Finns. When the Finns saw that, and found that they were betrayed, they fell into confusion, and lost all discipline and order. At this moment the garrison sallied

têre burch. Tham navt ne fljuchte, werth afmakad, ånd thêr fljuchte fvnd sin ende into tha polum fon et Krylinger wald.

Nêischrift.

Thâ tha stjurar an da kreke lêjon was thêr en spotter fon ut Stavora mank, thêr sêide, Mêdêa mei lakkja, sa wi hyr ut hjra burch reda. Thêrvmbe håvon tha fåmna thju krêke Mêdêa mêi lakkja* hêten.

Tha bêrtnissa thêr afternêi skêd send, mêi alra mannalik hügja. Tha fåmna hagon tham nei hjara wysa to tella ånd wel biskriwa lêta. Thêrvmbe rêkenjath wi hirmitha vsa arbêd fvlbrocht. Held.

---

* Medemi'lacus.

ENDE FON 'T BOK.

forth from the citadel. Those who resisted were killed, and those who fled found their death in the marshes of the Krylinger wood.

Postscript.

When the sailors were in the creek, there was a wag from Stavoren among them, who said, Medea may well laugh if we rescue her from her citadel. Upon this, the maidens gave to the creek the name Medea mêilakkia (Lake of Medea). The occurrences that happened after this everybody can remember. The maidens ought to relate it in their own way, and have it well inscribed. We consider that our task is fulfilled. Hail!

---

* Medemi lacus, Lake of Medea's laughter.

THE END OF THE BOOK.

THA SKRIFTA FON ADELBROST AND APOLLONIA.

Min nôm is Adelbrost svn fon Apol ånd fon Adela. Thrvch min folk ben ik kêren to Grêvetman ovira Linda wrda. Thêrvmbe wil ik thit bok forfolgja vp alsa dênera wisa as mine mem sproken heth.

Nêi that thene Mâgy felt was ånd Fryasburch vp stel brocht, most er en moder kêren wertha. Bi-ra lêva nêde thju Moder hira folgstera navt nômth. Hira lersta wille was sok ånd narne to findne. Sjugun mônatha åfter werth er en mêna acht bilidsen ånd wel to Grênegâ* ut êrsêke that anna Saxanamarka pâlth. Min mem werth kêren, men hju nilde nên Moder wêsa. Hju hêde heth lif minar tåt hrêd, thêrthruch hêden hja ekkorum lyaf krêjen ånd nw wildon hja åk gådath wertha. Fêlon wildon min mem fon er bislut ofbrenga; men min mem sêide, en Êremoder åcht alsa rên in-ra mod to wêsana as hja buta blikt ånd êven mild far al hjara bern. Nêidam ik Apol nw lyaf håv hoppa ella in wralda, så ne kån ik så-ne Moder navt nêsa. Så sprek ånd kêth Adela, men tha ôra burchfåmna wildon algåder Moder wêsa. Alrek ståt thong fori sinera åjne fåm ånd nilde navt fyra. Ther-thrvch nis er nêne kêren ånd heth rik thus bandlås. Hyr åfter müg-it bigripa.

Ljudgêrt, tham kêning thêr hêmesdêga fallen is, was bi thêre Moder-is lêva kêren blikbêr trvch alle ståtha mith lyafde ånd trjvw. Heth wêre sin torn vmbe vppin eth gråte hof to Dok-hêm† to hêmande, ånd bi thêre Moder-is lêva wrd-im ther gråte êr biwêsen, hwand et wêre immer sa ful mith bodon ånd riddarum fon hêinde ånd fêre as-m-å to fora na nêde sjan. Tach nw wêr-er ênsêm and

---

* Grênegâ, Groningen.   Dokhêm, Dokkum.

THE WRITINGS OF ADELBROST AND APOLLONIA.

My name is Adelbrost, the son of Apol and Adela. I was elected by my people as Grevetman over the Linda-oorden. Therefore I will continue this book in the same way as my mother has spoken it.

After the Magy was killed and Fryasburgt was restored, a mother had to be chosen. The mother had not named her successor, and her will was nowhere to be found. Seven months later a general assembly was called at Grênegâ (Groningen), because it was on the boundary of Saxamarken. My mother was chosen, but she would not be the mother. She had saved my father's life, in consequence of which they had fallen in love with each other, and she wished to marry. Many people wished my mother to alter her decision, but she said an Eeremoeder ought to be as pure in her conscience as she appears outwardly, and to have the same love for all her children. Now, as I love Apol better than anything else in the world, I cannot be such a mother. Thus spoke and reasoned Adela, but all the other maidens wished to be the mother. Each state was in favour of its own maiden, and would not yield. Therefore none was chosen, and the kingdom was without any restraint. From what follows you will understand Liudgert, the king who had lately died, had been chosen in the lifetime of the mother, and seemingly with the love and confidence of all the states. It was his turn to live at the great court of Dokhem, and in the lifetime of the mother great honour was done to him there, as there were more messengers and knights there than had ever been seen there before. But now he was lonely and forsaken,

---

* Grênegâ is Groningen. † Dokhem is Dokkum.

vrlêten, hwand alrek wêre ange that-er him mâster skolde mâkja boppa heth rjucht ând welda ê-lik tha slâvona kêninggar. Elk forst wânde forth that-er enoch dêde as er wâkade ovir sin âjn stât; ând thi ên ne jêf nawet tâ antha ôthera. Mith-êra burchfamna gvnget jeta ârger to. Alrek thisra bogade vppira âjne wisdom ând sahwersa tha Grêvetmanna awet dêdon buta hjam, sâ wrochten hja mistryvwa bitwiska tham ând sinum ljudum. Skêder en sêke thêr fêlon stâtha trof ând hêde mân thju rêd êner fâm in wnnen, sâ kêthon alle ôthera that hju sproken hêde to fêre fon hjra âjne stât. Thrvch althus dênera renka brochton hja twyspalt in ovira stâtha ând torendon hja that band sâdêne fon ên, that et folk fon tha ênne stât nythich wêre vppet folk fon en ora stât ând fâret alderminesta lik fêrhêmande biskôwade. Thju fêre thêra is wêst that tha Gola jeftha Trowyda vs al-êt lând of wnnen hâven al ont thêra Skelda ând thi Magy al to thêre Wrsâra. Ho-r thêrby to gvngen is, heth min mem vntlêth, owers nas thit bok navt skrêven ne wrden, afskên ik alle hâpe vrlêren hâv tha-et skil helpa thâ bâta. Ik ne skryw thus navt inna wân, thet ik thêrthrvch thet lând skil winna jeftha bihaldane, that is minra achtne vndvalik, ik skryw allêna fâr et âfter kvmande slacht, til thju hja algâdur wêta müge vp hvdêna wisa wy vrlêren gvnge, ând tha alra mannalik hyr ut lêra mêi that elk kwâd sin gêja têlath.

My heth mân Apollônja hêten. Twyia thritich dega nêi mâm hira dâd heth mân Adelbrost min brother vrslêjen fonden vppa wârf, sin hawed split ând sina lithne ût ên hrêten. Min tât thêr siak lêide is fon skrik vrsturven. Thâ is Apol min jungere brother fon hyr nêi thêre westsyde fon Skênlând fâren. Thêr heth er en burch ebuwad, Lindasburch* hêten, vmbe dâna to wrekana vs lêth. Wr.alda heth-im thêr to fêlo jêra lênad. Hy heth fîf svna wnnen. Altham brengath thêne Magy skrik

---

* Lindasburch, op kaap Lindanaes, Noorwegen.

because every one was afraid that he would set himself above the law, and rule them like the slave kings. Every headman imagined that he did enough if he looked after his own state, and did not care for the others. With the Burgtmaagden it was still worse. Each of them depended upon her own judgment, and whenever a Grevetman did anything without her, she raised distrust between him and his people. If any case happened which concerned several states, and one maid had been consulted, the rest all exclaimed that she had spoken only in the interest of her own state. By such proceedings they brought disputes among the states, and so severed the bond of union that the people of one state were jealous of those of the rest, or at least considered them as strangers; the consequence of which was that the Gauls or Truwenden (Druids) took possession of our lands as far as the Scheldt, and the Magy as far as the Wesara. How this happened my mother has explained, otherwise this book would not have been written, although I have lost all hope that it would be of any use. I do not write in the hope that I shall win back the land or preserve it: in my opinion that is impossible. I write only for the future generations, that they may all know in what way we were lost, and that each may learn that every crime brings its punishment.

My name is Apollonia. Two-and-thirty days after my mother's death my brother Adelbrost was found murdered on the wharf, his skull fractured and his limbs torn asunder. My father, who lay ill, died of fright. Then my younger brother, Apol, sailed from here to the west side of Schoonland. There he built a citadel named Lindasburgt, in order there to avenge our wrong. Wr-alda accorded him many years for that. He had five sons, who all caused fear

---

* Lindasburch, on Cape Lindanaes, Norway.

ånd min brother gôma. After måm ånd brother-is dâd send tha fromesta fon-ut-a låndum to ekkôrum kvmen, hja havon en bånd sloten Adelbånd hêten. Til thju vs nên leth witherfåra ne skolde, håvath hja my ånd Adelhirt min jungste brother vpper burch brocht, my by tha fâmna ånd min brother by tha wêrar. Thâ ik thritich jêr werê heth man my to Burchfâm kêren, ånd thâ min brother fiftich wêre, werth-er keren to Grêvetman. Fon måm-is syde wêre min brother thene sexte, men fon tåt his syde thene thride. Nêi rjucht machton sine åfterkvmande thus nên overa Linda åfter hjara nômun navt ne fora, men alra månnalik wildet håva to êre fon mina måm. Thêr to boppa heth mån vs åk en ofskrifte jêven fon thet bok thêra Adela follistar. Thêr mitha ben ik thet blydeste, hwand thrvch min måm hjra wisdom kêm-et in wralda. In thas burch håv ik jeta ôra skrifta fvnden, thêr navt in 't bok ne stan, åk lovsprêka ovir min måm, altham wil ik åfter skriva.

Thit send tha nêilêtne skrifta Brunnos, ther skrywer wêsen is to thisre burch. After that tha Adela follistar ella hêde lêta overskryva elk in sin rik, hwat wryt was in vppa wâgarum thêra burgum, bisloton hja en Moder to kjasane. Thêrto wårth en mêna acht bilêid vp thisra hêm. After tha forme rêd Adelas wårth Tüntja bifolen. Ak skoldet slåcht håve. Thach nw frêge min Burgtfåm thet wort, hju hede immerthe wênich wêst thåt hju Moder skolde wertha, ut êrsêke thåt hju hyr vpper burch sat, hwana mêst alle Moderum kêren wêron. Tha hju thet word gund was, êpende hju hira falxa wêra ånde kêth: I alle skinth årg to heftane an Adelas rêd, tha thåt ne skil thêrvmde min mvla navt ne sluta ner snôra. Hwa tach is Adela ånd hwåna kvmt et wêi thåtster sokke håge love to swikth. Lik ik hjuddêga is hju to fara hyr burchfam wêst.

to Magy, and brought fame to my brother. After the death of my mother and my brother, all the bravest of the land joined together and made a covenant, called the Adelbond. In order to preserve us from injury, they brought me and my youngest brother, Adelhirt, to the burgt—me to the maidens, and him to the warriors. When I was thirty years old I was chosen as Burgtmaagd, and my brother at fifty was chosen Grevetman. From mother's side my brother was the sixth, but from father's side the third. By right, therefore, his descendants could not put "overa Linda" after their names, but they all wished to do it in honour of their mother. In addition to this, there was given to us also a copy of "The Book of Adela's Followers." That gave me the most pleasure, because it came into the world by my mother's wisdom. In the burgt I have found other writings also in praise of my mother. All this I will write afterwards.

These are the writings left by Bruno, who was the writer of this burgt. After the followers of Adela had made copies, each in his kingdom, of what was inscribed upon the walls of the burgt, they resolved to choose a mother. For this purpose a general assembly was called at this farm. By the first advice of Adela, Teuntje was recommended. That would have been arranged, only that my Burgtmaagd asked to speak: she had always supposed that she would be chosen mother, because she was at the burgt from which mothers had generally been chosen. When she was allowed to speak, she opened her false lips and said: You all seem to place great value on Adela's advice, but that shall not shut my mouth. Who is Adela, and whence comes it that you respect her so highly? She was what I am now, a Burgtmaagd of this

Tha is hju thêr vmbe wiser jefta bêtre as ik ånd alle ôthera, jefta is hju mår stelet vppvsa˙sêd ånd plêgum. Hwêre thåt et fal, så skolde hju wel Moder wrden wêsa, thå hju thêrto kêren is, men nêan hju wilde reḍer ennen bosta ha mith all joi ånd nochta thêr er anebonden send, in stêd fon ênsum over hjam ånd et folk to wåkane. Hju is êl klarsjande, god, men min âgne ne send fêr fon vrthjustred to wêsane. Ik håv sjan thåt hju hir fryadelf herde minth, nw god, thåt is lovelik, men ik håv forther sjan thåt Tüntja Apol-is nift is. Wyder wil ik navt ne sedsa.

Tha forsta bigripen êl god, hwêr hju hly sochte, men emong et folk kêm twyspalt, ånd nêidam heth maradêl fon hyr wei kêm, wilde-t Tüntja thiu êre navt ne guna. Rêdne wrde stopth, tha saxne tågon uta skådne, men thêr ne wårth nêne Moder kêren. Kirt åfter hêde annen vsera bodne sin makker fåleth. Til hjuddêga hêde der frod wêsen, thêrvmbe hede min burchfåm orlovi vmb-im buta tha låndpåla to helpane. Thach in stêd fon im to helpane nêi thet Twiskland, alsa fljuchte hju selva mith im overe Wrsara ånd forth nêi tha Mågy. Thi Mågy tham sina Fryas svna hagja wilde stald-iri as Moder to Godaburch et Skênland, mên hju wilde mår, hju sêid-im thåt sahwersa hi Adela vpruma koste, hi måster skolde wertha over êl Fryas land. Hju wêr en fyand fon Adele sêide hju, hwand thrvch hjra renka nas hju nên Moder wrden. Sahwersa hy hir Texland forspreka wilde, sa skolde hjra boda sina wichar to wêiwyser thjanja. Al thissa sêka heth hjra boda selva bilyad.

Thet Othera Skrift.

Fiftian monatha nêi thêre lerste acht wêr-et Frjunsklp jeftha Winnemônath. Alleramånnelik jef to an mery

place; is she, then, wiser and better than I and all the others? or is she more conversant with our laws and customs? If that had been the case, she would have become mother when she was chosen; but instead of that, she preferred matrimony to a single life, watching over herself and her people. She is certainly very clear-sighted, but my eyes are far from being dim. I have observed that she is very much attached to her husband, which is very praiseworthy; but I see, likewise, that Teuntje is Apol's niece. Further I say nothing.

The principal people understood very well which way the wind blew with her; but among the people there arose disputes, and as most of the people came from here, they would not give the honour to Teuntje. The conferences were ended, knives were drawn, and no mother was chosen. Shortly afterwards one of our messengers killed his comrade. As he had been a man of good character hitherto, my Burgtmaagd had permission to help him over the frontier; but instead of helping him over to Twiskland (Germany), she fled with him herself to Wesara, and then to the Magy. The Magy, who wished to please his sons of Frya, appointed her mother of Godaburgt, in Schoonland; but she wished for more, and she told him that if he could get Adela out of the way he might become master of the whole of Frya's land. She said she hated Adela for having prevented her from being chosen mother. If he would promise her Texland, her messenger should serve as guide to his warriors. All this was confessed by her messenger.

The Second Writing.

Fifteen months after the last general assembly, at the festival of the harvest month, everybody gave himself

mery fru ånd bly, ånd nimman nêde diger than to åkane sina nocht. Thach Wr.alda wild vs wysa, thåt wåkendom navt vrgamlath wrde ne mêi. To midne fon-et] fêst fyrja kêm nêvil to hullande vsa wrda in thikke thjusternise. Nocht runde wêi, tha wåkendom nilde navt ne kêra. Tha strandwåkar wêron fon hjara nêd fjura hlåpen ånd vppa tha topådum nas nênen to bisja. Thå nêvil ewêi tåch, lokte svnne thrvch tha rêta thêra wolkum vp irtha. Alrek kêm wither ut to juwgande ånd to jolande, thet jungk folk tåch sjongande mitha gürbåm* ånd thisse overfulde luft mith sina liaflika ådam. Men thahwila thêr alrek in nocht båjada, was vrrêd lånd mith horsum ånd ridderum. Lik alle årga wêron hja helpen thrvch thjusternisse, ånd hinne glupath thrvch Linda waldis påda. To fåra Adelas dure tagon twilif mangêrtne mith twilif låmkes ånd twilif knåpa mith twilif hoklinga, en junge Saxmån birêd en wilde bufle thêr er selva fensen hêde ånd tåmad. Mith allerlêja blomma wêron hja siarad, ånd tha linnen tohnekna thêra mångêrtne wêron omborad mith gold ut-er Rêne.

Thå Adela to hira hus ut vppet slecht kêm, fol en blomrêin del vppira hole, alle juwgade herde ånd tha tothorne thêra knåpum gûldon boppa ella ut. Arme Adela, årm folk, ho kirt skil frü hir bydja. Thå thju lônge skåre ut sjocht wêre kêm er en hloth mågjara ridderum linrjucht to rinnande vp Adelas hêm. Hira tåt ånd gåde wêron jeta vppa stoppenbenke sêten. Thju dure stond êpen ånd thêr binna stand Adelbrost hira svna. As er sach ho sina eldra in frêse wêron, gripter sine bôge fon-ere wåch wêi ånd skåt nêi tha foresta thêra råwarum; this swikt ånd trulde vppet gårs del; overne twade ånd thride was en êlik lôt biskêren. Intwiska hêdon sina eldra hjara wêpne fat, ånd tagon vndyger to Jonis. Tha råwera skoldon hjam ring

---

* Gürbam. C. Niebuhr Reize enz. I. 174. Eene zakpijp bij de Egyptenaren *Sumåra el Kürbe* genoemd.

up to pleasure and merry-making, and no one thought of anything but diversion; but Wr-alda wished to teach us that watchfulness should never be relaxed. In the midst of the festivities the fog came and enveloped every place in darkness. Cheerfulness melted away, but watchfulness did not take its place. The coastguard deserted their beacons, and no one was to be seen on any of the paths. When the fog rose, the sun scarcely appeared among the clouds; but the people all came out shouting with joy, and the young folks went about singing to their bagpipes, filling the air with their melody. But while every one was intoxicated with pleasure, treachery had landed with its horses and riders. As usual, darkness had favoured the wicked, and they had slipped in through the paths of Linda's wood. Before Adela's door twelve girls led twelve lambs, and twelve boys led twelve calves. A young Saxon bestrode a wild bull which he had caught and tamed. They were decked with all kinds of flowers, and the girls' dresses were fringed with gold from the Rhine.

When Adela came out of her house, a shower of flowers fell on her head; they all cheered loudly, and the fifes of the boys were heard over everything. Poor Adela! poor people! how short will be your joy! When the procession was out of sight, a troop of Magyar soldiers rushed up to Adela's house. Her father and her husband were sitting on the steps. The door was open, and within stood Adelbrost her son. When he saw the danger of his parents, he took his bow from the wall and shot the leader of the pirates, who staggered and fell on the grass. The second and third met a similar fate. In the meantime his parents had seized their weapons, and went slowly to Jon's house. They would soon have been taken, but

---

Gürbam. C. Niebuhr, Travels, vol. i. p. 174. The bagpipe is called by the Egyptians *Sumdra el Kürbe*.

fensen ha, men Adela kêm, vppere burch hêde hja alle wêpne to hantêra lêrad, sjugun irthfêt wêre hju lông ånd hira gêrt så fêlo, thryja swikte hja tham or hjra hole ånd as er del kêm wêr en ridder gårsfallich. Follistar kêmon omme herne thêre lône wêi. Tha råwar wrdon fålath ånd fensen. Thach to lêt, en pil hêde hjra bosme trefth. Vrrêdelika Magy! In fenin was sin pint dipth ånd thêrof is hju sturven.

Thêre Burchfams Lov.

Jes ferhêmande åthe, thusande send al kumen ånd jet måra send vp wêi.

Wel, hja willath Adelas wisdom hêra.

Sekur is hju forstine, hwand hju is immer thja forste wêst.

O wach hwêrto skolde hja thjanja. Hira hemeth is linnen, hira tohnekka* wol, thåt hjv selva spon ånd wêvade. Hwêrmêi skolde hja hjra skênhêd håga. Navt mith pårlum, hwand hjra tuskar send witter; navt mith gold, hwand hjra hêr is blikkander; navt mith stêna, wel send hjra ågon saft as lamkes ågon, thach to lik sa glander thåt mån thêr skrômlik in sja ne mêi.

Men hwat kålt ik fon skên. Frya wêre wis navt skêner.

Ja åthe, Frya thêr sjugun skênhêde hêde, hwêrfon hjra toghåtera men êne elk håchstens thria urven håve. Men al wêre hju lêdlik, thach skolde hju vs djura wêsa.

Jef hju wygandlik sy. Hark åthe, Adela is thet ênge bern vsar grêvetman. Sjugun jrthfet is hju håch, jeta grâter then hjra licheme is hjra wishêd ånd hjra mod is lik bêde to sêmine.

Lok thêr, thêr wêre ênis en fênbrônd, thrju bern wêron vp jenske gråfstên sprongen. Wind blos fel. Alrek krêta ånd thju måm wêre rêdalås. Thêr kvmt Adela: ho stêitst ånd têmethste hropth hju, tragd help to lê-

---

* To hnekka, eene hooge, *tot aan de nek* reikende, japon.

Adela came. She had learned in the burgt to use all kinds of weapons. She was seven feet high, and her sword was the same length. She waved it three times over her head, and each time a knight bit the earth. Reinforcements came, and the pirates were made prisoners; but too late—an arrow had penetrated her bosom! The treacherous Magy had poisoned it, and she died of it.

The Elegy of the Burgtmaagd.

Yes, departed friend, thousands are arrived, and more are coming. They wish to hear the wisdom of Adela. Truly, she was a princess, for she had always been the leader. O Sorrow, what good can you do!

Her garments of linen and * wool she spun and wove herself. How could she add to her beauty? Not with pearls, for her teeth were more white; not with gold, for her tresses were more brilliant; not with precious stones, for her eyes, though soft as those of a lamb, were so lustrous that you could scarcely look into them. But why do I talk of beauty? Frya was certainly not more beautiful; yes, my friends, Frya, who possessed seven perfections, of which each of her daughters inherited one, or at most three. But even if she had been ugly, she would still have been dear to us. Is she warlike? Listen, my friend. Adela was the only daughter of our Grevetman. She stood seven feet high. Her wisdom exceeded her stature, and her courage was equal to both together. Here is an instance. There was once a turf-ground on fire. Three children got upon yonder gravestone. There was a furious wind. The people were all shouting, and the mother was helpless. Then came Adela. What are you all standing still here for? she cried. Try to

---

* *To knekka*, a high petticoat reaching up to the neck.

nande ånd Wr.alda skil jo krefta jêva. Thêr hipth hja nêi-t krylwod, gript'elsne trêjon, tragd en breg to makjande, nw helpath åk tha ôthera ånd tha bern send hred.

Jêrlikes kêmon tha bern hyr blomma ledsa.

Thêr kêmon thrê Fonysjar skipljuda thêr hja wrêvela wilde, men Adela kêm, hju hêde hjara hwop (hrop) hêrad, in swim slêith hju tha lêtha ånd til thju hja selva jechta skolde, thet hja vnwêrthelike manna wêron, bint hju alsêmen an en spinrok fest. Tha fêrhêmanda hêra kêmon hjara thjud askja. Tha hja sagon ho skots hja misdên wêron, kêm torn vp, thach mån tellade ho-t bêrd was.

Hwat hja forth dêdon, hja buwgdon to fåra Adela ånd keston thju slyp hyrar tohnekka.

Kvm fêrhêmande åthe, tha wald füglon fljuchtath to fåra tha fêlo forsykar. Kvm åthe så mêist hjara wishêd hêra.

By tha gråfstên hwer fon in tha lovsprêke meld wårth, is måm hira lik bigråven. Vppira gråfstên heth mån thissa worda hwryten.

NE HLAP NAVT TO HASTICH HWAND HYR LÊID ADELA.

Thju formlêre thêr is hwryten inutere wâch thêr burchtore, nis navt wither eskrêven in thåt bok thêra Adela follistar. Hwêrvmbe thet lêten is nêt ik navt to skriwand. Tha thit bok is min ajn, thêrvmbe wil ik hja thêr inna setta to wille minra mågum.

FORMLÊRE.

Alle god minnanda Fryas bern sy held. Hwand thrvch

help them, and Wr-alda will give you strength. Then she ran to the Krylwood and got some elder branches, of which she made a bridge. The others then came to assist her, and the children were saved. The children bring flowers to the place every year. There came once three Phœnician sailors, who began to ill-treat the children, when Adela, having heard their screams, beat the scoundrels till they were insensible, and then, to prove to them what miserable wretches they were, she tied them all three to a spindle.

The foreign lords came to look after their people, and when they saw how ridiculously they had been treated they were very angry, till they were told what had happened. Upon that they bowed themselves before Adela, and kissed the hem of her garment. But come, distant living friend. The birds of the forest fled before the numerous visitors. Come, friend, and you shall hear her wisdom. By the gravestone of which mention has already been made her body is buried. Upon the stone the following words are inscribed:—

TREAD SOFTLY, FOR HERE LIES ADELA.

The old legend which is written on the outside wall of the city tower is not written in "The Book of Adela's Followers." Why this has been neglected I do not know; but this book is my own, so I will put it in out of regard to my relations.

The Oldest Doctrine.

Hail to all the well-intentioned children of Frya!

tham skil et sêlich wertha vp jrtha. Lêr ånd kêth to tha
folkum. Wr.alda is thet alderaldesta jeftha overaldesta,
hwand thet skop alla thinga. Wr.alda is ella in ella,
hwand thet is êvg ånd vnendlik. Wr.alda is overal ain-
wardich, men narne to bisja, thêrvmbe wårth thet wêsa
gåst hêten. Al hwat wi fon him sja müge send tha skepsela thêr thrvch sin lêva kvme ånd wither henne ga,
hwand inut Wr.alda kvmath alle thinga ånd kêrath alle
thinga. Fon ut Wr.alda kvmth t anfang ånd et ende, alra
thinga gêith in im vppa. Wr.alda is thet êne ella mach-
tige wêsa, hwand alle ôre macht is fon him lênad ånd
kêrath to him wither. In ut Wr.alda kvmath alle krefta
ånd alle krefta kêrath to him wither. Thêrvmbe is hi
allêna theth skeppande wêsa ånd thêr nis nawet eskêpen
buta him.

Wr.alda lêide êvge setma thet is êwa in al et skêpne,
ånd thêr ne send nên gode setma jeftha hja moton thêrnêi
tavlikt wêsa. Men afskên ella in Wr.alda sy, tha boshêd
thêra månniska nis navt fon him. Boshêd kvmth thrvch
lômhêd vndigerhed ånd domhêd. Thêrvmbe kån hju wel
tha månniska skåda, Wr.alda nimmer. Wr.alda is thju
wishêd, ånd tha êwa thêr hju tavlikt heth, send tha boka
werût wy lêra müge, ånd thêr nis nêne wishêd to findande
ner to garjande buta tham. Tha månniska mügon fêlo
thinga sja, men Wr.alda sjath alle thinga. Tha månniska
mügon fêlo thinga lêra, men Wr.alda wêt alle thinga.
Tha månniska mügon fêlo thinga vntslûta, men to fåra
Wr.alda is ella êpned. Tha månniska send månnalik
ånd berlik, men Wr.alda skept bêde. Tha månniska
minnath ånd håtath, tha Wr.alda is allêna rjuchtfêrdich.
Thêrvmbe is Wr.alda allêne god, ånd thêr ne send nêne
goda bûta him. Mith thet Jol wandelath ånd wixlat
allet eskêpne, men god is allêna vnforanderlik. Thruch
that Wr.alda god is, alsa ne mei hi åk navt foranderja;

Through them the earth shall become holy. Learn and announce to the people Wr-alda is the ancient of ancients, for he created all things. Wr-alda is all in all, for he is eternal and everlasting. Wr-alda is omnipresent but invisible, and therefore is called a spirit. All that we can see of him are the created beings who come to life through him and go again, because from Wr-alda all things proceed and return to him. Wr-alda is the beginning and the end. Wr-alda is the only almighty being, because from him all other strength comes, and returns to him. Therefore he alone is the creator, and nothing exists without him. Wr-alda established eternal principles, upon which the laws of creation were founded, and no good laws could stand on any other foundation. But although everything is derived from Wr-alda, the wickedness of men does not come from him. Wickedness comes from heaviness, carelessness, and stupidity; therefore they may well be injurious to men, but never to Wr-alda. Wr-alda is wisdom, and the laws that he has made are the books from which we learn, nor is any wisdom to be found or gathered but in them. Men may see a great deal, but Wr-alda sees everything. Men can learn a great deal, but Wr-alda knows everything. Men can discover much, but to Wr-alda everything is open. Mankind are male and female, but Wr-alda created both. Mankind love and hate, but Wr-alda alone is just. Therefore Wr-alda is good, and there is no good without him. In the progress of time all creation alters and changes, but goodness alone is unalterable; and since Wr-alda is good, he cannot

ånd thrvch thet er bilywath, thêrvmbe is hy allêna wêsa ånd al et ora skin.

Thet othera dêl Fonre Formlêr.

Emong Findas folk send wanwysa, thêr thrvch hjara overfindingrikhêd alsa årg send, thåt hja hjara selva wis måkja ånd tha inewida bitjuga, thåt hja thet besta dêl send fon Wr.alda; thåt hjara gåst thet beste dêl is fon Wr.aldas gåst ånd thet Wr.alda allêna mêi thånkja thrvch helpe hjaris bryn.*

Thåt aider skepsle en dêl is fon Wr.aldas vnendlik wêsa; thåt håvon hja fon vs gåbad.

Men hjara falxe rêdne ånd hjara tåmlåse båchfarenhêd heth ra vppen dwålwêi brocht. Wêre hjara gåst Wr.aldas gåst, så skolde Wr.alda êl dvm wêsa in stêde fon licht and wis. Hwand hjara gåst slåvth him selva immer of vmbe skêne bylda to måkjande, thêr y åfternêi anbid. Men Findas folk is en årg folk, hwand afskên tha wanwysa thêra hjara selva wis måkja thåt hja drochtne send, sa håvon hja to fåra tha vnewida falxa drochtne eskêpen, to kêthande allerwêikes, thåt thissa drochtne Wr.alda eskêpen håve, mith al hwat thêr inne is; gyriga drochtne fvl nyd ånd torn, tham êrath ånd thjanath willath wêsa thrvch tha månniska, thêr blod ånd offer willa ånd skåt askja. Men thi wanwisa falxa manna, tham hjara selva godis skalka jeftha prestera nôma lêta, bürath ånd såmnath ånd gethath aldam to fåra drochtne thêr er navt ne send, vmbet selva to bihaldande. Aldam bidrywath hja mith en rum emod, thrvchdam hja hjara selva drochtne wåne, thêr an ninman andert skeldich ne send. Send thêr svme tham hjara renka froda ånd bår måkja, alsa wrdon hja thrvch hjara rakkera fåt ånd vmbira laster vrbarnad, ella mith fêlo ståtska plêgum, hjara falxa drochtne to-n êre. Men in trvth,

---

* Cf. Hegel a. h. l.

change. As he endures, he alone exists; everything else is show.

The Second Part of the Oldest Doctrine.

Among Finda's people there are false teachers, who, by their over-inventiveness, have become so wicked that they make themselves and their adherents believe that they are the best part of Wr-alda, that their spirit is the best part of Wr-alda's spirit, and that Wr-alda can only think by the help of their brains.

That every creature is a part of Wr-alda's eternal being, *that* they have stolen from us; but their false reasoning and ungovernable pride have brought them on the road to ruin. If their spirit was Wr-alda's spirit, then Wr-alda would be very stupid, instead of being sensible and wise; for their spirit labours to create beautiful statues, which they afterwards worship. Finda's people are a wicked people, for although they presumptuously pretend among themselves that they are gods, they proclaim the unconsecrated false gods, and declare everywhere that these idols created the world and all that therein is—greedy idols, full of envy and anger, who desire to be served and honoured by the people, and who exact bloody sacrifices and rich offerings; but these presumptuous and false men, who call themselves God's servants and priests, receive and collect everything in the name of the idols that have no real existence, for their own benefit.

They do all this with an easy conscience, as they think themselves gods not answerable to any one. If there are some who discover their tricks and expose them, they hand them over to the executioners to be burnt for their calumnies, with solemn ceremonies in honour of the false gods;

allêna vmbe thât hja ra navt skâda ne skolde. Til thju vsa bern nw wêpned müge wêsa tojenst hjara drochtenlika lêre, alsa hâgon tha fâmna hjam fon buta to lêrande hwat hyr skil folgja.

Wr.alda was êr alle thinga, ånd nêi alle thinga skil er wêsa. Wr.alda is alsa êvg ånd hi is vnendlik, thervmb nis thêr nawet buta him. Thrvch ut Wr.aldas lêva warth tid ånd alle thinga bern, ånd sin lêva nimth tid ånd alle thinga wêi. Thissa sêka moton klêr ånd bâr mâkad wrda by alle wisa, sâ thåt hja-t an ôthera bithjuta ånd biwisa müge. Is-t sâ får wnnen, sa sêith mån forther: Hwat thus vsa ommefang treft, alsa send wy en dêl fon Wr.aldas vnendelik wêsa, alsa tha ommefang fon al et eskêpne, thach hwat angâ vsa dânte, vsa ainskipa, vsa gåst ånd al vsa bithånkinga, thissa ne hêra navt to thet wêsa. Thit ella send fljuchtiga thinga tham thrvch Wr.aldas lêva forskina, thach thêr thrvch sin wishêd sâdâne ånd navt owers navt ne forskina. Men thrvchdam sin lêva stêdes forthga, alsa ne mêi thêr nawet vppa sin stêd navt bilywa. Thêrvmbe forwixlath alle eskêpne thinga fon stêd, fon dânte ånd åk fon thånkwisa. Thervmbe ne mêi irtha selva, ner eng skepsle ni sedsa: ik ben, men wel ik was. Ak ne mêi nên månniska navt ne sedsa ik thånk, men blåt, ik thochte. Thi knåp is grâter ånd owers as tha-r bern wêre. Hy heth ora gêrtne, tochta ånd thånkwisa. Thi man en tât is ånd thånkth owers as thâ-r knåp wêre. Êvin tha alda fon dêgum. Thât wêt allera mannelik. Sâhwersa allera mannalik nw wêt ånd jechta mot, thåt hy alon wixlath, sâ mot hy åk bijechta, that er jahweder âgeblik wixlath, åk thahwila-r sêid: ik ben, ånd thåt sina thånk bylda wixle, tha hwile-r sêid: ik thånk.

Instêde thåt wy tha årga Findas althus vnwerthlik afternêi snakka ånd kålta, ik ben, jeftha wel, ik ben thet beste dêl Wr.aldas, ja thrvch vs allêna mêi-r thånkja,

but really in order to save themselves. In order that our children may be protected against their idolatrous doctrine, the duty of the maidens is to make them learn by heart the following: Wr-alda existed before all things, and will endure after all things. Wr-alda is also eternal and everlasting, therefore nothing exists without him. From Wr-alda's life sprang time and all living things, and his life takes away time and every other thing. These things must be made clear and manifest in every way, so that they can be made clear and comprehensible to all. When we have learned thus much, then we say further: In what regards our existence, we are a part of Wr-alda's everlasting being, like the existence of all created beings; but as regards our form, our qualities, our spirit, and all our thoughts, these do not belong to the being. All these are passing things which appear through Wr-alda's life, and which appear through his wisdom, and not otherwise; but whereas his life is continually progressing, nothing can remain stationary, therefore all created things change their locality, their form, and their thoughts. So neither the earth nor any other created object can say, I am; but rather, I was. So no man can say, I think; but rather, I thought. The boy is greater and different from the child; he has different desires, inclinations, and thoughts. The man and father feels and thinks differently from the boy, the old man just the same. Everybody knows that. Besides, everybody knows and must acknowledge that he is now changing, that he changes every minute even while he says, I am, and that his thoughts change even while he says, I think. Instead, then, of imitating Finda's wicked people, and saying, I am the best part of Wr-alda, and through us alone he can think,

så willath wy kêtha wral ånd allerwêikes wêr et nêdlik sy:
wy Fryas bern send forskinsla thrvch Wr.aldas lêva; by-t
anfang min ånd blåt, thach immer wårthande ånd nåkande
to fvlkvmenlikhêd, svnder å sa god to wrda as Wr.alda
selva. Vsa gåst nis navt Wr.aldas gåst, hi is thêrfon
allêna en afskinsle. Tha Wr.alda vs skop, heth er vs in
thrvch sine wishêd-bryn-sintûga, hūgia ånd fêlo goda ainskipa lênad. Hyrmêi mugon wy sina êwa, bitrachta.
Thêrof mügon wy lêra ånd thêrvr mügon wy rêda, ella
ånd allêna to vs ain held. Hêde Wr.alda vs nêne sinna
jêven, sa ne skolde wy narne of nêta ånd wy skolde jeta
reddalasser as en sêkwale wêsa, thêr forthdryven wårth
thrvch ebbe ånd thrvch flod.

Thit Stat vp Skrivfilt Skrêven. Tal and Andworde ora Famna to-n Forbyld.

En vnsels gyrich mån kêm to bårande by Tråst thêr fåm
wêre to Stavia. Hy sêide vnwêder hêde sin hus wêi brocht.
Hy hêde to Wr.alda bêden, men Wr.alda nêdim nêne helpe
lênad. Bist en åfte Fryas, frêje Tråst. Fon elder t elder,
andere thene mån. Thån sêide hju wil ik åwet in thin
mod sêja in bitrouwa, thåt et kyma groja ånd früchda
jêva mêi. Forth sprêk hju ånde kêth. Thå Frya bern
was, stand vs moder naked ånd blåt, vnbihod to jenst tha
strêlum thêre svnne. Ninman macht hju frêja ånd thêr
wêre ninman thêr hja help macht lêna. Thå gvng Wr.alda
to ånd wrochte in hjara mod nigung ånd liavde anggost ånd
skrik. Hju sach rondomme, hjara nigung kås thet beste ånd
hju sochte skul vndera wårande linda. Men rêin kêm ånd
t onhlest wêre thåt hju wet wrde. Thach hju hêde sjan

we proclaim everywhere where it is necessary, We, Frya's children, exist through Wr-alda's life—in the beginning mean and base, but always advancing towards perfection without ever attaining the excellence of Wr-alda himself. Our spirit is not Wr-alda's spirit, it is merely a shadow of it. When Wr-alda created us, he lent us his wisdom, brains, organs, memory, and many other good qualities. By this means we are able to contemplate his creatures and his laws; by this means we can learn and can speak of them always, and only for our own benefit. If Wr-alda had given us no organs, we should have known nothing, and been more irrational than a piece of sea-weed driven up and down by the ebb and flood.

THIS IS WRITTEN ON PARCHMENT—"SKRIVFILT." SPEECH AND ANSWER TO OTHER MAIDENS AS AN EXAMPLE.

An unsociable, avaricious man came to complain to Troost, who was the maid of Stavia. He said a thunder-storm had destroyed his house. He had prayed to Wr-alda, but Wr-alda had given him no help. Are you a true Frisian? Troost asked. From father and forefathers, replied the man. Then she said, I will sow something in your conscience, in confidence that it will take root, grow, and bear fruit. She continued, When Frya was born, our mother stood naked and bare, unprotected from the rays of the sun. She could ask no one, and there was no one who could give her any help. Then Wr-alda wrought in her conscience inclination and love, anxiety and fright. She looked round her, and her inclination chose the best. She sought a hiding-place under the sheltering lime-trees, but the rain came, and the difficulty was that she got wet. She had seen,

ho thet wêter to tha hellanda blâdar of drupte. Nw mâkade hju en hrof mith hellanda sidum, vp stôka mâkade hju tham. Men stornewind kêm ånd blos rein thêr vnder. Nw hêde hja sjan thåt tha stam hly jef, åfter gong hja to ånd mâkade en wâch fon plâga ånd sâdum, thet forma an êne syda ånd forth an alle syda. Storne wind kêm to bek jeta wodander as to fora ånd blos thju hrof ewêi. Men hju ne bârade navt over Wr.alda ner to jenst Wr.alda. Men hja mâkade en reitne hrof ånd leide stêne thêr vppa. Bifvnden håvande ho sêr thet dvath vmb allêna to tobbande, alsa bithjude hju hira bern ho ånd hwêrvmbe hju alsa hêde dên. Thissa wrochton ånd tochton to sêmine. A sadenera wise send wy an hûsa kêmen mith stoppenbånkum, en slecht ånd warande linda with tha svnnestrêlum. To tha lesta håvon hja en burch mâkad ånd forth alle ôthera. Nis thin hus thus navt sterk noch wêst, alsa mot i trachda vmbet ôre bêter to mâkjande. Min hus wêre sterk enoch, sêider, men thet hâge wêter heth et vp bêrad ånd stornewind heth et ore dên. Hwêr stand thin hus thån, frêje Tråst. Alingen thêre Rêne, andere thene man. Ne stand et thån navt vppen nol jeftha therp, frêje Tråst. Nean sêider, min hus stand ênsum by tha overe, allêna håv ik et buwad, men ik ne macht thêr allêna nên therp to makane. Ik wist wel, sêide Tråst, tha fâmna håv et my meld. Thv hest al thin lêva en grûwel had an tha månniska, ut frêse thåtste awet jêva jeftha dva moste to fara hjam. Thach thêr mitha ne mêi mån navt fêr ne kvma. Hwand Wr.alda thêr mild is, kêrath him fona gyriga. Fåsta het vs rêden ånd buppa tha dura fon alle burgum is t in stên ut wryten: bist årg båtsjochtig sêide Fåsta, bihod thån jvwe nêsta, bithjod thån jvwe nêsta, help thån juwe nesta, så skilun hja t thi witherdva. Is i thina rêd navt god noch, ik nêt får thi nên bêtera. Skåmråd wårth then mån ånd hi drupte stolkes hinne.

how the water ran down the pendent leaves; so she made a roof of leaves fastened with sticks, but the wind blew the rain under it. She observed that the stem would afford protection. She then built a wall of sods, first on one side, and then all round. The wind grew stronger and blew away the roof, but she made no complaint of Wr-alda. She made a roof of rushes, and put stones upon it. Having found how hard it is to toil alone, she showed her children how and why she had done it. They acted and thought as she did. This is the way in which we became possessed of houses and porches, a street, and lime-trees to protect us from the rays of the sun. At last we have built a citadel, and all the rest. If your house is not strong enough, then you must try and make another. My house was strong enough, he said, but the flood and the wind destroyed it. Where did your house stand? Troost asked. On the bank of the Rhine, he answered. Did it not stand on a knoll? Troost asked. No, said the man; my house stood alone on the bank. I built it alone, but I could not alone make a hillock. I knew it, Troost answered; the maidens told me. All your life you have avoided your neighbours, fearing that you might have to give or do something for them; but one cannot get on in the world in that way, for Wr-alda, who is kind, turns away from the niggardly. Fâsta has advised us, and it is engraved in stone over all our doors. If you are selfish, distrustful towards your neighbours, teach your neighbours, help your neighbours, and they will return the same to you. If this advice is not good enough for you, I can give you no better. The man blushed for shame, and slunk away.

Nw wil ik selva skriwa êrost fon over min Burch and than over hwat ik hav muge sjan.

Min burch lêid an-t north-ende thêre Liudgârda. Thju tore heth sex syda. Thrya thrittich fêt is hju hâch. Flât fon boppa. En lyth huske thêr vppa, hwâna mân tha stâra bisjath. An aider syd thêre tore stât en hus, long thrya hondred, brêd thrya sjugun fêt, êlika hâch bihalva thju hrof, thêr rondlik is. Altham fon hyrbakken stên, ând fon buta ne send nênen ôthera. Om tha burch is en hringdik, thêrom en grâft diap thrya sjugun fêt, wyd thrya twilif fêt. Siath hwa fonêre tore del, sa siath hi thju dânte fon et Jol. Vppa grvnd twisk tha sûdlika hûsa thêre, send allerlêja krûda fon hêinde ând fêr, thêrof moton tha fâmna tha krefta lêra. Twisk tha nortlika hûsa is allêna fjeld. Tha thrju nortlika hûsa send fol kêren ând ôther bihof. Twa sûdar send to fâra tha fâmkes vmbe to skola ând to hêma. Thet sûdlikoste hus is thêre Burchfâm his hêm. Inna tore hangt thju foddik. Tha wagar thêre tore send mith kestlika stêna smukad. In vppa thêre sûderwach is thêne Tex wrytten. An tha fêre syde thêra finth mân thju formlêre; anna winstere syde tha êwa. Tha ora sêka finth mân vppa ôra thrja. Tojenst tha dik by-t hus thêr fâm stêt thju owne ând thju molmâk thrvch fjuwer bufla kroden. Buta vsa burchwal is-t hêm, thêr vppa tha burchhêra ânda wêrar hême. Thju ringdik thêra is en stonde grât, nên stjurar, men svnna stonde, hwêrfon twya twilif vppen etmelde kvma. In vpper binnasyde fona dik is en flât, fif fêt vndera krûn. Thêr vppa send thrya hondred krânboga, todekt mith wod ând lêther. Bihalva tha hûsa thêra inhêmar send thêr binna alingne tha

Now I will write myself, first about my Citadel, and then about what I have been able to see.

My city lies near the north end of the Liudgaarde. The tower has six sides, and is ninety feet high, flat-roofed, with a small house upon it out of which they look at the stars. On either side of the tower is a house three hundred feet long, and twenty-one feet broad, and twenty-one feet high, besides the roof, which is round. All this is built of hard-baked bricks, and outside there is nothing else. The citadel is surrounded by a dyke, with a moat thirty-six feet broad and twenty-one feet deep. If one looks down from the tower, he sees the form of the Juul. In the ground among the houses on the south side all kinds of native and foreign herbs grow, of which the maidens must study the qualities. Among the houses on the north side there are only fields. The three houses on the north are full of corn and other necessaries; the two houses on the south are for the maidens to live in and keep school. The most southern house is the dwelling of the Burgtmaagd. In the tower hangs the lamp. The walls of the tower are decorated with precious stones. On the south wall the Tex is inscribed. On the right side of this are the formulæ, and on the other side the laws; the other things are found upon the three other sides. Against the dyke, near the house of the Burgtmaagd, stand the oven and the mill, worked by four oxen. Outside the citadel wall is the place where the Burgtheeren and the soldiers live. The fortification outside is an hour long—not a seaman's hour, but an hour of the sun, of which twenty-four go to a day. Inside it is a plain five feet below the top. On it are three hundred crossbows covered with wood and leather.

Besides the houses of the inhabitants, there are along

dik jeta thrya twilif nêdhûsa to fâra tha omhêmar. Thet fjeld thjanath to kåmp ånd to wêde. Anna sûdsyde fon tha bûtenste hringdik is thju Lindgårde omtûnad thrvch thet gråte Lindawald. Hjara dånte is thrju hernich, thet brêde buta, til thju svnne thêr in sia mêi. Hwand thêr send fêlo fêrlandeska thrêja ånd blommen thrvch tha stjurar mith brocht. Alsa thju dånte vsar burch is, send alle ôthera; thach vs-is is thju gråteste; men thi fon Texland is tha aldergråteste. Thju tore fon Fryasburch is alsa håch thåt hju tha wolka torent, nêi thêre tore is al et ôthera.

By vs vppa burch ist alsa dêlad. Sjugun jonge fåmna wåkath by thêre foddik. Aider wåk thrja stonda. In ha ôre tid moton hja huswårk dva, lêra ånd slêpa. Send hja sjugun jêr wåkande wêsen, alsa send hja fry. Thån mügon hja emong tha månniska gå, vp-ra sêd to letane ånd rêd to jêvane. Is hwa thrju jêr fåm wêst, så mêi hju alto met mith tha alda fåmna mith gå.

Thi skrywer mot tha fåmkes lêra lêsa, skrywa ånd rêkenja. Tha grysa jeftha grêva moton lêra hjam rjucht ånd plicht, sêdkunda, krûdkunda, hêlkunda, skêdnesa, tellinga ånd sanga, bijunka allerlêja thinga thêr hjam nêdlik send vmbe rêd to jêva. Thju Burchfåm mot lêra hjam ho hja thêrmith to wårk gå mota by thå månniska. Êr en Burchfåm hjra stêd innimt, mot hju thrvch thet lånd fåra en fvl jêr. Thrê grêva burchhêra ånd thrja alda fåmna gan mith hiri mitha. Alsa is-t åk my gvngon. Min fårt is alingen thêre Rêne wêst, thjus kåd opward, alingen thêre ôre syde ofward. Ho håger ik upkêm, to årmer likte mi tha månniska. Wral inna Rêne hêde mån utstekka makad. Thet sôn thåt thêr ain kêm, wr mith wêter wr skêpfachta gåten vmbe gold to winnande. Men tha mångêrta ne drogon thêr nêne golden krone fon. Êr wêron thêr

the inside of the dyke thirty-six refuge-houses for the people who live in the neighbourhood. The field serves for a camp and for a meadow. On the south side of the outer fortification is the Liudgaarde, enclosed by the great wood of lime-trees. Its shape is three-cornered, with the widest part outside, so that the sun may shine in it, for there are a great number of foreign trees and flowers brought by the seafarers. All the other citadels are the same shape as ours, only not so large; but the largest of all is that of Texland. The tower of the Fryaburgt is so high that it rends the sky, and all the rest is in proportion to the tower. In our citadel this is the arrangement: Seven young maidens attend to the lamp; each watch is three hours. In the rest of their time they do housework, learn, and sleep. When they have watched for seven years, they are free; then they may go among the people, to look after their morals and to give advice. When they have been three years maidens, they may sometimes accompany the older ones.

The writer must teach the girls to read, to write, and to reckon. The elders, or "Greva," must teach them justice and duty, morals, botany, and medicine, history, traditions, and singing, besides all that may be necessary for them to give advice. The Burgtmaagd must teach them how to set to work when they go among the people. Before a Burgtmaagd can take office, she must travel through the country a whole year. Three grey-headed Burgtheeren and three old maidens must go with her. This was the way that I did. My journey was along the Rhine—on this side up, and on the other side down. The higher I went, the poorer the people seemed to be. Everywhere about the Rhine the people dug holes, and the sand that was got out was poured with water over fleeces to get the gold, but the girls did not wear golden crowns of it. Formerly they were

mâr wêst, men sont wi Skênland miste, send hja nêi tha berga gvngon. Thêr delvath hja yserirtha, thêr hja yser of mâkja. Boppa thêre Rêne twisk thet berchta, thêr hâv ik Mârsâta sjan. Tha Mârsâta thât send mânniska thêr invppa mâra hêma. Hjara husa send vp pâlum buwad. Thât is vret wilde kwik ânda bose mânniska. Thêr send wolva, bâra ând swârte grislika lawa.* And hja send tha swetsar† jeftha pâlingar fonda hêinde Krêkalandar, thêra Kâlta folgar ând tha vrwildere Twiskar, alle gyrich nêi râv ând but. Tha Mârsâta helpath hjara selva mith fiska ând jâga. Tha huda wrdat thrvch tha wiva tomâkad ând birhet mith skors fon berkum. Tha litha huda saft lik fâmnafilt. Thju burchfâm et Fryasburch‡ sêide vs thât hja gode ênfalde mânniska weron. Thach hêd ik hja êr navt sprêken hêred, ik skolde mênath hâve thât hja nên Fryas wêre, men wilda, sâ bryst sâgon hja ut. Hjara fachta ând kruda wrdon thrvch tha Rênhêmar vrwandelath ând thrvch tha stjurar buta brocht. Alingen thêre Rêne wêr et alên, til Lydasburch.§ Thêr was en grâte flyt.‖ Invppa thisra flyt wêron âk mânniska, thêr husa vp pâla hêde. Men thât nêr nên Fryas folk, men thât wêron swarte ând bruna mânniska, thêr thjanath hêde to rojar vmbe tha butafârar to honk to helpane. Hja moston thêr bilywa til thju thju flâte wither wêi brûda.

To tha lersta kêmon wi to-t Alderga. By-t suderhâva-hâved stêt thju Wâraburch, en stênhus, thêrin send aller-lêja skulpa, hulka, wêpne ând klathar wârad, fon fêre landum, thrvch tha stjurar mith brocht. En fjardêl dâna is-t Alderga. En grâte flyt omborad mith lothum, husa ând gârdum ella riklik sjarad. Invpper flyt lêi en grâte flâte rêd, mith fônon fon allerlêja farwa. Et Fryas dêi hon-gon tha skilda omma tha borda to. Svme blikton

---

* Leeuwen in Europa, Herodotus, VII. 125.
† Swetsar, Switsers.   ‡ Fryasburch, Freiburg.
§ Lydasburch, Leiden, de burcht.   ‖ Flyt, jeftha mâre, de Mare.

more numerous, but since we lost Schoonland they have gone up to the mountains. There they dig ore and make iron. Above the Rhine among the mountains I have seen Marsaten. The Marsaten are people who live on the lakes. Their houses are built upon piles, for protection from the wild beasts and wicked people. There are wolves, bears, and horrible lions.* Then come the Swiss,† the nearest to the frontiers of the distant Italians, the followers of Kalta and the savage Twiskar, all greedy for robbery and booty. The Marsaten gain their livelihood by fishing and hunting. The skins are sewn together by the women, and prepared with birch bark. The small skins are as soft as a woman's skin. The Burgtmaagd at Fryasburgt (Freiburg)‡ told us that they were good, simple people; but if I had not heard her speak of them first, I should have thought that they were not Frya's people, they looked so impudent. Their wool and herbs are bought by the Rhine people, and taken to foreign countries by the ship captains. Along the other side of the Rhine it was just the same as at Lydasburcht (Leiden).§ There was a great river or lake, and upon this lake also there were people living upon piles. But they were not Frya's people; they were black and brown men who had been employed as rowers to bring home the men who had been making foreign voyages, and they had to stay there till the fleet went back.

At last we came to Alderga. At the head of the south harbour lies the Waraburgt, built of stone, in which all kinds of clothes, weapons, shells, and horns are kept, which were brought by the sea-people from distant lands. A quarter of an hour's distance from there is Alderga, a great river surrounded by houses, sheds, and gardens, all richly decorated. In the river lay a great fleet ready, with banners of all sorts of colours. On Frya's day the shields were hung on board likewise. Some shone

---

* Lions in Europe, see Herodotus, vii. 125.
† Swetsar are Swiss. ‡ Fryasburch is Freiburg.
§ Lydasburch is Leyden, the city. ‖ *Flyt, jeftha mâre*, is a lake or sea.

lik svnna. Tha skilda thêr witking ånd thêra skolta bi tha nachtum wêron mith gold vmborad. Abefta thêre flyt was en gråft gråven, to hlåpande dåna alingen thêre burch Forâna* ånd forth mith en ênga muda† in sê. To fâra thêre flâte wêre thit tha utgvng ånd et Fly tha ingvng. A bêde syda thêre gråft send skêne husa mith hel blikanda farwa målad. Tha gårdne send mit altid grêne hågvm omtunad. Ik håv thêr wiva sian, thêr filtne tohnekna drogon as t skriffilt wêre. Lik to Stavere wêron tha mångêrtne mith golden kronum vppira holum ånd mith hringum‡ om årma ånd fêt sjarad. Sudward fon Forâna lêid Alkmârum. Alkmârum is en mâre jefta flyt, thêrin lêid en êland, vppa thåt êland moton tha swarte ånd bruna månniska hwila êvin as to Lydahisburch. Thju Burchfåm fon Forâna sêide my, thåt tha burchhêra dêistik to-rå gvngon vmb ra to lêrande, hwat åfte frydom sy, ånd ho tha månniska an thêre minne agon to lêvane vmbe sêjen to winnande fon Wr.aldas gåst. Was thêr hwa thêr hêra wilde ånd bigripa machte, sa wårth er halden, alont er fvl lêrad wêre. Thåt wrde dên vmbe tha fêrhêmande folka wis to måkane, ånd vmbe vral åtha to winnande. Êr hêd ik anda Såxanamarka to thêr burch Månnagårda forda§ wêst. Thach thêr hêd ik mår skåmelhêd sjan, as-k hyr rikdom spêrde. Hju andere: så hwersa thêr an da Såxanamarka en frêjar kvmath en mangêrte to bi frêjande, alsa frêjath tha mångêrtne thêr, kanst thin hus fry wêra tojenst tha bannane Twisklandar, håst nach nêne fålad, ho fêlo bufle håst al fånsen ånd ho fêlo båra ånd wolva huda håst ål vppa thêre mårk brocht? Dåna ist kvmen thåt tha Saxmanna thju buw anda wiva vrlêten håve. Thåt fon hvndred to sêmine nên êne lêsa mêi ner skriwa ne kån. Dåna is-t kvmen, thåt nimman nên sprêk vppa sin skild neth, men blåt en mislikande dånte fon en diar, thåt er fålad

---

* Forana, Vroonen.   † Engamuda, Egmond.
‡ Diod. Sic. V. 27, van de Galliers.   § Mannagårdaforda, Munster.

like the sun. The shields of the sea-king and the admiral were bordered with gold. From the river a canal was dug going past the citadel Forana (Vroonen), with a narrow outlet to the sea. This was the egress of the fleet; the Fly was the ingress. On both sides of the river are fine houses built, painted in bright colours. The gardens are all surrounded by green hedges. I saw there women wearing felt tunics, as if it were writing felt.[1] Just as at Staveren, the girls wore golden crowns on their heads, and rings on their arms and ankles. To the south of Forana lies Alkmarum. Alkmarum is a lake or river in which there is an island. On this island the black and brown people must remain, the same as at Lydasburgt. The Burgtmaagd of Forana told me that the burgtheeren go every day to teach them what real freedom is, and how it behoves men to live in order to obtain the blessing of Wr-alda's spirit. If there was any one who was willing to listen and could comprehend, he was kept there till he was fully taught. That was done in order to instruct the distant people, and to make friends everywhere. I had been before in the Saxenmarken, at the Mannagardaforde castle (Munster). There I saw more poverty than I could discover wealth here. She answered: So whenever at the Saxenmarken a young man courts a young girl, the girls ask: Can you keep your house free from the banished Twisklanders? Have you ever killed any of them? How many cattle have you already caught, and how many bear and wolfskins have you brought to market? And from this it comes that the Saxons have left the cultivation of the soil to the women, that not one in a hundred can read or write; from this it comes, too, that no one has a motto on his shield, but only a misshapen form of some animal that he has killed;

---

[1] *Felt*, very thin and compressed, with a smooth surface.
* Forana is Vroonen. † Engamuda is Egmond.
‡ Diodorus Siculus, v. 27, on the Gauls. § Mannagárdaforda is Munster.

heth. And åndlik, dåna is-t kvmen, thåt hja sêr wichandlik ewrden send, men to met êvin dvm send as et kwik, thåt hja fånsa, ånd êvin erm as tha Twisklåndar, hwêr mith hja, orloge. To fåra Fryas folk is irtha ånd sê eskêpen. Al vsa rinstråma runath vppa sê to. Thåt Lydas folk ånd thåt Findas folk skil ekkorum vrdelgja, ånd wy moton tha lêthoga landa bifolka. In-t fon ånd omme fåra lêid vs held. Wilst nw thåt tha boppalånder dêl håve an vsa rikdom ånd wisdom, så skil ik thi en rêd jêva. Lêt et tha mangêrtne to wênhêd wrde hjara frêjar to frêjande, êr hja ja segsa : hwêr håst al in wralda ommefåren, hwad kånst thin bern tella wra fêra landa ånd wra fêrhêmanda folka? Dvath hja alsa, så skilun tha wickandlika knåpa to vs kvma. Hja skilun wiser wårtha ånd rikkår ånd wi ne skilun nên bihof longer navt nåve an thåt wla thjud. Tha jongste thêr fåmna fon thêra thêr by mi wêron, kêm uta Saxsanamarka wêi. As wi nw to hongk kêmon, heth hju orlovi frêjad vmbe nêi hjra hus to gåne. Afternêi is hju thêr Burchfåm wrden, ånd dåna is-t kvmen thåt er hjudêga så felo Saxmånna by tha stjurar fåre.

ENDE FON THET APOLLONIA BOK.

and lastly, from this comes also that they are very warlike, but sometimes as stupid as the beasts that they catch, and as poor as the Twisklanders with whom they go to war. The earth and the sea were made for Frya's people. All our rivers run into the sea. The Lydas people and the Findas people will exterminate each other, and we must people the empty countries. In movement and sailing is our prosperity. If you wish the highlanders to share our riches and wisdom, I will give you a piece of advice. Let the girls, when they are asked to marry, before they say yes, ask their lovers: What parts of the world have you travelled in? What can you tell your children about distant lands and distant people? If they do this, then the young warriors will come to us; they will become wiser and richer, and we shall have no occasion to deal with those nasty people. The youngest of the maids who were with me came from the Saxenmarken. When we came back she asked leave to go home. Afterwards she became Burgtmaagd there, and that is the reason why in these days so many of our sailors are Saxons.

END OF APOLLONIA'S BOOK.

THA SKRIFTA FON FRETHORIK AND WILJOW.

Min nôm is Frêthorik to nomath oera Linda, thât wil segsa ovir tha Linda. To Ljudwardja bin ik to Asga kêren. Ljudwardja is en ny thorp, binna thene ringdik fon thêr burch Ljudgarda, hwêrfon tha nôma an vnêr kvmen is. Vnder mina tida is er fül bêred. Fül hêd ik thêr vr skrêven, men âfternêi send mi âk fêlo thinga meld. Fon ên ând ôther wil ik en skêdnese âfter thit bok skrywa, tha goda mânniska to-n êre tha ârga to vnêre.

In min jüged hêrd ik grêdwird alomme, ârge tid kêm, ârge tid was kvmen, Frya hêd vs lêton, hjra wâkfâmkes, hêde hju abefta halden, hwand drochten likande bylda wêron binna vsa lândpâla fvnden.

Ik brônde fon nysgyr vmbe thi bylda to bisjan. In vsa bûrt strompele en ôld fâmke to tha husa uta in, immer to kêthande vr ârge tid. Ik gryde hja ling syde. Hju strik mi omme kin to. Nw wrd ik drist ând frêje jef hju mi ârge tid ând tha bylda rêis wisa wilde. Hju lakte godlik ând brocht mi vpper burch. En grêve mân frêje my jef ik al lêsa ând skrywa kv. Nê sêid ik. Thân most êrost to ga ând lêra, sêid-er owers ne mêi-t jow navt wysen wrde. Dystik gvng ik bi tha skriwer lêra. Acht jêr lêtter hêrd ik, vsa burchfâm hêde hordom bidryven ând svme burchhêra hêdon vrrêd plêgad mith tha Magy, ând fêlo mânniska wêron vp hjara syde. Vral kêm twispalt. Thêr wêron bern, thêr vpstandon ajen hjara eldrum. Inna gluppa

THE WRITINGS OF FRÊTHORIK AND WILJOW.

My name is Frêthorik, surnamed oera Linda, which means over the Linden. In Ljudwardia I was chosen as Asga. Ljudwardia is a new village within the fortification of the Ljudgaarda, of which the name has fallen into disrepute. In my time much has happened. I had written a good deal about it, but afterwards much more was related to me. I will write an account of both one and the other after this book, to the honour of the good people and to the disgrace of the bad.

In my youth I heard complaints on all sides. The bad time was coming; the bad time did come—Frya had forsaken us. She withheld from us all her watch-maidens, because monstrous idolatrous images had been found within our landmarks. I burnt with curiosity to see those images. In our neighbourhood a little old woman tottered in and out of the houses, always calling out about the bad times. I came to her; she stroked my chin; then I became bold, and asked her if she would show me the bad times and the images. She laughed good-naturedly, and took me to the citadel. An old man asked me if I could read and write. No, I said. Then you must first go and learn, he replied, otherwise it may not be shown to you. I went daily to the writer and learnt. Eight years afterwards I heard that our Burgtmaagd had been unchaste, and that some of the burgtheeren had committed treason with the Magy, and many people took their part. Everywhere disputes arose. There were children rebelling against their parents; good

wrdon tha froda månniska morth. Thet alde fåmke, thêr ella bår måkade, wårth dåd fvnden in en grupe. Min tåt, thêr rjuchter wêre, wilde hja wrêken hå. Nachtis wårth er in sin hus vrmorth. Thrju jêr lêtter wêr thene Mågy bås svnder strid. Tha Saxmånna wêron frome ånd frod bilywen. Nêi tham fljuchton alle gode månniska. Min måm bistvrv-et. Nw dêd ik lik tha ôthera. Thi Mågy bogade vppa sinra snôdhêd. Men Irtha skold im tbåna, thåt hja nên Mågy ner afgoda to lêta ne mochte to thêre hêlge skêta, hwêrut hju Frya bêrade. Êvin sa thet wilde hors sina månna sked, nêi thåt thet sina ridder gersfallich måkad heth, êvin så skodde Irtha hjara walda ånd berga. Rinstråma wrdon ovira fjelda sprêd. Sê kokade. Berga spydon nêi tha wolkum, ånd hwad hja spyth hêde, swikton tha wolka wither vp jrtha. By-t anfang there Arnemônath nigade jrtha northward, hju sêg del, ôl lêgor ånd lêgor. Anna Wolfamônath lêidon tha Dênemarka fon Fryas lånd vnder-ne sê bidobben. Tha walda thêr bylda in wêron, wrdon vphyvath ånd thêr windum spel. Thet jêr åfter kêm frost inna Herdemônath ånd lêid ôld Fryas lånd vnder en plônke skul. In Sellamônath kêm stornewind ut et northa wêi, mith forande berga fon ise ånd stênum. Tha spring kåm, hyf jrtha hjra selva vp. Ise smolt wêi. Ebbe kêm ånd tha walda mith byldum drêvon nêi sê. Inner Winna jeftha Minnamônath gvng aider thurvar wither hêm fåra. Ik kêm mith en fåm to thêre burch Ljudgårda. Ho drove sach et ut. Tha walda thêra Lindawrda wêron mêst wêi. Thêr tha Ljudgårde wêst hêde, was sê. Sin hef fêtere thene hringdik. Ise hêde tha tore wêi brocht ånd tha husa lêide in thrvch ekkôrum. Anna helde fonna dik fond ik in sten.

people were secretly murdered. The little old woman who had brought everything to light was found dead in a ditch. My father, who was a judge, would have her avenged. He was murdered in the night in his own house. Three years after that the Magy was master without any resistance. The Saxmen had remained religious and upright. All the good people fled to them. My mother died of it. Now I did like the others. The Magy prided himself upon his cunning, but Irtha made him know that she would not tolerate any Magy or idol on the holy bosom that had borne Frya. As a wild horse tosses his mane after he has thrown his rider, so Irtha shook her forests and her mountains. Rivers flowed over the land; the sea raged; mountains spouted fire to the clouds, and what they vomited forth the clouds flung upon the earth. At the beginning of the Arnemaand (harvest month) the earth bowed towards the north, and sank down lower and lower. In the Welvenmaand (winter month) the low lands of Fryasland were buried under the sea. The woods in which the images were, were torn up and scattered by the wind. The following year the frost came in the Hardemaand (Louwmaand, January), and laid Fryasland concealed under a sheet of ice. In Sellemaand (Sprokkelmaand, February) there were storms of wind from the north, driving mountains of ice and stones. When the spring-tides came the earth raised herself up, the ice melted; with the ebb the forests with the images drifted out to sea. In the Winne, or Minnemaand (Bloeimaand, May), every one who dared went home. I came with a maiden to the citadel Liudgaarde. How sad it looked there. The forests of the Lindaoorden were almost all gone. Where Liudgaarde used to be was sea. The waves swept over the fortifications. Ice had destroyed the tower, and the houses lay heaped over each other. On the slope of the dyke I found a stone

vsa skriver hêd er sin nôm inwryten, thât wêre my en bâken. Sâ-t mith vsa burch gvngen was, was-t mith mitha ôra gvngon. Inna hâga lânda wêron hja thrvch jrtha, inna dêna landa thrvch wêter vrdên. Allêna Fryasburch to Texland wârth vnedêrad fvnden. Men al et lând thet northward lêid hêde, wêre vnder sê. Noch nis-t navt boppa brocht. An thâs kâd fon-t Flymâre wêron nêi meld wrde thrichtich salta mâra kvmen, vnstonden thrvch tha walda, thêr mith grvnd ånd al vrdrêven wêron. To Westflyland fiftich. Thi grâft thêr fon-t Alderga thweres to het land thrvchlâpen hêde, was vrsôndath ånd vrdên. Tha stjurar ånd ôr fârande folk, thêr to honk wêron, hêde hjara selva mith mâga ånd sibba vppira skepum hret. Men thåt swarte folk fon Lydasburch ånd Alikmarum hêde alên dên. Thawil tha swarta sûdward dryvon, hêdon hja fêlo mångêrtne hret, ånd nêidam nimman ne kêm to aska tham, hildon hja tham to hjara wiva. Tha månniska thêr to bek kêmon, gvngon alle binna tha hringdika thêra burgum hêma, thrvchdam et thêr buta al slyp ånd broklând wêre. Tha gamla husa wrde byên klust. Fona boppalândum kâpade mån ky ånd skêp, ånd inna tha grâte husa thêr to fâra tha fâmna sêton hêde, wrde nw lêken ånd filt mâkad, vmbe thes lêvens willa. Thåt skêd 1888* jer nêi thåt Atlând svnken was.

In 282 jer† nêdon wi nên Êremoder navt hat, and nw ella tomet vrlêren skinde, gvng mån êne kjasa. Thet hlot falde vp Gosa to nômath Makonta. Hju wêre Burchfâm et Fryasburch to Texlând. Hel fon hawed ånd klâr fon sin, êlle god, ånd thrvchdam hira burch allêna spârad was, sach alrik thêrut hira hropang. Tjan jêr lêttere kêmon tha stjurar fon Forana ånd fon Lydas burch. Hja wildon tha swarta månniska mith wif ånd bern to thet lånd utdryva. Thêrwr wildon hja thêre Moder is rêd biwinna. Men Gosa

---

* 2193 = 1888 − 305 voor Chr.
† Sedert 587 voor Chr. Verg. pag. 110. 112.

on which the writer had inscribed his name. That was a sign to me. The same thing had happened to other citadels as to ours. In the upper lands they had been destroyed by the earth, in the lower lands by the water. Fryasburgt, at Texland, was the only one found uninjured, but all the land to the north was sunk under the sea, and has never been recovered. At the mouth of the Flymeer, as we were told, thirty salt swamps were found, consisting of the forest and the ground that had been swept away. At Westflyland there were fifty. The canal which had run across the land from Alderga was filled up with sand and destroyed. The seafaring people and other travellers who were at home had saved themselves, their goods, and their relations upon their ships. But the black people at Lydasburgt and Alkmarum had done the same; and as they went south they saved many girls, and as no one came to claim them, they took them for their wives. The people who came back all lived within the lines of the citadel, as outside there was nothing but mud and marsh. The old houses were all smashed together. People bought cattle and sheep from the upper lands, and in the great houses where formerly the maidens were established cloth and felt were made for a livelihood. This happened 1888 years after the submersion of Atland.

For 282 years we had not had an Eeremoeder, and now, when everything seemed lost, they set about choosing one. The lot fell upon Gosa, surnamed Makonta. She was Burgtmaagd at Fryasburgt, in Texland. She had a clear head and strong sense, and was very good; and as her citadel was the only one that had been spared, every one saw in that her call. Ten years after that the seafarers came from Forana and Lydasburgt. They wished to drive the black men, with their wives and children, out of the country. They wished to obtain the opinion of the mother upon the subject. She asked them:

---

* 2193 – 1888 is 305 before Christ.
† Since 587 before Christ. See pages 110 and 112.

frêje, kânst ên ånd ôr to bek fora nêi hjra lândum, thån âchste spod to mâkjande, owers ne skilun hja hjara mâga navt wither ne finda. Nê sêide hja. Thâ sêide Gosa: Hja hâvon thin salt provad ånd thin brâd êten. Hjara lif ånd lêva hâvon hja vnder jow hod stâlad. I moste jow anje hirta bisêka. Men ik wil thi en rêd jeva. Hald hjam alond jow wâldich biste vm ra wither honk to fora. Men hald hjam bi jow burgum thêr bûta. Wâk ovir hjara sêd ånd lêr hjam as jef hja Fry'as svna wêre. Hjra wiva send hyr tha steriksta. As rêk skil hjara blod vrfljuchta, til er tha lesta navt owers as Fryas blod in hjara åfterkv- mande skil bilywa. Sâ send hja hyr bilêwen. Nw winst ik wel thåt mina åfterkvmande thêr vp letta, ho fêr Gosa wêrhêd sprek. Thâ vsa lânda wither to bigana wêr, kêmon thêr banda erma Saxmanna ånd wiva nêi tha vvrdum fon Stavere ånd thåt Alderga, vmbe golden ånd ôra sjarhêd to sêkane fon ut tha wasige bodeme. Thach tha stjurar nil- don hja navt to lêta. Tha gvngon hja tha lêthoga thorpa bihêma to West Flyland, vmbe ra lif to bihaldane.

Nw wil ik skriwa ho tha Gêrtmanna and fêlo Hêlênja folgar tobek kêmon.

Twa jêr nêi thåt Gosa Moder wrde,* kêm er en flâte to thet Flymara in fala. Thet folk hropte ho.n.sêen. Hja foron til Stavere, thêr hropton hja jeta rêis. Tha fôna wêron an top ånd thes nachtes skâton hja barnpila† anda loft. Thâ dêirêd wêre rojadon svme mith ên snâke to thêre hava in. Hja hropton wither ho.n.sêen. Tha hja landa hipte-n jong kerdel wal vp. In sina handa hêdi-n skild, thêrvp was brâd ånd salt lêid. Afterdam kêm en grêva, hi sêide wi kvmath

---

* 303. v. Chr.
† Barnpila. De *falarica* by Livius XXI. 8.

Can you send them all back to their country? If so, then lose no time, or they will find no relatives alive. No, they said. Gosa replied: They have eaten your bread and salt; they have placed themselves entirely under your protection. You must consult your own hearts. But I will give you one piece of advice. Keep them till you are able to send them back, but keep them outside your citadels. Watch over their morals, and educate them as if they were Frya's sons. Their women are the strongest here. Their blood will disappear like smoke, till at last nothing but Frya's blood will remain in their descendants. So they remained here. Now, I should wish that my descendants should observe in how far Gosa spoke the truth. When our country began to recover, there came troops of poor Saxon men and women to the neighbourhoods of Staveren and Alderga, to search for gold and other treasures in the swampy lands. But the sea-people would not permit it, so they went and settled in the empty village of the West Flyland in order to preserve their lives.

Now I will relate how the Geertman and many followers of Hellenia came back.

Two years after Gosa had become the mother (303 B.C.) there arrived a fleet at Flymeer. The people shouted "Ho-n-sêen" (What a blessing). They sailed to Staveren, where they shouted again. Their flags were hoisted, and at night they shot lighted arrows into the air. At daylight some of them rowed into the harbour in a boat, shouting again, "Ho-n-sêen." When they landed a young fellow jumped upon the rampart. In his hand he held a shield on which bread and salt were laid. After him came a grey-headed man, who said we come from

---

* 303 before Christ.
† *Barnpila*, De falarica, Livy, xxi. 8.

fona fere Krêkalandum wêi, vmb vsa sêd to warjande, nw winstath wi i skolde alsa mild wêsa vs alsa fül lånd to jêvane thât wi thêrvp müge hêma. Hi telade-n êle skêdnese thêr ik âfter bêtre skryva wil. Tha grêva niston navt hwat to dvande, hja sandon bodon allerwêikes; âk ta my. Ik gvng to ånd sêide: nw wi-n Moder håve agon wi hjra rêd to frêjande. Ik selva gvng mitha. Thju Moder, thêr ella wiste, sêide, lêt hja kvme, så mügon hja vs lånd helpa bihalda: men lêt hjam navt up êne stêd ne bilyva, til thju hja navt waldich ne wrde ovir vs. Wi dêdon as hju sêid hêde. That wêre êl nêi hjra hêi. Fryso reste mith sinå ljudum to Stavere, that hja wither to êne sêstêde måkade, sa god hja machte. Wichhirte gvng mith sinum ljudum astward nêi there Êmude. Svme thêra Johnjar, thêr mênde thât hja font Alderga folk sproten wêre, gvngen thêr hinne. En lyth dêl thêr wânde thât hjara êthla fon tha sjugon êlanda wei kêmon, gvngon hinne ând setton hjara selva binna tha hringdik fon thêre burch Walhallagâra del. Ljudgert thene skolte bi nachte fon Wichhirte wårth min åthe åfternêi min frjund. Fon ut sin dêibok håv ik thju skêdnese thêr hir åfter skil folgja.

Nei thât wi 12 mel 100 ånd twia 12 jêr bi tha fif wêtrum sêten hêde, thahwila vsa sêkåmpar alle sêa bifåren hêde thêr to findane, kêm Alexandre (*) tham kêning mith en weldich hêr fon boppa allingen thêr strâm vsa thorpa bifâra. Nimman ne mâcht in wither worda. Thach wi stjurar thêr by tha sê såton, wi skêpt vs mith al vsa tilbêre hava in ând brûda hinna. Tha Alexandre fornom thât im så ne grâte flâte vntfåra was, wårth er wodinlik, to swêrande hi skolde alle thorpa an logha offerja jef wi navt to bek kvma nilde. Wichhirte lêide siak to bedde. Thâ Alexandre thât fornom heth er wacht alont er bêter wêre. Afternêi kêm er to him sêr kindlyk snakkande, thach hi thrjvchde lik

---

* Alexander aan den Indus 327 v. Chr. 327.
† 1224 = 1551 v. Chr.

the distant Greek land to preserve our customs. Now we wish you to be kind enough to give us as much land as will enable us to live. He told a long story, which I will hereafter relate more fully. The old man did not know what to do. They sent messengers all round, also to me. I went, and said now that we have a mother it behoves us to ask her advice. I went with them myself. The mother, who already knew it all, said: Let them come, they will help us to keep our lands, but do not let them remain in one place, that they may not become too powerful over us. We did as she said, which was quite to their liking. Fryso remained with his people at Staveren, which they made again into a port as well as they could. Wichhirte went with his people eastwards to the Emude. Some of the descendants of Jon who imagined that they sprang from the Alderga people went there. A small number, who fancied that their forefathers had come from the seven islands, went there and set themselves down within the enclosure of the citadel of Walhallagara. Liudgert, the admiral of Wichhirt, was my comrade, and afterwards my friend. Out of his diary I have taken the following history.

After we had been settled 12 times 100 and twice 12 years in the Five Waters (Punjab), whilst our naval warriors were navigating all the seas they could find, came Alexander* the King, with a powerful army descending the river towards our villages. No one could withstand him; but we sea-people, who lived by the sea, put all our possessions on board ships and took our departure. When Alexander heard that such a large fleet had escaped him, he became furious, and swore that he would burn all the villages if we did not come back. Wichhirte was ill in bed. When Alexander heard that, he waited till he was better. After that he came to him, speaking very kindly—but he deceived,

---

* Alexander at the Indus, 327 before Christ.
† 327 + 1224 is 1551 before Christ.

hi êr dên hêde. Wichhirte andere thêr âfter, o aldergrâteste thêra kêningar. Wi stjurar kvmath allerwêikes, wi hâven fon jow grâte dêdun hêred. Thêrvmbe send wi fvl êrbidenese to fara jowa wêpne, tha jet mar vr thina witskip. Men wi ôthera wy send frybern Fryas bern. Wy ne mügon nêne slâfona navt ne wrde. Jef ik wilde, tha ôra skolde rêder sterva willa, hwand alsa ist thrvch vsa êwa bifôlen. Alexandre sêide: ik wil thin lând navt ne mâkja to min bût, ner thin folk to mina slâfona. Ik wil blât thât ste my thjanja skolste vmb lân. Thêrvr wil ik swêra by vs bêdar godum, that nimman vr my wrogja skil. Tha Alexandre âfternei brâd ând salt mith im dêlade, heth Wichhirte that wiste dêl kâsen. Hi lêt tha skêpa hala thrvch sin svne. Tha thi alle tobek wêron, heth Alexandre thi alle hêred. Thêr mitha wilde hi sin folk nêi tha helge Gônga fâra, thêr hi to land navt hêde müge nâka. Nw gvng er to ând kâs altham ut sin folk ând ut sina salt-atha thêr wenath wêron vvr-ne sê to fârane. Wichhirte was wither siak wrden, thêrvmbe gvng ik allêna mitha ând Nearchus fon thes keningis wêga. Thi tocht hlip svnder fardêl to-n-ende, uthâvede tha Johnjar immerthe an vnmin wêron with tha Phonisjar, alsa Nêarchus thêr selva nên bâs ovir bilywe ne kv. Intwiska hêde tham kêning navt stile nêst. Hi hêde sina salt-atha bâma kapja lêta ând to planka mâkja. Thrvch help vsar timberljud hêder thêr of skêpa mâkad. Nw wilder selva sêkêning wertha, ând mith êl sin hêr thju Gonga vpfâra. Thach tha salt-atha thêr fon thet bergland kêmon, wêron ang to fara sê. As hja hêradon thât hja mith moste, stakon hja tha timberhlotha ane brônd. Thêr thrvch wrde vs êle thorp anda aska lêid. Thet forma wânde wy thât Alexandre thât bifalen hêde ând jahwêder stand rêd vmb sê to kjasane. Men Alexander wêre wodin, hi wilde tha salt-atha thrvch sin ajn folk ombrensa lêta. Men Nêar-

as he had done before. Wichhirte answered: Oh greatest of kings, we sailors go everywhere; we have heard of your great deeds, therefore we are full of respect for your arms, and still more for your wisdom; but we who are free-born Fryas children, we may not become your slaves; and even if I would, the others would sooner die, for so it is commanded in our laws. Alexander said: I do not desire to take your land or make slaves of your people, I only wish to hire your services. That I will swear by both our Gods, so that no one may be dissatisfied. When Alexander shared bread and salt with him, Wichhirte had chosen the wisest part. He let his son fetch the ships. When they were all come back Alexander hired them all. By means of them he wished to transport his people to the holy Ganges, which he had not been able to reach. Then he chose among all his people and soldiers those who were accustomed to the sea. Wichhirte had fallen sick again, therefore I went alone with Nearchus, sent by the king. The voyage came to an end without any advantage, because the Joniers and the Phœnicians were always quarrelling, so that Nearchus himself could not keep them in order. In the meantime, the king had not sat still. He had let his soldiers cut down trees and make planks, with which, with the help of our carpenters, he had built ships. Now he would himself become a sea-king, and sail with his whole army up the Ganges; but the soldiers who came from the mountainous countries were afraid of the sea. When they heard that they must sail, they set fire to the timber yards, and so our whole village was laid in ashes. At first we thought that this had been done by Alexander's orders, and we were all ready to cast ourselves into the sea: but Alexander was furious, and wished his own people to kill the soldiers. However, Nearchus,

chus tham navt allêna sin êroste forst men ak sin frjund wêre, rêde him owers to dvande. Nw bêrad er as wen der lavade thet vnluk et dên hêde. Tha hi ne thvrade sin tocht navt vrfata. Nw wild er to bek kêra, thach êr hi thât dêde, lêt hi thet forma bisêka hwa-r skeldich wêron. Dry-r thât wiste lêt er altham svnder wêpne bilywa, vmb en ny thorp to mâkjande. Fon sin ajn folk lêt er wepned vmbe tha ôra to tâmma, ând vmbe êne burch to bvwande. Wy moston wiv ând bern mith nimma. Kêmon wi anda muda thêre Êuphrat, sa machton wi thêr en stêd kiasa jeftha omkêra, vs lân skold vs êvin blyd to dêlath wrde. An tha nya skêpa, thêr tha brônd vntkvma wêron, let-er Johniar ând Krêkalandar gâ. Hi selva gvng mith sin ôra folk allingen thêre kâd thrvch tha dorra wostêna, thât is thrvch et land thât Irtha vphêid hêde uta sê, tha hju thju strête after vsa êthela vphêide as hja inna Râde sê kêmon.

Tha wy to ny Gêrtmanja kêmon (ny Gêrtmanja is en hâva thêr wi selva makad hede, vmbe thêr to wêterja) mêton wi Alexandre mith sin hêr. Nêarchus gvng wal vp ând bêide thrja dêga. Tha gvng et wither forth. Tha wi bi thêre Êuphrat kêmon, gvng Nêarchus mith sina salt-alta ând fêlo fon sin folk wal vp. Tha hi kêm hring wither. Hi sêide, thi kêning lêt jow bidda, i skille jet en lithge tocht to sinra wille dvan, alont et ende fona Râde sê. Thêrnêi skil jawehder sâ fül gold krêja as er bêra mêi. Tha wi thêr kêmon, lêt er vs wysa hwêr thju strête êr wêst hêde. Thêr nêi wylader ên ând thritich dêga, alan ut sjande vvra wostêne.

Tho tha lesta kêm er en hloth mânniska mith forande twa hondred êlephanta thvsend kêmlun tolêden mith wodin balkum, râpum ând allerlêja ark vmbe vsa flâte nêi tha Middelsê to tyande. Thât bisâwd-vs, ând likt

who was not only his chief officer, but also his friend, advised him not to do so. So he pretended to believe that it had happened by accident, and said no more about it. He wished now to return, but before going he made an inquiry who really were the guilty ones. As soon as he ascertained it, he had them all disarmed, and made them build a new village. His own people he kept under arms to overawe the others, and to build a citadel. We were to take the women and children with us. When we arrived at the mouth of the Euphrates, we might either choose a place to settle there or come back. Our pay would be guaranteed to us the same in either case. Upon the new ships which had been saved from the fire he embarked the Joniers and the Greeks. He himself went with the rest of his people along the coast, through the barren wilderness; that is, through the land that Irtha had heaved up out of the sea when she had raised up the strait as soon as our forefathers had passed into the Red Sea.

When we arrived at New Gertmania (New Gertmania is the port that we had made in order to take in water), we met Alexander with his army. Nearchus went ashore, and stayed three days. Then we proceeded further on. When we came to the Euphrates, Nearchus went ashore with the soldiers and a large body of people; but he soon returned, and said, The King requests you, for his sake, to go a voyage up the Red Sea; after that each shall receive as much gold as he can carry. When we arrived there, he showed us where the strait had formerly been. There he spent thirty-one days, always looking steadily towards the desert.

At last there arrived a great troop of people, bringing with them 200 elephants, 1000 camels, a quantity of timber, ropes, and all kinds of implements necessary to drag our fleet to the Mediterranean Sea. This astounded us, and seemed

vs bal to, men Nêarchus teld vs, sin kêning wilde tha ôthera kêninggar tâna that i weldiger wêre, sa tha kêninggar fon Thyris êr wêsen hêde. Wi skoldon men mith helpa, sêkur skolde vs thât nên skâda navt dva. Wi moston wel swika, ând Nêarchus wiste ella sâ pront to birjuchte thât wi inna Middelsê lêide êr thrja mônatha forby wêron. Tha Alexandre fornom ho-t mith sinra onwerp ofkvmen was, wârth er sa vrmêten thât er tha drage strête utdiapa wilde Irtha to-n spot. Men Wr.alda lêt sine sêle lâs, thêrvmbe vrdronk er inna win ând in sina ovirmodichhêd, êr thât er bijinna kvste. After sin dâd wrde thet rik dêlad thrvch sina forsta. Hja skolde alrek en dêl to fara sina svnum wârja, thach hja wêron vnmênis. Elk wilde sin dêl bihalda ând selva formâra. Tha kêm orloch ând wi ne kvste navt omme kêra. Nêarchus wilde nw, wi skolde vs del setta an Phonisi his kâd, men thât nilde nimman navt ne dva. Wi sêide, rêder willath wi wâga nêi Fryasland to gâna. Tha brocht-er vs nei thêre nya hâva fon Athenia, hwêr alle âfte Fryas bern formels hin têin wêron. Forth gvngon wi salt-âtha liftochta ând wêpne fâra. Among tha fêlo forsta hêde Nêarchus en frjund mith nôme Antigonus. Thisse strêdon bêde vmb ên dol, sâ hja sêidon as follistar to fâra-t kêninglike slachte ând forth vmbe alle Krêkalanda hjara alda frydom wither to jêvane. Antigonus hêde among fêlo ôtherum ênnen svn, thi hête Demêtrius, âfter tonômad thene stêda winner. Thisse gvng ênis vpper stêde Salâmis of. Nêi thât er thêr en stût mêi strêden hêde most er mith thêre flâte strida fon Ptholemeus. Ptholemeus, alsa hête thene forst thêr welda ovir Êgiptaland. Dêmêtrius wn thêre kêse, tha navt thrvch sina salt-âtha, men thrvch dam wy him helpen hêde. Thit hêde wi dên thrvch athskip to fâra Nêarchus, hwand wi him far bastard blod bikânde thrvch sin friska hûd ând blâwa âgon mith

most extraordinary; but Nearchus told us that his king wished to show to the other kings that he was more powerful than any kings of Tyre had ever been. We were only to assist, and that surely could do us no harm. We were obliged to yield, and Nearchus knew so well how to regulate everything, that before three months had elapsed our ships lay in the Mediterranean Sea. When Alexander ascertained how his project had succeeded, he became so audacious that he wished to dig out the dried-up strait in defiance of Irtha; but Wr-alda deserted his soul, so that he destroyed himself by wine and rashness before he could begin it. After his death his kingdom was divided among his princes. They were each to have preserved a share for his sons, but that was not their intention. Each wished to keep his own share, and to get more. Then war arose, and we could not return. Nearchus wished us to settle on the coast of Phœnicia, but that no one would do. We said we would rather risk the attempt to return to Fryasland. Then he brought us to the new port of Athens, where all the true children of Frya had formerly gone. We went, soldiers with our goods and weapons. Among the many princes Nearchus had a friend named Antigonus. These two had only one object in view, as they told us—to help the royal race, and to restore freedom to all the Greek lands. Antigonus had, among many others, one son named Demetrius, afterwards called the "City Winner." He went once to the town of Salamis, and after he had been some time fighting there, he had an engagement with the fleet of Ptolemy. Ptolemy was the name of the prince who reigned over Egypt. Demetrius won the battle, not by his own soldiers, but because we helped him. We had done this out of friendship for Nearchus, because we knew that he was of bastard birth by his white skin, blue eyes, and

wit hêr. After nêi gvng Dêmêtrius lâs vp Hrodus* thêr
hinne brochton wi sina salt-âtha ånd liftochta wr. Thâ
wi tha leste rêis to Hrodus kêmon, was orloch vrtyan.
Dêmêtrius was nêi Athenia fâren. Tha vs kêning thât
vnderstande, lêd-er vs tobek. Tha wi anda hâve kêmon,
wêre êl et thorp in row bidobben. Friso thêr kêning wêr
ovir-a flåte, hêde en svn ånd en toghater tûs, så bjustre
fres, as jef hja pås ut Fryasland wêi kvmen wêren, ånd så
wonderskên as nimman mocht hügja. Thjv hrop thêrvr
gvng vvr alle Krêkalanda ånd kêm in tha åra fon Dêmêtrius. Dêmêtrius wêre vvl ånd vnsêdlik, ånd hi thogte
thåt-im ella fry stvnde. Hi lêt thju toghater avber skûkja.
Thju moder ne thvrade hjra joi† navt wachtja, joi nomath
tha stjurar wiva hira måna, thåt is blideskip, ak segsath
hja swêthirte. Tha stjurar hêton hjra wiva trâst, ånd fro
jefta frow thât is frü åk frolik, thât is êlik an frü. Thrvchdam hju hjra man navt wachtja thurade, gvng hju mith
hjra svne nêi Dêmêtrius ånd bad, hi skolde hja hjra toghater wither jêva. Men as Dêmêtrius hira svn sa, lêt-er
tham nêi sinra hove fora, ånd dêde alên mith him, as-er
mith tham his suster dên hêde. Anda moder sand hi en
buda gold, thach hju stirt-et in sê. As hju thûs kêm, warth
hju wansinnich, allerwêikes run hju vvra strête: nåst min
kindar navt sjan, o wach, lêt mi to jow skul sêka, wand
min joi wil mi dêja for tha-k sina kindar wêi brocht hâv.
Tha Dêmêtrius fornom, thåt Friso to honk wêre, sand-i en
bodja to him segsande, thåt hi sina bern to him nomen hêde
wmbe ra to fora to-n hâge stât vmbe to lånja him to fåra
sina thjanesta. Men Friso thêr stolte ånd herdfochtich wêre,
sand en bodja mith en brêve nêi sinum bern tha, thêrin
månde hi hjam, hja skolde Dêmêtrius to willa wêsa, vrmithis
tham hjara luk jêrde. Thach thene bodja hêde jeta-n ora
brêve mith fenin, thêrmêi bifâl-er hja skolde that innimma,

---

* 305 voor Chr.
† Joi 'en trâst. Te Scheveningen hoort men nog: joei en troos. Joi,
Fransch *joye.*

fair hair. Afterwards, Demetrius attacked Rhodes, and we transported thither his soldiers and provisions. When we made our last voyage to Rhodes, the war was finished. Demetrius had sailed to Athens. When we came into the harbour, the whole village was in deep mourning. Friso, who was king over the fleet, had a son and a daughter so remarkably fair, as if they had just come out of Fryasland, and more beautiful than any one could picture to himself. The fame of this went all over Greece, and came to the ears of Demetrius. Demetrius was vile and immoral, and thought he could do as he pleased. He carried off the daughter. The mother did not dare await the return of her *joi* (the sailors wives call their husbands *joi* or *zoethart* (sweetheart). The men call their wives *troost* (comfort) and *fro* or *frow*, that is, *vreuyde* (delight) and frolic; that is the same as *vreugde*.

As she dared not wait for her husband's return, she went with her son to Demetrius, and implored him to send back her daughter; but when Demetrius saw the son he had him taken to his palace, and did to him as he had done to his sister. He sent a bag of gold to the mother, which she flung into the sea. When she came home she was out of her mind, and ran about the streets calling out: Have you seen my children. Woe is me! let me find a place to hide in, for my husband will kill me because I have lost his children.

When Demetrius heard that Friso had come home, he sent messengers to him to say that he had taken his children to raise them to high rank, and to reward him for his services. But Friso was proud and passionate, and sent a messenger with a letter to his children, in which he recommended them to accept the will of Demetrius, as he wished to promote their happiness; but the messenger had another letter with poison, which he ordered them to take:

---

* 305 before Christ.

† *Joi en tråst.* At Scheveningen you still hear "Joei en troos." *Joi* is the French *joye*.

hwand sêid-er-vnwillinglik is thin lif bivvllad; thât ne skil jow navt to rêkned ni wrde, thach sâhwersa jow jowe sêle bivvlath sa ne skil jow nimmerthe to Walhâlla ne kvma, jow sêle skil thân ovir irtha ommewâra, svnder â thet ljucht sja to mugande, lik tha flâramusa ând nachtula skilstv alra dystik in thina hola skula, thes nachtis utkvma, then vp vsa grâva grâja ând hûla, thahwila Frya hjra haved fon jow ofwenda mot. Tha bern dêde lik-ra bifâlen warth. Dêmêtrius lêt ra likka in sê werpa ând to tha mânniska wrde sêid, thât hja fljucht wêron. Nw wilde Friso mith alleman nêi Fryasland fâra, thêr-i êr wêst hêde, men tha mêst nilde thât navt ne dva. Nw gvng Friso to ând skât thet thorp mith-a kêninglika fârrêdskûrum anda brônd. Hjud ne kv ni thvrade ninman ne bilywa, ând alle wêron blyde, that hja bûta wêre, bihalva wif ând bern hêdon wi ella abefta lêten, thach wi wêron to lêden mith liftochtum ând orluchtuch.

Friso nêde nach nên fretho. Tha wi by tha alda hâve kêmon gvnger mith sina drista ljudum to ând skât vnwarlinga tha brônd inna skêpa, thêr-i mith sina pilum bigâna kv. After sex dêgum sâgon wi tha orlochflâte fon Dêmêtrius vp vs to kvma. Friso bifâl vs, wi moston tha lithste skêpa âfterhâde in êne brêde line, tha stora mith wif ând bern fârut. Forth bâd-er wi skoldon tha krânboga fon for nimma ând anda âftestêwen fâstigja, hwand sêid-er, wi achon al fljuchtande to fjuchtane. Nimman ne mêi him formêta vmb en enkeldera fyand to forfolgjande, alsa sêid-er is min bislut. Tha hwila wi thêrmitha al dvande wêron, kêm wind vs vppa kop, to thêra lâfa ând thêra wiva skrik, thrvchdam wi nêne slâvona navt nêde as thêra thêr vs bi ajn willa folgan wêre. Wi ne machton hja thus navt thruch roja ni vntkvma. Men Wr. alda wiste wel, hwêrvmb-er

THE BOOK OF ADELA'S FOLLOWERS. 175

But, said he, your bodies have been defiled against your will. That you are not to blame for; but if your souls are not pure, you will never come into Walhalla. Your spirits will haunt the earth in darkness. Like the bats and owls, you will hide yourselves in the daytime in holes, and in the night will come and shriek and cry about our graves, while Frya must turn her head away from you. The children did as their father had commanded. The messenger had their bodies thrown into the sea, and it was reported that they had fled. Now Friso wished to go with all his people to Frya's land, where he had been formerly, but most of them would not go. So Friso set fire to the village and all the royal storehouses; then no one could remain there, and all were glad to be out of it. We left everything behind us except wives and children, but we had an ample stock of provisions and warlike implements.

Friso was not yet satisfied. When we came to the old harbour, he went off with his stout soldiers and threw fire into all the ships that he could reach with his arrows. Six days later we saw the war-fleet of Demetrius coming down upon us. Friso ordered us to keep back the small ships in a broad line, and to put the large ships with the women and children in front. Further, he ordered us to take the crossbows that were in the fore part and fix them on the sterns of the ships, because, said he, we must fight a retreating battle. No man must presume to pursue a single enemy—that is my order. While we were busy about this, all at once the wind came ahead, to the great alarm of the cowards and the women, because we had no slaves except those who had voluntarily followed us. Therefore we could not escape the enemy by rowing. But Wr-alda knew well why he

sâ dêde, ånd Friso thêr-et fata, lêt tha bårnpila ring inna krånboga lidsa. To lik bâd-er thåt nimman skiata ne machte, êr hy skåten hêde. Forth sêid-er thåt wi alle nêi thåt midloste skip skiata moste, is thåt dol god biracht sêid-er, så skilun tha ôra him to helpane kvma ånd thån mot alrik skiata sa-r alderbesta mêi. As wi nw arhalf ketting fon-ra of wêre, bigoston tha Phonisiar to skiata. Men Friso n-andere navt bi fåra tha êroste pil del falde a sex fadema fon sin skip. Nw skât-er. Tha ôra folgade, thet likte en fjurrêin ånd thrvchdam vsa pila mith wind mêi gvngon, bilêvon hja alle an brônd, ånd nåkade selva tha thridde låge. Allera månnelik gyradon ånd jûwgade. Men tha krêta vsar witherlågum wêron sa herde, thet-et vs thet hirte binêpen warth. As Friso mênde thåt et to koste, lêt-er ofhalde ånd wi spode hinne. Thach nêi that wi twa dêga forth pilath hêde, kêm thêr en ôre flâte ant sjocht, fon thrittich skêpun, thêr vs stêdis in wnne. Friso lêt vs wither rêd makja. Men tha ôthera sandon en lichte snåka fvl rojar forut, tha bodon thêra bådon ut alera nôma jef hja mith fåra machte. Hja wêron Johniar, thrvch Dêmêtrius wêron hja wåldantlik nêi there alda håve skikad. Thêr hêdon hja fon thêre kêse hêrad ånd nw hêdon hja thet stolta swêrd antjan, ånd wêron vs folgad. Friso thêr fül mitha Johnjar faren hêde sêide jå, men Wichhirte vsa kêning sêide nê, Tha Johnjar send afgoda thjanjar sêid-er, ik selva håv hêrad, ho hja thi an hropte. Friso sêide thet kvmath thrvch tha wandel mith tha åfta Krêkalandar. Thåt håv ik våken selva dên. Thach ben ik alsa herde Fryas as tha finste fon jow. Friso wêre thene mån thêr vs to Fryasland wisa moste. Thus gvngon tha Johnjar mith. Ak likt-et nei Wr.aldas hêi, hwand êr thrja mônathe om hlåpen wêron, gvngon wi allingen Britannja, ånd thrja dêga lêter machton wi ho.n.sêen hropa.

did this; and Friso, who understood it, immediately had the fire-arrows placed on the crossbows. At the same time he gave the order that no one should shoot before he did, and that we should all aim at the centre ship. If we succeeded in this, he said, the others would all go to its assistance, and then everybody might shoot as he best was able. When we were at a cable and a half distance from them the Phœnicians began to shoot, but Friso did not reply till the first arrow fell six fathoms from his ship. Then he fired, and the rest followed. It was like a shower of fire; and as our arrows went with the wind, they all remained alight and reached the third line. Everybody shouted and cheered, but the screams of our opponents were so loud that our hearts shrank. When Friso thought that it was sufficient he called us off, and we sped away; but after two days' slow sailing another fleet of thirty ships came in sight and gained upon us. Friso cleared for action again, but the others sent forward a small rowing-boat with messengers, who asked permission to sail with us, as they were Joniers. They had been compelled by Demetrius to go to the old haven; there they had heard of the battle, and girding on their stout swords, had followed us. Friso, who had sailed a good deal with the Joniers, said Yes; but Wichirte, our king, said No. The Joniers, said he, are worshippers of heathen gods; I myself have heard them call upon them. That comes from their intercourse with the real Greeks, Friso said. I have often done it myself, and yet I am as pious a Fryas man as any of you. Friso was the man to take us to Friesland, therefore the Joniers went with us. It seems that this was pleasing to Wr-alda, for before three months were past we coasted along Britain, and three days later we could shout huzza.

THIT SKRIFT IS MIJ OWER NORTLAND JEFTHA SKÊNLAND
JÊVEN.

Vndera tida thåt vs land del sêg, wêre ik to Skênland. Thêr gvng et alsa to. Thêr wêron gråte mâra, thêr fon tha bodeme lik en blêse vt setta, then spliton hja vt-ên. Uta rêta kêm stof as-t gliande yser wêre. Thêr wêron berga thêr tha krunna of swikte. Thesse truldon nêther ånd brochton walda ånd thorpa wêi. Ik self så thåt en berch fon tha ôra of torent wrde. Linrjucht sêg-er del. As ik afternêi sjan gvng, was thêr en mâre kvmen. Tha irtha bêterad was, kêm er en hêrtoga fon Lindasburch wêi, mit sin folk ånd en fåm, thju fåm kêthe allomme: Thene Mâgy is skeldich an al-eth lêt thåt wi lêden håve. Hja tågon immer forth en thet hêr wårth al grâter. Thene Mâgy fluchte hinne, mån fand sin lik, hi hêde sin self vrdên. Tha wrdon tha Finna vrdrêven nêi ênre stêd, thêr machton hja lêva. Thêr wêron fon basterde blode. Thissa machton biliwa, thach fêlo gvngon mith tha Finna mêi. Thi hêrtoga warth to kêning kêren. Tha kårka thêr êl bilêven wêron wrde vrdên. Sont komath tha gode North-ljud våken to Texland vmb there Moder-is rêd. Thå wi ne mügath hjam for nêne rjuchta Fryas mar ne halde. Inna Dênamarka ist sêkur as bi vs gvngon. Tha stjurar, tham hjara self thêr stoltelika sêkåmpar bêton, send vppira skêpa gvngon, ånd åfternêi sind hja to bek gvngon.

Held!

Hwersa thene Kroder en tid forth kroden heth, thån skilun tha åfterkomanda wâna thåt tha lêka ånd brêka, thêr tha Brokmanna mith brocht håve, åjen were an hjara êthla. Thêr vr wil ik wåka ånd thus så fül vr hjåra plêga skriva as ik sjan hå. Vr tha Gêrt-

This Writing has been given to me about Northland and Schoonland (Scandinavia).

When our land was submerged I was in Schoonland. It was very bad there. There were great lakes which rose from the earth like bubbles, then burst asunder, and from the rents flowed a stuff like red-hot iron. The tops of high mountains fell and destroyed whole forests and villages. I myself saw one mountain torn from another and fall straight down. When I afterwards went to see the place there was a lake there. When the earth was composed there came a duke of Lindasburgt with his people, and one maiden who cried everywhere, Magy is the cause of all the misery that we have suffered. They continued their progress, and their hosts increased. The Magy fled, and his corpse was found where he had killed himself. Then the Finns were driven to one place where they might live. There were some of mixed blood who were allowed to stay, but most of them went with the Finns. The duke was chosen as king. The temples which had remained whole were destroyed. Since that time the good Northmen come often to Texland for the advice of the mother; still we cannot consider them real Frisians. In Denmark it has certainly happened as with us. The sea-people, who call themselves famous sea-warriors, went on board their ships, and afterwards went back again.

Heil!

Whenever the Carrier has completed a period, then posterity shall understand that the faults and misdeeds that the Brokmannen have brought with them belonged to their forefathers; therefore I will watch, and will describe as much of their manners as I have seen. The Geertmannen I can

manna kân ik rêd hinne stappa. Ik nâv navt fül mithra omme gvngen. Tha sâ fêr ik sjan hâ send hja thât mast bi tâl ând sêd bilêwen. Thât ne mêi ik navt segsa fon tha ôthera. Thêr fon.a Krêkalânda wêi kvme, send kwâd ther tâl ând vppira sêd ne mêi mân êl navt boga. Fêlo hâvath brûna âgon ând hêr. Hja send nidich ând drist ând ang thrvch overbilâwichhêd. Hwêrsa hja sprêka, sâ nômath hja the worda fâr vppa thêr lerst kvma mosta. Ajen ald segath hja âd, âjen salt sâd, mâ fori mân, sel fori skil, sode fori skolde, to fül vmb to nomande. Ak forath hja mêst vrdvaliske ând bikirte nôma, hwêran mân nên sin an hefta ne mêi. Tha Johniar sprêkath bêtre, thach hja swygath thi h ând hwêri navt nêsa mot, wârth er ûtekêth. Hwersa imman en blyd mâkath âfter ênnen vrstvrven ând thet likt, sâ lâwath hja, thât thene gâst thes vrsturvene thêr inne fârath. Thêrvr hâvath hja alle bylda vrburgen fon Frya, Fâsta, Mêdêa, Thjanja, Hellênja ând fêlo ôthera. Hwerth thêr en bern ebern, sâ kvmath tha sibba et sêmne ând biddath an Frya thât hju hjara fâmkes mêi kvma lêta thât bern to sêenande. Hâvon hja bêden sa ne mêi nimman him rora ni hêra lêta. Kvmt et bern to grâjande ând halt thit en stvnde an, alsa is thât en kwâd têken ând man is an formoda, thât thju mâm hordom dên heth. Thêrvr hâv ik al ârge thinga sjan. Kvmt et bern to slêpande, sâ is thât en têken, thât tha fâmkes vr-et kvmen send. Lakt et inna slêp, sâ hâvon tha fâmkes thât bern luk to sêit. Olon lâwath hja an bosa gâsta, hexna, kolla, aldermankes ând elfun, as jef hja fon tha Finna wei kêmen. Hyrmitha wil ik enda ând nw mên ik tha-k mâr skrêven hâ, as ên minra êthla. Frêthorik.

Frêthorik min gâd is 63 jêr wrden. Sont 100 ând 8 jêr is hi thene êroste fon sin folk, thêr frêdsum

readily pass by. I have not had much to do with them, but as far as I have seen they have mostly retained their language and customs. I cannot say that of the others. Those who descend from the Greeks speak a bad language, and have not much to boast of in their manners. Many have brown eyes and hair. They are envious and impudent, and cowardly from superstition. When they speak, they put the words first that ought to come last. For old they say *at;* for salt, *sât;* and for man, *ma*—too many to mention. They also use abbreviations of names, which have no meaning. The Joniers speak better, but they drop the H, and put it where it ought not to be. When they make a statue of a dead person they believe that the spirit of the departed enters into it; therefore they have hidden their statues of Frya, Fâsta, Medea, Thiania, Hellenia, and many others. When a child is born, all the relatives come together and pray to Frya to send her servants to bless the child. When they have prayed, they must neither move nor speak. If the child begins to cry, and continues some time, it is a bad sign, and they suspect that the mother has committed adultery. I have seen very bad things come from that. If the child sleeps, that is a good sign—Frya's servants are come. If it laughs in its sleep, the servants have promised it happiness. Moreover, they believe in bad spirits, witches, sorcerers, dwarfs, and elves, as if they descended from the Finns. Herewith I will finish, and I think I have written more than any of my forefathers. Frethorik.

Frethorik, my husband, lived to the age of 63. Since 108 years he is the first of his race who died a

sturven is, alle ôthera send vndera slêga swikt, thêrvr thật alle kâmpade with ajn ånd fêrhêmande vmb rjucht ånd plicht.

Min nôm is Wil-jo, ik bin tha fâm thêr mith him fona Saxanamarka to honk for. Thrvch tâl ånd ommegang kêm et ut, thật wi alle bêde fon Adela his folk wêron, thâ kêm ljafde ånd âfternêi send wi man ånd wif wrden. Hi heth mi fyf bern lêten, two suna ånd thrju toghatera. Konerêd alsa hêt min forma, Hâchgâna min ôthera, mine aldeste toghater hêth Adela, thju ôthera Frulik ånd tha jongeste Nocht. Thâ-k nêi tha Saxanamarka for, hâv ik thrju boka hret. Thet bok thêra sanga, thêra tellinga, ånd thet Hêlênja bok. Ik skrif thit til thju mån navt thånka ne mêi thật hja fon Apollânja send; ik hâv thêr fūl lêt vr had ånd wil thus åk thju êra hâ. Ak hâv ik mâr den, tha Gosa-Makonta fallen is, hwames godhêd ånd klârsjanhêd to en sprêkword is wrden, thâ ben ik allêna nêi Texland gvngen vmbe tha skrifta vr to skrivane, thêr hju âfter lêten heth, ånd thâ tha lerste wille fonden is fon Frâna ånd tha nêilêtne skrifta fon Adela jefta Hellênja, hâv ik thật jetta rêis den. Thit send tha skrifta Hellênjas. Ik set hjam får vppa vmbe thật hja tha aldesta send.

Alle Afta Fryas Held.

In êra tida niston tha Slâvona folkar nawet fon fryhêd. Lik oxa wrdon hja vnder et juk brocht. In irthas wand wrdon hja jågath vmbe mêtal to delvane ånd ut-a herde bergum moston hja hûsa hâwa to forst ånd presterums hêm. Bi al hwat hja dêdon, thêr nas nawet to fâra hjara selva, men ella moste thjanja vmbe tha forsta ånd prestera jeta riker ånd weldiger to mâk-jane hjara selva to sâdene. Vnder thesse arbêd wrdon hja

peaceable death; all the others died by violence, because they all fought with their own people, and with foreigners for right and duty.

My name is Wiljo. I am the maiden who came home with him from Saxsenmarken. In the course of conversation it came out that we were both of Adela's race—thus our affection commenced, and we became man and wife. He left me with five children, two sons and three daughters. Konreed was my eldest son, Hachgana my second. My eldest daughter is called Adela, my second Frulik, and the youngest Nocht. When I went to Saxsenmarken I preserved three books—the book of songs, the book of narratives, and the Hellenia book.

I write this in order that people may not think they were by Apollonia. I have had a good deal of annoyance about this, and therefore now wish to have the honour of it. I also did more. When Gosa Makonta died, whose goodness and clear-sightedness have become a proverb, I went alone to Texland to copy the writings that she had left; and when the last will of Frana was found, and the writings left by Adela or Hellenia, I did that again. These are the writings of Hellenia. I have put them first because they are the oldest.

Hail to all true Frisians.

In the olden times, the Slavonic race knew nothing of liberty. They were brought under the yoke like oxen. They were driven into the bowels of the earth to dig metals, and had to build houses of stone as dwelling-places for princes and priests. Of all that they did nothing came to themselves, everything must serve to enrich and make more powerful the priests and the princes, and to satisfy them. Under this treatment they grew

grêv ånd stråm êr hja jêrich wêron, ånd sturvon svnder nochta afshên irtha tham overflodlik fvl jêf to båta al hjara bern. Men vsa britna kêmon ånd vsa bånnalinga thrvch tha Twisklånda vr in hjara marka fåra ånd vsa stjurar kemon in hjara håvna. Fon hjam hêradon hja kålta vr êlika frydom ånd rjucht ånd overa êwa, hwer bûta nimman omme ne mêi. Altham wrde vpsugon thrvch tha drova månniska lik dåwa thrvch tha dorra fjelde. As hju fvl wêron bijonnon tha alderdrista månniska to klippane mith hjara kêdne, alsa-t tha forsta wê dêde. Tha forste send stolte ånd wichandlik, thêrvmbe is thêr åk noch düged in hjara hirta, hja birêdon et sêmine ånd javon awet fon hjara overflodalikhêd. Men tha låfa skin fråna prestara ne machton thåt navt ne lyda, emong hjara forsinde godum hêdon hja åk wrangwråda drochtne eskêpen. Pest kêm inovera lånda. Nw sêidon hja, tha drochtna send tornich overa overhêrichhêd thêra bosa. Tha wrdon tha alderdrista månniska mith hjara kêdne wirgad. Irtha heth hjara blod dronken, mith thåt blod fode hju früchda ånd nochta, ånd alle tham thêr of êton wrdon wis.

16 wåra 100 jêr lêden* is Atland svnken, ånd to thêra tidum bêrade thêr awat hwêr vppa nimman rêkned nêde. In-t hirte fon Findas lånd vppet berchta lêid en del, thêr is kêthen Kasamyr,† thet is sjeldsum. Thêr werth en bern e-bern, sin måm wêre thju toghater enis kêning ånd sin tåt wêre-n håvedprester. Vmb skôm to vnkvma mosten hja hjara åjen blod vnkvma. Thêrvmbe wårth er bûta thêre stêde brocht bi årma månniska. In twiska was-t im navt forhêlad ne wrden, thêr vmbe dêd er ella vmbe wisdom to gêtane ånd gårane. Sin forstån wêre så gråt thåt er ella forstånde hwat er så ånd hêrade. Thåt folk skowde him mit êrbêdenese and tha prestera wr don ang vr sina frêga. Thå-r jêrich wrde gvnger nêi sinum

---

* 2193 − 1600 = 593 v. Chr.   † Kasamyr, Kashmir.

gray and old before their time, and died without any enjoyment; although the earth produces abundantly for the good of all her children. But our runaways and exiles came through Twiskland to their boundaries, and our sailors came to their harbours. From them they heard of liberty, of justice, and laws, without which men cannot exist. This was all absorbed by the unhappy people like dew into an arid soil. When they fully understood this, the most courageous among them began to clank their chains, which grieved the princes. The princes are proud and warlike; there is therefore some virtue in their hearts. They consulted together and bestowed some of their superfluity; but the cowardly hypocritical priests could not suffer this. Among their false gods they had invented also wicked cruel monsters. Pestilence broke out in the country; and they said that the gods were angry with the domineering of the wicked. Then the boldest of the people were strangled in their chains. The earth drank their blood, and that blood produced corn and fruits that inspired with wisdom those who ate them.

Sixteen hundred years ago (she writes, 593 B.C.), Atland was submerged; and at that time something happened which nobody had reckoned upon. In the heart of Findasland, upon a mountain, lies a plain called Kasamyr (Cashmere) that is "extraordinary." There was a child born whose mother was the daughter of a king, and whose father was a high-priest. In order to hide the shame they were obliged to renounce their own blood. Therefore it was taken out of the town to poor people. As the boy grew up, nothing was concealed from him, so he did all in his power to acquire wisdom. His intellect was so great that he understood everything that he saw or heard. The people regarded him with respect, and the priests were afraid of his questions. When he was of full age he went to his

---

* 2193 − 1600 is 593 years before Christ.   † *Kasamyr* is Kashmere.

aldrum. Hja moston herda thinga hêra, vmb-im kwit to werthane javon hja him vrflod fon kestlika stênum; men hja ne thvradon him navt avbêr bikânnâ as hjara âjne blod. Mith drovenese in vrdelven overa falxe skôm sinra aldrum gvnger ommedwâla. Al forth fârande mête hi en Fryas stjurar thêr as slâv thjanade, fon tham lêrd-i vsa sêd ând plêgum. Hi kâpade him fry, ând to ther dâd send hja frjunda bilêwen. Alomme hwêr er forth hinne tâch, lêrd-i an tha ljuda thât hja nêne rika ner prestera tolêta moston, thât hja hjara selva hode moston âjen falxe skôm, ther allerwêikes kvad dvat an tha ljavde. Irtha sêid-er skânkath hjara jêva nêi mêta men hjara hûd klâwat, thât mân thêrin âch to delvane to êrane ând to sêjane, sâ mân thêrof skêra wil. Thach sêid-er nimman hovat thit to dvande fori ennen ôthera hit ne sy, thât et bi mêne wille jef ut ljavade skêd. Hi lêrde thât nimman in hjara wand machte frota vmbe gold her silver ner kestlika stêna, hwêr nid an klywath ând ljavde fon fljuchth. Vmbe jow manghêrta ând wiva to sjarane, sêid-er, jêvath hjara rin strâma ênoch. Nimman sêid-er is weldich alle mânniska mêtrik ând êlika luk to jân. Tha thât it alra mânniska plicht vmbe tha mânniska alsa mêtrik to mâkjane ând sa fêlo nocht to jân, as to binâka is. Nêne witskip sêid-er ne mêi mân minachtja, thach êlika dêla is tha grâteste witskip, thêr tid vs lêra mêi. Thêrvmbe thât hjv argenese fon irtha wêrath ând ljavde feth.

Sin forme nôm wêre Jes-us,* thach tha prestera thêr-im sêralik hâton hêton him Fo thât is falx, thât folk hête him Kris-en thât is herder, ând sin Fryaske frjund hêta him Bûda, vmbe that hi in sin hâvad en skât fon wisdom hêde ând in sin hirt en skât fon ljavde.

To tha lersta most-er fluchta vr tha wrêka thêra prestera, men vral hwêr er kêm was sine lêre him fârut gvngen

---

* Jes-us, evenmin te verwarren met Jezus, als Krisen (Krishna) met Christus.

parents. They had to listen to some hard language; and to get rid of him they gave him a quantity of jewels, but they dared not openly acknowledge him. Overcome with sorrow at the false shame of his parents, he wandered about. While travelling he fell in with a Frisian sailor who was serving as a slave, and who taught him our manners and customs. He bought the freedom of the slave, and they remained friends till death. Wherever he went he taught the people not to tolerate rich men or priests, and that they must guard themselves against false shame, which everywhere did harm to love and charity. The earth, he said, bestowed her treasures on those who scratch her skin; so all are obliged to dig, and plough, and sow if they wish to reap, but no one is obliged to do anything for another unless it be out of goodwill. He taught that men should not seek in her bowels for gold, or silver, or precious stones, which occasion envy and destroy love. To embellish your wives and daughters, he said, the river offers her pure stream. No man is able to make everybody equally rich and happy, but it is the duty of all men to make each other as equally rich and as happy as possible. Men should not despise any knowledge; but justice is the greatest knowledge that time can teach, because she wards off offences and promotes love.

His first name was Jessos, but the priests, who hated him, called him Fo, that is, false; the people called him Krishna, that is, shepherd; and his Frisian friend called him Buddha (purse), because he had in his head a treasure of wisdom, and in his heart a treasure of love.

At last he was obliged to flee from the wrath of the priests; but wherever he went his teaching had preceded him, whilst his enemies followed him like

---

* *Jes-us*—not to be confounded with Jesus any more than Krisen (Krishna) with Christ.

ånd vral hwêr-er gvng folgadon him sina lêtha lik sine skåde nêi. Thâ Jes-vs alsa twilif jêr om fåren hêde, sturv-er, men sina frjunda wåradon sine lêre ånd kêthon hwêr-et åron fvnde.

Hwat mênst nw thåt tha prestera dêdon, thåt mot ik jo melde, åk mot-i thêr sêralik acht vp jân, forth mot-i over hjara bidryv ånd renka wåka mith alle kråftum, thêr Wr.alda in jo lêid heth. Thahwila Jes-us lêre vr irtha for, gvngon tha falxe prestera nêi-t lånd sinra berta sin dåd avbêra, hja sêidon thåt hja fon sinum frjundum wêron, hja bêradon gråte rowa, torennande hjara klåthar to flardum ånd to skêrande hjara hola kål. Inna hôla thêra berga gvngon hja hêma, thach thêrin hêdon hja hjara skåt brocht, thêr binna måkadon hja blydon åfter Jes-us, thessa blydon jåvon hja antha vnârg thânkanda ljuda, to longa lersta sêidon hja thåt Jes-us en drochten wêre, thåt-i thåt selva an hjam bilêden hêde, ånd thåt alle thêr an him ånd an sina lêra låwa wilde, nêimels in sin kêningkrik kvme skolde, hwêr frü is ånd nochta send. Vrmites hja wiston thåt Jes-us åjen tha rika to fjelda tågen hêde, så kêthon hja allerwêikes, that årmode hå ånd ênfald så thju düre wêre vmbe in sin rik to kvmane, thåt thêra thêr hyr vp irtha thåt måste lêden hêde, nêimels tha måsta nochta håva skolde. Thahwila hja wiston thåt Jes-us lêrad hêde thåt mân sina tochta welda ånd bistjura moste, så lêrdon hja thåt mân alle sina tochta dêja moste, ånd thåt tha fvlkvminhêd thêra månniska thêrin bistande thåt er êvin vnforstoren wrde så thåt kalde stên. Vmbe thåt folk nw wis to måkjande thåt hja alsa dêdon, alsa bêradon hja årmode overa strêta ånd vmb forth to biwisane thåt hja al hjara tochta dåd hêde, nåmon hja nêne wiwa. Thach sahwêrsa en toghater en misstap hêde, så wårth hja that ring forjân, tha wrakka sêidon hja most mân helpa and vmbe sin åjn

his shadow. When Jessos had thus travelled for twelve years he died; but his friends preserved his teaching, and spread it wherever they found listeners.

What do you think the priests did then? That I must tell you, and you must give your best attention to it. Moreover, you must keep guard against their acts and their tricks with all the strength that Wr-alda has given you. While the doctrine of Jessos was thus spreading over the earth, the false priests went to the land of his birth to make his death known. They said they were his friends, and they pretended to show great sorrow by tearing their clothes and shaving their heads. They went to live in caves in the mountains, but in them they had hid all their treasures, and they made in them images of Jessos. They gave these statues to simple people, and at last they said that Jessos was a god, that he had declared this himself to them, and that all those who followed his doctrine should enter his kingdom hereafter, where all was joy and happiness. Because they knew that he was opposed to the rich, they announced everywhere that poverty, suffering, and humility were the door by which to enter into his kingdom, and that those who had suffered the most on earth should enjoy the greatest happiness there. Although they knew that Jessos had taught that men should regulate and control their passions, they taught that men should stifle their passions, and that the perfection of humanity consisted in being as unfeeling as the cold stones. In order to make the people believe that they did as they preached, they pretended to outward poverty; and that they had overcome all sensual feelings, they took no wives. But if any young girl had made a false step, it was quickly forgiven; the weak, they said, were to be assisted, and to save

sêle to bihaldane most mån fül anda cherke jân. Thus todvande hêde hja wiv ånd bern svnder hûshalden ånd wrdon hja rik svnder werka, men that folk wårth fül ârmer ånd mâr êlåndich as â to fâra. Thas lêre hwêrbi tha prestera nên ôre witskip hova as drochtlik rêda, fråna skin ånd vnrjuchta plêga, brêd hiri selva ut fon-t asta to-t westa ånd skil åk vr vsa landa kvma.

Men astha prestera skilun wåna, thåt hja allet ljucht fon Frya ånd fon Jes-us lêre vtdåvath håva, så skilum thêr in alle vvrda månniska vpstonda, tham wêrhêd in stilnise among ekkorum wårath ånd to fâra tha prestera forborgen håve. Thissa skilun wêsa ut forsta blod, fon presterum blod, fon Slåvonum blod, ånd fon Fryas blod. Tham skilun hjara foddikum ånd thåt ljucht bûta bringa, så thåt allera månnalik wêrhêd mêi sjan; hja skilun wê hropa overa dêda thêra prestera ånd forsta. Tha forsta thêr wêrhêd minna ånd rjucht tham skilun fon tha prestera wika, blod skil strâma, men thêrut skil-et folk nye kråfta gåra. Findas folk skil sina findingrikhêd to mêna nitha wenda, thåt Lydas folk sina kråfta ånd wi vsa wisdom. Tha skilun tha falxa prestera wêi fågath wertha fon irtha. Wr.alda his gåst skil alomme ånd allerwêikes êrath ånd bihropa wertha. Tha êwa thêr Wr.alda bi-t anfang in vs mod lêide, skilun allêna hêrad wertha, thêr ne skilun nêne ôra måstera, noch forsta, ner båsa navt nêsa, as thêra thêr bi mêna wille kêren send. Thån skil Frya juwgja ånd Irtha skil hira jêva allêna skånka an tha werkande månnisk. Altham skil anfanga fjuwer thusand jêr nêi Atland svnken is ånd thusand jêr lêter skil thêr longer nên prester ner tvang vp irtha sa.

Dela tonômath Hellênja, wåk!

their souls men must give largely to the Church. Acting in this way, they had wives and children without households, and were rich without working; but the people grew poorer and more miserable than they had ever been before. This doctrine, which requires the priests to possess no further knowledge than to speak deceitfully, and to pretend to be pious while acting unjustly, spreads from east to west, and will come to our land also.

But when the priests fancy that they have entirely extinguished the light of Frya and Jessos, then shall all classes of men rise up who have quietly preserved the truth among themselves, and have hidden it from the priests. They shall be of princely blood of priests, Slavonic, and Frya's blood. They will make their light visible, so that all men shall see the truth; they shall cry woe to the acts of the princes and the priests. The princes who love the truth and justice shall separate themselves from the priests; blood shall flow, but from it the people will gather new strength. Finda's folk shall contribute their industry to the common good, Linda's folk their strength, and we our wisdom. Then the false priests shall be swept away from the earth. Wr-alda's spirit shall be invoked everywhere and always; the laws that Wr-alda in the beginning instilled into our consciences shall alone be listened to. There shall be neither princes, nor masters, nor rulers, except those chosen by the general voice. Then Frya shall rejoice, and the earth will only bestow her gifts on those who work. All this shall begin 4000 years after the submersion of Atland, and 1000 years later there shall exist no longer either priest or oppression.

Dela, surnamed Hellenia, watch!

Så lûda Frånas ûtroste wille. Alle welle Fryas held. An tha nôme Wr.aldas, fon Frya, ånd thêre fryhêd grête ik jo, ånd bidde jo, sahwersa ik falla machte êr ik en folgster nômath hêde, så bifêl ik jo Tüntja thêr Burchfåm is to thêre burch Mêdêasblik, til hjud dêgum is hja tha besta.

Thet- heth Gôsa nêi lêten. Alle månniska held. Ik nåv nêne êremoder binomad thrvchdam ik nêne niste, ånd et is jo bêter nêne Moder to håvande as êne hwêr vp-i jo navt forlêta ne mêi. Arge tid is forbi fåren, men thêr kvmt en ôthere. Irtha heth hja navt ne bårad ånd Wr.alda heth hja navt ne skêren. Hju kvmt ut et åsta ut-a bosma thêra prestera wêi. Så fêlo lêd skil hju broda, thåt Irtha-t blod algådvr navt drinka ne kån fon hira vrslêjana bernum. Thjustrenesse skil hju in overne gåst thêra månniska sprêda, lik tongar-is wolka oviret svnneljucht. Alom ånd allerwêikes skil lest ånd drochten bidryf with fryhêd kåmpa ånd rjucht. Rjucht ånd fryhêd skilun swika ånd wi mith tham. Men thesse winst skil hjara vrlias wrochta. Fon thrju worda skilun vsa åfterkvmande an hjara ljuda ånd slåvona tha bithjutnesse lêra. Hja send mêna ljavde, fryhêd ånd rjucht. Thåt forma skilun hja glora, åfternêi with thjustrenesse kåmpa al ont et hel ånd klår in hjawlikes hirt ånd holle wårth. Thån skil tvang fon irtha fågad wertha, lik tongarswolka thrvch stornewind, ånd alle drochten bidryv ne skil thêr åjen nawet navt ne formüga. Gôsa.

THE BOOK OF ADELA'S FOLLOWERS.

Thus runs Frana's last will: All noble Frisians, Heil! In the name of Wr-alda, of Frya, and of Freedom, I greet you; and pray you if I die before I have named a successor, then I recommend to you Teuntja, who is Burgtmaagd in the citadel of Medeasblik; till now she is the best.

This Gosa has left behind her: Hail to all men! I have named no Eeremoeder, because I know none, and because it is better for you to have no mother than to have one you cannot trust. One bad time is passed by, but there is still another coming. Irtha has not given it birth, and Wr-alda has not decreed it. It comes from the East, out of the bosom of the priests. It will breed so much mischief that Irtha will not be able to drink the blood of her slain children. It will spread darkness over the minds of men like storm-clouds over the sunlight. Everywhere craft and deception shall contend with freedom and justice. Freedom and justice shall be overcome, and we with them. But this success will work out its own loss. Our descendants shall teach their people and their slaves the meaning of three words; they are *universal love*, *freedom*, and *justice*. At first they shall shine, then struggle with darkness, until every man's head and heart has become bright and clear. Then shall oppression be driven from the earth, like the thunder-clouds by the storm-wind, and all deceit will cease to have any more power. Gosa.

THET SKRIFT FON KONERÊD.

Min êthla hâvon in åfter thit bok skrêven. Thit wil ik boppa ella dva, vmbe thåt er in min ståt nên burch ovir is, hwêrin tha bêrtnesa vp skrêven wrde lik to fåra. Min nôme is Konerêd, min tåt-his nôme was Frêthorik, min mem his nôme Wiljow. After tåt his dåd ben ik to sina folgar kêren, ånd tha-k fiftich jêr tålde kås men mij to vrste grêvetmån. Min tåt heth skrêven ho tha Linda-wrda ånd tha Ljudgårdne vrdilgen send. Lindahêm is jeta wêi, tha Linda-wrda far en dêl, tha northlikka Ljudgårdne send thrvch thene salta sê bidelven. That brûwsende hef slikt an tha hringdik thêre burch. Lik tåt melth heth, så send tha hâvalåsa månniska to gvngen ånd håvon hûskes bvwad binna tha hringdik thêra burch. Thêrvmbe is that ronddêl nw Ljvdwerd hêten. Tha stjurar segath Ljvwrd, men thåt is wansprêke. Bi mina jüged was-t ôre lånd, thåt bûta tha hringdik lêid, al pol ånd brok. Men Fryas folk is diger ånd flitich, hja wrdon mod ner wirg, thrvchdam hjara dol to tha besta lêide. Thrvch slåta to delvane ånd kådika to måkjane fon tha grvnd thêr ût-a slåta kêm, alsa håvon wi wither en gode hêm bûta tha hringdik, thêr thju dânte het fon en hof, thrê pêla åstwarth, thrê pêla sûdwarth ånd thrê pêla wêstwarth mêten. Hjud dêgum send wi to dvande å-pêla to hêjande, vmb êne hâve to winnande ånd mith ên vmb-vsa hringdik to biskirmande. Jef et werk rêd sy, så skilun wi stjurar utlvka. Bi min jüged stand-et hyr bjûstre om-to, men hjud send tha hûskes

THE WRITING OF KONERÊD.

My forefathers have written this book in succession. I will do this, the more because there exists no longer in my state any citadel on which events are inscribed as used to be the case. My name is Konerêd (Koenraad). My father's name was Frethorik, my mother's name was Wiljow. After my father's death I was chosen as his successor. When I was fifty years old I was chosen for chief Grevetman. My father has written how the Lindaoorden and Liudgaarden were destroyed. Lindahem is still lost, the Lindaoorden partially, and the north Lindgaarden are still concealed by the salt sea. The foaming sea washes the ramparts of the castle. As my father has mentioned, the people, being deprived of their harbour, went away and built houses inside the ramparts of the citadel; therefore that bastion is called Lindwerd. The sea-people say Linwerd, but that is nonsense. In my youth there was a portion of land lying outside the rampart all mud and marsh; but Frya's people were neither tired nor exhausted when they had a good object in view. By digging ditches, and making dams of the earth that came out of the ditches, we recovered a good space of land outside the rampart, which had the form of a hoof three poles eastward, three southwards, and three westwards. At present we are engaged in ramming piles into the ground to make a harbour to protect our rampart. When the work is finished we shall attract mariners. In my youth it looked very queer, but now there stands a row of houses.

al hûsa thêr an rêja stân. And lek ånd brek thêr mith ermode hir in glupt wêron, send thrvch flit a-buta drêven. Fon hir ut mêi allera månnalik lêra, thåt Wr.alda vsa Alfoder, al sina skepsela fot, mits thåt hja mod halde ånd månlik ôtherum helpa wille.

Nv wil ik vr Friso skriva.

Friso thêr al weldich wêre thrvch sin ljud, wårth åk to vrste grêve kêren thrvch Staverens ommelandar. Hi spot mith vsa wisa fon lånd-wêr ånd sêkåmpa, thêrvmbe hether en skol stift hwêr in tha knåpa fjuchta lêra nêi Krêkalandar wysa. Thån ik låv thåt i thåt dên heth vmb thåt jongk-folk an sin snôr to bindane. Ik håv min brother thêr åk hin skikt, tha-s nv thjan jêr lêden. Hwand tocht ik nv wi nêne Moder lônger navt nåve, vmbe tha ênen åjen tha ôre to bi skirmande, åch ik dubbel to wåkane thåt hi vs nên måster ne wårth.

Gosa neth vs nêne folgstere nômeth, thêr vr nil ik nên ordêl ne fella, men thêr send jeta alda årg thenkande månniska, thêr mêne thåt hju-t thêr-vr mith Friso ênis wrden is. Thå Gosa fallen was, thå wildon tha ljud fon alle wrda êne ôthere Moder kjasa. Men Friso thêr to dvande wêre vmb-en rik to fara him selva to måkjane, Friso ne gêrde nên rêd ner bodo fon Texland. As tha bodon thêra Landsåtum to him kêmon, sprek-i ånde kêth. Gosa sêid-er was fêrsjande wêst ånd wiser as alle grêva êtsêmne ånd thach nêde hju nên ljucht nêr klårhêd in thjuse sêke ne fvnden, thêrvmbe nêde hju nene mod hån vmb êne folgstere to kjasane, ånd vmb êne folgstere to kjasane thêr tvyvelik wêre, thêr heth hju bald in sjan, thêrvmbe heth hju in hjara ûtroste wille skrêven, thåt is jow bêtre nêne Moder to håvande as êne hwêr vpp-i jo selva navt forlêta ne mêi. Friso hêde fül sjan, bi orloch was er vpbrocht, ånd fon

Leaks and deficiencies produced by poverty have been remedied by industry. From this men may learn that Wr-alda, our universal father, protects all his creatures, if they preserve their courage and help each other.

Now I will write about Friso.

Friso, who was already powerful by his troops, was chosen chief Grevetman of the districts round Staveren. He laughed at our mode of defending our land and our sea-fights; therefore he established a school where the boys might learn to fight in the Greek manner, but I believe that he did it to attach the young people to himself. I sent my brother there ten years ago, because I thought, now that we have not got any mother, it behoves me to be doubly watchful, in order that he may not become our master.

Gosa has given us no successors. I will not give any opinion about that; but there are still old suspicious people who think that she and Friso had an understanding about it. When Gosa died, the people from all parts wished to choose another mother; but Friso, who was busy establishing a kingdom for himself, did not desire to have any advice or messenger from Texland. When the messengers of the Landsaten came to him, he said that Gosa had been far-seeing and wiser than all the counts together, and yet she had been unable to see any light or way out of this affair; therefore she had not had the courage to choose a successor, and to choose a doubtful one she thought would be very bad; therefore she wrote in her last will, It is better to have no mother than to have one on whom you cannot rely. Friso had seen a great deal. He had been brought up in the wars, and he had just learned and gathered as much of the tricks and

tha hrenkum ånd lestum thêra Golum ånd forstum hêder krek sa fül lêred ånd geth, as-er nêdich hêde vmbe tha ôra grêva to wêiande hwêr hi hjam wilde. Sjan hir ho-r thêrmith to gvngen is.

Friso hêde hir-ne ôther wif nimth, thju toghater fon Wil-frêthe, bi sin lêve was-er vrste Grêva to Staveren wêst. Thêr bi hêder twên svna wnnen ånd twa toghatera. Thrvch sin bilêid is Kornêlja sin jongste toghater mith min brother mant. Kornêlja is wan Fryas and mot Kornhêlja skrêven wrde. Wêmod sin aldeste heth er au Kavch bonden. Kavch thêr åk bi him to skole gvng is thi svnv fon Wichhirte thene Gêrtmanna kåning. Men Kavch is åk wan Fryas ånd mot Kåp wêsa. Men kvade tåle håvon hja mar mithbrocht as gode sêda.

Nw mot ik mith mine skêdnese a-befta kêra.

Aftre gråte flod hwêr vr min tåt skrêven heth, wêron fêlo Juttar ånd Lêtne mith ebbe uta Balda jefta kvade sê* fored. Bi Kåt his gat drêvon hja in hjara kåna mith yse vppa tha Dênemarka fåst ånd thêr vp send hja sitten bilêwen. Thêr nêron narne nên månniska an-t sjocht. Thêrvmbe håvon hja thåt lånd int, nêi hjara nôme håvon hja thåt land Juttarland hêten. Afternêi kêmon wel fêlo Denemarker to bek fon tha håga landum, men thissa setton hjara selva sûdliker del. And as tha stjurar to bek kêmon thêr navt vrgvngen navt nêron, gvng thi êna mith tha ôthera nei tha sê jefta êlandum.† Thrvch thisse skikking mochton tha Juttar thåt land halda, hwêr-vppa Wr.alda ra wêjad hêde. Tha Sêlandar stjurar tham hjara selva mith blåte fisk navt helpa ner nêra nilde, ånd thêr en årge grins hêde an tha Gola, tham gvngon dåna tha Phonisjar skêpa biråwa. An tha sûdwester herne fon Skênland, thêr lêid Lindasburcht tonômath Lindasnôse, thrvch vsa Apol stift, alsa in thit bok ‡ biskrêwen ståt. Alle kådhêmar ånd

---

* Balda jefta kvada sê, de Baltische zee. Juttarland, Jutland.
† Zeeland, de Deensche Eilanden. ‡ Zie bl. 124.

THE BOOK OF ADELA'S FOLLOWERS.   199

cunning ways of the Gauls and the princes as he required, to lead the other counts wherever he wished. See here how he went to work about that.

Friso had taken here another wife, a daughter of Wilfrêthe, who in his lifetime had been chief count of Staveren. By her he had two sons and two daughters. By his wish Kornelia, his youngest daughter, was married to my brother. Kornelia is not good Frisian; her name ought to be written Korn-helia. Weemoed, his eldest daughter, he married to Kauch. Kauch, who went to school to him, is the son of Wichhirte, the king of the Geertmen. But Kauch is likewise not good Frisian, and ought to be Kaap (Koop). So they have learned more bad language than good manners.

Now I must return to my story.

After the great flood of which my father wrote an account, there came many Jutlanders and Letlanders out of the Baltic, or bad sea. They were driven down the Kattegat in their boats by the ice as far as the coast of Denmark, and there they remained. There was not a creature to be seen; so they took possession of the land, and named it after themselves, Jutland. Afterwards many of the Denmarkers returned from the higher lands, but they settled more to the south; and when the mariners returned who had not been lost, they all went together to Zeeland. By this arrangement the Jutlanders retained the land to which Wr-alda had conducted them. The Zeeland skippers, who were not satisfied to live upon fish, and who hated the Gauls, took to robbing the Phœnician ships. In the south-west point of Scandinavia there lies Lindasburgt, called Lindasnôse, built by one Apol, as is written in the book. All the people

---

* *Balda jefta kvade sê* is the Baltic.   *Juttarland* is Jutland.
† *Zeeland* is the Danish Islands.   ‡ See page 124.

ommelandar dâna wêron eft Fryas bilêyen, men thrvch tha lust thêre wrêke âjen tha Golum ånd âjen tha Kâltana folgar gvngon hja mitha Sêlandar sâma dvan, men that sâma dva neth nen stek navt ne halden. Hwand tha Sêlandar hêde felo mislika plêga ånd wenhêde ovir nommen fon tha vvla Mâgjarum, Fryas folk to-n spot. Forth gvng ek to fara him selva râwa, thach jef et to pase kêm thân standon hja mânlik ôtherum trvlik by. Thach to tha lesta bijondon tha Sêlandar brek to krêjande an goda skêpa. Hjara skipmâkar weron omkvmen ånd hjara walda wêron mith grvnd ånd al fon-t land of fâged. Nw kêmon thêr vnwarlingen thry skêpa by tha ringdik fon vsa burch mêra. Thrvch tha inbrêka vsra landum wêron hja vrdvaled ånd tha Flymvda misfaren. Thi kâpmon thêr mith gvngen was, wilde fon vs nya skêpa hâ, thêrto hêdon hja mithbrocht allerlêja kestlika wêra, thêr hja râwed hêdon fon tha Kâltanarlandum ånd fon tha Phonisjar* skêpum. Nêidam wy selva nêne skêpa navt n-êde, jêf ik hjam flingka horsa ånd fjvwer wêpende rinbodon mith nei Friso. Hwand to Stâveren ånd allingen thåt Aldergâ thêr wrdon tha besta wêrskêpa maked fon herde êken wod thêr nimmerthe nên rot an ne kvmth. Thahwila tha sêkampar by my byde, wêron svme Juttar nêi Texland fâren ånd dânâ wêron hja nêi Friso wêsen. Tha Sêlandar hêdon felo fon hjara storeste knâpum râwed, thi moston vppa hjara benka roja, ånd fon hjara storeste toghtera vmb thêr by bern to têjande. Tha stora Juttar ne moohton et navt to wêrane, thrvchdam hja nêne gode wêpne navt nêde. Thâ hja hjara lêth telad hêde ånd thêrvr fêlo wordon wixlad wêron, frêje Friso to tha lesta jef hja nêne gode have in hjara gâ navt n-êde. O-jes, anderon hja, êne besta ên, êne thrvch Wr.alda skêpen. Hju is net krek lik jow bjarkrûk thêr, hira hals is eng, thâ in hira bâlg kånnath wel thvsanda grâte kâna lidsa, men wi nâvath nêna burch ner burchwêpne, vmbe tha râwskêpa thêr ut

* Phonisiar, hier Puniers, Carthagers.

who live on the coasts, and in the neighbouring districts, had remained true Frisians; but by their desire for vengeance upon the Gauls, and the followers of Kaltona, they joined the Zeelanders. But that connection did not hold together, because the Zeelanders had adopted many evil manners and customs of the wicked Magyars, in opposition to Frya's people. Afterwards, everybody went stealing on his own account; but when it suited them they held all together. At last the Zeelanders began to be in want of good ships. Their shipbuilders had died, and their forests as well as their land had been washed out to sea. Now there arrived unexpectedly three ships, which anchored off the ringdyk of our citadel. By the disruption of our land they had lost themselves, and had missed Flymond. The merchant who was with them wished to buy new ships from us, and for that purpose had brought all kinds of valuables, which they had stolen from the Celtic country and Phœnician ships. As we had no ships, I gave them active horses and four armed couriers to Friso; because at Stavere, along the Alberga, the best ships of war were built of hard oak which never rots. While these sea rovers remained with us, some of the Jutmen had gone to Texland, and thence to Friso. The Zeelanders had stolen many of their strongest boys to row their ships, and many of their finest daughters to have children by. The great Jutlanders could not prevent it, as they were not properly armed. When they had related all their misfortunes, and a good deal of conversation had taken place, Friso asked them at last if they had no good harbours in their country. Oh, yes, they answered; a beautiful one, created by Wr-alda. It is like a bottle, the neck narrow, but in the belly a thousand large boats may lie; but we have no citadel and no defences to keep out

---

* *Phonisjar* are Punics or Carthaginians.

to haldane. Thân mosten jow gvnst mâkja sêide Friso. God rêden anderon tha Juttar, men wi n-âvath nêne ambachtisljud ner bvwark, wi alle send fiskar ånd juttar. Tha ora send vrdrvnken jefta nêi tha hâga landum fljucht. Midlar hwila hja thus kâlta, kêmon mina bodon mitha Sêlândar hêra et sina hove. Hir most nw letta ho Friso alle to bidobbe wiste to nocht fon bêde partja ånd to bâte fon sin âjn dol. Tha Sêlandar sêider to, hja skoldon jêrlikes fiftech skêpa hâve, nêi fâsta mêtum ånd nêi fâsta jeldum, to hrêd mith ysere kêdne ånd krânbogum ånd mith fvlle tjuch alsa far wêrskêpa hof ånd nêdlik sy, men tha Juttar skoldon hja thån mith frêthe lêta, ånd all-et folk thåt to Fryasbern hêred. Jâ hi wilde mar dva, hi wilde al vsa sêkåmpar utnêda thåt hja skolde mith fjuchta ånd râwa. Thâ tha Sêlandar wêi brit wêron, thâ lêt-er fjuwertich alda skêpa to laja mith burchwêpne, wod, hirbaken stên, timberljud, mirtselêra ånd smêda vmbe thêr mith burga to bvwande. Witto, that is witte sin svn, sand hi mith vmb to to sjanande. Hwat thêr al fâr fallen is, n-is my navt ni meld, men sa fül is my bâr wrden, an byde sida thêre haves mvde is êne withburch bvwed, thêr in is folk lêid that Friso uta Saxanamarka tâch. Witto heth Sjuchthirte bifrêjad ånd to sin wiv nomen. Wilhem alsa hête hira tat, hi was vreste Aldermån thêra Juttar, that is vrste Grêvetman jefta Grêve. Wilhem is kirt after sturven ånd Witto is in sin stêd koren.

Ho Friso forther dêde.

Fon sin êrosta wif hêder twên sviaringa bihalda, thêr sêr klok wêron. Hetto, that is hête, thene jongste skikt er as

the pirate ships. Then you should make them, said Friso. That is very good advice, said the Jutlanders; but we have no workmen and no building materials; we are all fishermen and trawlers. The others are drowned or fled to the higher lands. While they were talking in this way, my messengers arrived at the court with the Zeeland gentlemen. Here you must observe how Friso understood deceiving everybody, to the satisfaction of both parties, and to the accomplishment of his own ends. To the Zeelanders he promised that they should have yearly fifty ships of a fixed size for a fixed price, fitted with iron chains and crossbows, and full rigging as is necessary and useful for men-of-war, but that they should leave in peace the Jutlanders and all the people of Frya's race. But he wished to do more; he wanted to engage all our sea rovers to go with him upon his fighting expedition. When the Zeelanders had gone, he loaded forty old ships with weapons for wall defences, wood, bricks, carpenters, masons, and smiths, in order to build citadels. Witto, or Witte, his son, he sent to superintend. I have never been well informed of what happened; but this much is clear to me, that on each side of the harbour a strong citadel has been built, and garrisoned by people brought by Friso out of Saksenmarken. Witto courted Siuchthirte and married her. Wilhem, her father, was chief Alderman of the Jutmen—that is, chief Grevetman or Count. Wilhem died shortly afterwards, and Witto was chosen in his place.

What Friso did further.

Of his first wife he still had two brothers-in-law, who were very daring. Hetto—that is, heat—the youngest, he sent as messenger to Kattaburgt, which

senda boda nêi Kattaburch thåt djap inna Saxanamarka lêid. Hi hêde fon Friso mith krêjen sjugon horsa buta sin åjn, to lêden mith kestlika sêkum, thrvch tha sêkåmpar råwed. Bi jahweder hors wêron twên jonga sêkåmpar ånd twên jonga hrutar mith rika klådarum klåth ånd jeld in hiara bûdar. Êvin as er Hetto nêi Kattabúrch skikte, skikter Bruno, thåt is brûne, thene ôthera svjaring nêi Mannagårda wrda, Mannagårda wrda is får in thit bok* Mannagårda forda skrêven, men thåt is misdên. Alle rikdoma thêr hja mith hede wrdon nêi omstand wêi skånkt an tha forsta and forstene ånd an tha utforkêrne mangêrtne. Kêmon thå sine knapa vppa thêre mêid vmbe thêr mith et jongkfolk to dônsjane, sa lêton hja kvra mith krûdkok kvma ånd bårgum jeftha tonnum fon tha besta bjar. After thissa bodon lêt-er immer jongkfolk over tha Saxanarmarka fåra, thêr alle jeld inna budar hêde ånd alle mêida jeftha skånkadja mith brochton, ånd vppa thêre mêid têradon hja alon vnkvmmerlik wêi. Jef-t nv bêrde thåt tha Saxana knåpa thêr nydich nêi utsågon, thån lakton hja godlik ånd sêidon, aste thvrath thene mêna fyand to bikåmpane, så kånst thin brêid jet fül riker mêida jån ånd jet forstelik têra. Al bêda sviaringa fon Friso send bostigjad mith toghaterum thêra romriksta forstum, ånd åfkernêi kêmon tha Saxanar knåpa ånd mangêrtne by êlle keddum nêi thåt Flymar del.

Tha burchfåmna ånd tha alda fåmna thêr jeta fon hjar êre gråthêd wiste, nygadon navt vr nêi Frisos bedriv, thêrvmbe ne kêthon hja nên god fon him. Men Friso snôder as hja lêt-ra snåka. Men tha jonga fåmna spônd-er mith goldne fingrum an sina sêk. Hja sêidon alomme wy nåvath longer nên Moder mår, men thåt kvmth dåna thåt wit jêroch send. Jvd past vs ne kåning, til thju wi vsa landa wither winna, thêr tha Modera vrlêren håve thrvch hjara

---

* Zie bl. 11.

lies far in the Saxsenmarken. Friso gave him to take seven horses, besides his own, laden with precious things stolen by the sea-rovers. With each horse there were two young sea-rovers and two young horsemen, clad in rich garments, and with money in their purses. In the same way as he sent Hettò to Kattaburgt, he sent Bruno —that is, brown—the other brother-in-law, to Mannagarda oord. Mannagarda oord was written Mannagarda ford in the earlier part of this book, but that is wrong. All the riches that they took with them were given away, according to circumstances, to princes, princesses, and chosen young girls. When his young men went to the tavern to dance with the young people there, they ordered baskets of spice, gingerbread, and tuns of the best beer. After these messengers he let his young people constantly go over to the Saxsenmarken, always with money in their purses and presents to give away, and they spent money carelessly in the taverns. When the Saxsen youths looked with envy at this they smiled, and said, If you dare go and fight the common enemy you would be able to give much richer presents to your brides, and live much more princely. Both the brothers-in-law of Friso had married daughters of the chief princes, and afterwards the Saxsen youths and girls came in whole troops to the Flymeer.

The burgtmaidens and old maidens who still remembered their greatness did not hold with Friso's object, and therefore they said no good of him; but Friso, more cunning than they, let them chatter, but the younger maidens he led to his side with golden fingers. They said everywhere, For a long time we have had no mother, but that comes from our being fit to take care of ourselves. At present it suits us best to have a king to win back our lands that we have lost through the imprudence of our mothers.

---

* See page 11.

vndigerhêd. Forth kêthon hja, alrek Fryasbern is frydom jêven, sin stem hêra to lêtane bi fara thêr bisloten wârth bi t kjasa ênre forste, men ast alsa wyd kvma machte thật i jo wither ne kåning kjasa, så wil ik åk min mêne segse. Nêi al hwat ik skoja mêi, så is Friso thêr to thrvch Wr.alda kêren, hwand hi heth im wonderlik hir hinne wêiad. Friso wêt tha hrenka thêra Golum, hwam his tâle hi sprêkt, hi kån thus åjen hjara lestum wâka. Thån is thêr jeta awet to skojande, hok Grêva skolde mån to kåning kjasa svnder that tha ôra thêr nidich vr wêron. Aldulkera tâlum wârth thrvch tha jonga fâmnn kethen, men tha alde fâmma afskên fê an tal, tapadon hjara rêdne ut en ôthera bårg. Hja kêthon allerwêikes ånd to alla mannalik: Friso kêthon hja dvath så tha spinna dvan, thes nachtis spôuth-i netta nêi alle sidum ånd thes dêis vrskalkth-i thêr sina vnåftertochtlika frjunda in. Friso sêith that-er nêne prestera ner poppa forsta lyde ne mêi, men ik seg, hi ne mêi nimman lyda as him selva. Thêrvmbe nil hi navt ne dåja thåt thju burch Stavia wither vp hêjath warth. Thêrvmbe wil hi nêne Moder wêr hâ. Jud is Friso jow rêd jêvar, men morne wil hi jow kåning wertha, til thju hi over jo alle rjuchta mei. Inna bosm thes folk-is antstondon nw twa partyja. Tha alda ånd årma wildon wither êne Moder hâ, men thåt jongkfolk, thåt fvl strêd-lust wêre wilde ne tåt jeftha kåning hâ. Tha êrosta hêton hjara selva moder his svna ånd tha ôthera hêton hjara selva tåt his svna, men tha Moder his svna ne wrde wrde navt ni meld, hwand thrvchdam thêr fêlo skêpa måked wrde, was thêr ovirflod to fåra skipmåkar, smêda, sylmåkar, rêpmåkar ånd to fåra alle ôra ambachtisljud. Thêr to boppa brochton tha sêkåmpar allerlêja syrhêda mith. Thêr fon hêdon tha wiva nocht, tha fâmna nocht, tha mangêrtne nocht, ånd thêrof hêdon al hjara mêgum nocht, ånd al hjara frjundum ånd åthum.

Further they said, Every child of Frya has permission to let his voice be heard before the choice of a prince is decided; but if it comes to that, that you choose a king, then also we will have our say. From all that we can see, Wr-alda has appointed Friso for it, for he has brought him here in a wonderful way. Friso knows the tricks of the Gauls, whose language he speaks; he can therefore watch against their craftiness. Then there is something else to keep the eye upon. What count could be chosen as king without the others being jealous of him? All such nonsense the young maidens talked; but the old maidens, though few in number, tapped their advice out of another cask. They said always and to every one: Friso does like the spiders. At night he spreads his webs in all directions, and in the day he catches in them all his unsuspecting friends. Friso says he cannot suffer any priests or foreign princes, but we say that he cannot suffer anybody but himself; therefore he will not allow the citadel of Stavia to be rebuilt; therefore he will not have the mother again. To-day Friso is your counsellor, to-morrow he will be your king, in order to have full power over you. Among the people there now existed two parties. The old and the poor wished to have the mother again, but the young and the warlike wished for a father and a king. The first called themselves mother's sons, the others father's sons, but the mother's sons did not count for much; because there were many ships to build, there was a good time for all kinds of workmen. Moreover, the sea-rovers brought all sorts of treasures, with which the maidens were pleased, the girls were pleased, and their relations and friends.

Tha Friso bi fjuwertich jêr et Stâveren hushalden hêde sturf-er.* Thrvch sin bijelda hêde-r fêlo stâta wither to manlik ôtherum brocht, thach jef wi thêr thrvch bêter wrde thvr ik navt bijechta. Fon alle Grêva thêr bifâra him wêron n-as thêr nimman sâ bifâmed lik Friso wêst. Tha sâ as-k êr sêide, tha jonge fâmna kêthon sina love, thahwila tha alda fâmna ella dêdon vmb-im to achtjane ând hâtlik to mâkjane bi alle mânniska. Nw ne machton tha alda fâmna him thêr mitha wel navt ne stôra in sina bijeldinga, men hja hâvon mith hjara bâra thach alsa fül utrjucht thât-er sturven is svnder thât er kâning wêre.

Nw wil ik skriwa vr Adel sin svnv.

Friso thêr vsa skidnese lêred hêde ut-et bok thêra Adellinga, hêde ella dên vmbe hjara frjundskip to winnande. Sin êroste svnv thêr hi hir won by Swêthirte sin wif, heth-er bi stonda Adel hêten. And afskên hi kâmpade mith alle sin weld, vmbe nêne burga to forstâlane ner wither vp to bvwande, thach sand hi Adel nêi thêre burch et Texland til thju hi diger bi diger kvd wertha machta, mith ella hwat to vsa êwa, tâle ând sedum hêreth. Tha Adel twintich jêr tâlde lêt Friso him to sin âjn skol kvma, ând as er thêr utlêred was, lêt-er him thrvch ovir alle stâta fâra. Adel was-ne minlika skalk, bi sin fâra heth-er fêlo âtha wnnen. Dâna is-t kvmen thât et folk him Atha-rik hêten heth, awet hwat him âfternêi sa wel to puse kêm, hwand as sin tât fallen was, bilêv-er in sin stêd svnder that er vr-et kjasa ên er ôthera Grêva sprêka kêm.

Thahwila Adel to Texland inna lêre wêre, was thêr tefta en êlle ljawe fâm in vpper burch. Hju kêm fon ut tha Saxanamarkum wêi, fon ut-êre stâtha thêr is kêthen Svôbaland thêr thrvch wârth hju to Texland Svôbene† hêten, afskên

---

* 263 v. Chr. † Hamconius, p. 8. Suobinna.

THE BOOK OF ADELA'S FOLLOWERS.   209

When Friso had been nearly forty years at Staveren he died. Owing to him many of the states had been joined together again, but that we were the better for it I am not prepared to certify. Of all the counts that preceded him there was none so renowned as Friso; for, as I said before, the young maidens spoke in his praise, while the old maidens did all in their power to make him hateful to everybody. Although the old women could not prevent his meddling, they made so much fuss that he died without becoming king.

Now I will write about his son Adel.

Friso, who had learned our history from the book of the Adelingen, had done everything in his power to win their friendship. His eldest son, whom he had by his wife Swethirte, he named Adel; and although he strove with all his might to prevent the building or restoring any citadels, he sent Adel to the citadel of Texland in order to make himself better acquainted with our laws, language, and customs. When Adel was twenty years old Friso brought him into his own school, and when he had fully educated him he sent him to travel through all the states. Adel was an amiable young man, and in his travels he made many friends, so the people called him Atharik—that is, rich in friends—which was very useful to him afterwards, for when his father died he took his place without a question of any other count being chosen.

While Adel was studying at Texland there was a lovely maiden at the citadel. She came from Saxenmarken, from the state of Suobaland, therefore she was called at Texland Suobene, although her name

---

* 263 before Christ.   † Hamconius, page 8. Suobinna.

hjra nôme Ifkja wêre. Adel hêde hja ljaf krêjen ånd hju hêde Adel ljaf, men sin tåt bêd-im hi skolde jet wachtja. Adel was hêrich, men alsa ring sin tåt fallen was ånd hi sêten, sand hi bistonda bodon nei Berth-holda hira tåt hin, as-er sine toghter to wif håva machte. Bertholda wêr-ne forste fon vnforbastere sêd, hi hêde Ifkja nêi Texland inna lêre svnden inner håpe that hja ênis to burchfåm kêre wrde skolde in sine åjn land. Thach hi hêde hjara bêder gêrte kånna lêred, thêrvmbe gvng-er to ånd jef hjam sina sêjen. Ifkja wêr-ne kante Fryas. Far sa fêre ik hja håv kånna lêred, heth hju alôn wrocht ånd wrot til thju Fryasbern wither kvma machte vndera selva êwa ånd vnder ênen bôn. Vmbe tha månniska vppa hira syd to krêjande, was hju mith hira frjudelf fon of hira tåt thrvch alle Saxanamarka fåren and forth nêi Gêrtmånnja. Gêrtmannja alsa hêdon tha Gêrtmanna hjara ståt hêten, thêr hja thrvch Gosa hira bijeldinga krêjen hêde. Dåna gvngen hja nei tha Dênemarka. Fon tha Dênemarka gvngon hja skip nei Texland. Fon Texland gvngon hja nêi Westflyland en sa allingen tha sê nêi Walhallagåra hin. Fon Walhallagåra brûdon hja allingen thêra sûder Hrênum al ont hja mith gråta frêse boppa thêre Rêne bi tha Marsåta kêmon* hwêrfon vsa Apollånja skrêven heth. Tho hja thêr en stût wêst hêde, gvngon hja wither nêi tha delta.† As hja nw en tid lông nêi tha delta offåren wêron al ont hja inna strêk fon thêre alda burch Aken‡ kêmon, sind thêr vnwurlinga fjuwer skalka morth and naked uteklåt. Hja wêron en lith åfter an kvmen. Min brother thêr vral by was hêde hja often vrbêden, thach hja nêde navt ne hêred. Tha bônar thêr thåt dên hêde wêron Twisklåndar thêr juddêga drist wêi ovira Hrêna kvma to morda and to råwande. Tha Twislåndar thåt sind bannane ånd wêi britne Fryas-

---

* Zie bl. 150.   ‡ Aken, Aken.
† Delte nog in N. Holland in gebruik, laagte.

was Ifkja. Adel fell in love with her, and she with him, but his father wished him to wait a little. Adel did as he wished; but as soon as he was dead, sent messengers to Berthold, her father, to ask her in marriage. Berthold was a prince of high-principled feelings. He had sent his daughter to Texland in the hope that she might be chosen Burgtmaagd in her country, but when he knew of their mutual affection he bestowed his blessing upon them. Ifkja was a clever Frisian. As far as I have been able to learn, she always toiled and worked to bring the Frya's people back under the same laws and customs. To bring the people to her side, she travelled with her husband through all Saxenmarken, and also to Geertmannia—as the Geertmen had named the country which they had obtained by means of Gosa. Thence they went to Denmark, and from Denmark by sea to Texland. From Texland they went to Westflyland, and so along the coast to Walhallagara; thence they followed the Zuiderryn (the Waal), till, with great apprehension, they arrived beyond the Rhine at the Marsaten of whom our Apollonia has written. When they had stayed there a little time, they returned to the lowlands. When they had been some time descending towards the lowlands, and had reached about the old citadel of Aken, four of their servants were suddenly murdered and stripped. They had loitered a little behind. My brother, who was always on the alert, had forbidden them to do so, but they did not listen to him. The murderers that had committed this crime were Twisklanders, who had at that time audaciously crossed the Rhine to murder and to steal. The Twisklanders are banished and fugitive children of Frya,

---

* See page 150.
† *Delta*, still in use in North Holland for swampy land.

bern, men hjara wiva håvath hja fon tha Tartarum råwet. Tha Tartara is en brûn Findas folk, althus hêten thrvchdam hja alle folka to strida uttarta. Hja send al hrutar ånd råwar. Thêr fon send tha Twisklândar alsa blod thorstich wrden. Tha Twisklândar tham thju årgnise dên hêde, hêton hjara selva Frya jeftha Franka. Ther wêron sêide min brother råda bruna ånd wita mong. Thêre thêr råd jeftha brun wêron biton hjara hêre mith sjalkwêter* wit. Nêidam hjara ônthlita thêr brun by wêr, alsa wrdon hja thesto lêdliker thêr thrvch. Êvin as Apollånja biskojadon hja åfternêi Lydasburch ånd et Aldergå. Dåna tågon hju in over Ståverens wrde by hjara ljuda rond. Alsa minlik hêdon hja hjara selva anståled that tha månniska ra allerwêikes halda wilde. Thrê mônatha forther sand Adel bodon nêi alle åthum thêr hi biwnnen hêde ånd lêt tham bidda, hja skoldon inna Minna mônath lichta ljuda to him senda.†

---

* Diod Sic. V. 28.
† Hier heeft de afschrijver Hiddo oera Linda een blad te veel omgeslagen, en daardoor twee bladzijden overgeslagen.

but their wives they have stolen from the Tartars. The Tartars are a brown tribe of Finda's people, who are thus named because they make war on everybody. They are all horsemen and robbers. This is what makes the Twisklanders so bloodthirsty. The Twisklanders who had done the wicked deed called themselves Frijen or Franken. There were among them, my brother said, red, brown, and white men. The red and brown made their hair white with lime-water—but as their faces remained brown, they were only the more ugly. In the same way as Apollonia, they visited Lydasburgt and the Alderga. Afterwards they made a tour of all the neighbourhood of Stavera. They behaved with so much amiability, that everywhere the people wished to keep them. Three months later, Adel sent messengers to all the friends that he had made, requesting them to send to him their " wise men " in the month of May.†

---

* Diodorus Siculus, V. 28.
† Here the copyist, Hiddo oera Linda, has turned over a leaf too much, and has thus omitted two pages.

sin wif sêid er thêr fåm wêst hêde to Texlånd, hêde dåna en ovirskrift krêjen. To Texland warthat jeta fêlo skrifta fvnden, thêr navt in-t bok thêra Adelinga vrskrêven send. Fon thissa skriftum hêde Gosa ên bi hira utroste wille lêid, thêr thrvch tha aldeste fåm Albêthe avbêr måkt wertha most, alsa ringen Friso fallen was.

Hyr is that Skrift mith Gosas Rêd.

Tha Wr.alda bern jêf an tha modera fon thåt månniskelik slachte, thå lêid er êne tåle in aller tonga ånd vp aller lippa. Thjus mêide hêde Wr.alda an tha månniska jêven, til thju hja månlik ôthera thêrmith machte kånbêr måkja, hwat mån formyde mot ånd hwat mån bijagja mot vmbe sêlighêd to findane ånd sêlighêd to haldane in al êvghêd. Wr.alda is wis ånd god ånd al fårsjande. Nêidam er nw wist, thåt luk ånd sêlighêd fon irtha flya mot, jef boshêd düged bidroga mêi, alsa heth er an thju tål êne rjuchtfêrdige åjendomlikhêd fåst bonden. Thjus åjendomlikhêd is thêr an lêgen, thåt mån thêr mith nên lêjen sêge, ner bidroglika worda sprêka ne mêi svnder stem lêth noch svnder skåmråd, thrvch hvam mån tha bosa fon hirte bistonda vrkånna mêi. Nêidam vsa tåle thus to luk ånd to sêlighêd wêjath, ånd thus mith wåkt åjen tha bosa nygonga, thêrvmbe is hju mith alle rjucht godis tåle hêten, ånd alle tha jêna hwam hja an êre halda håvath thêr gôme fon. Tha hwat is bêrth. Alsa ring thêr mong vsa halfsusterum ånd halfbrotharum bidrogar vpkêmon, tham hjara selva fori godis skalkum utjavon, also ring is thåt owers wrden. Tha bidroglika prestera ånd tha wrangwrêja forsta thêr immer sêmin hêladon, wildon nêi wilkêr lêva ånd buta god-is êwa dvan. In hjara

his wife, he said, who had been maagd of Texland, had received a copy of it. In Texland many writings are still found which are not copied in the book of the Adelingen. One of these writings had been placed by Gosa with her last will, which was to be opened by the oldest maiden, Albetha, as soon as Friso was dead.

HERE IS THE WRITING WITH GOSA'S ADVICE.

When Wr-alda gave children to the mothers of mankind, he gave one language to every tongue and to all lips. This gift Wr-alda had bestowed upon men in order that by its means they might make known to each other what must be avoided and what must be followed to find salvation, and to hold salvation to all eternity. Wr-alda is wise and good, and all-foreseeing. As he knew that happiness and holiness would flee from the earth when wickedness could overcome virtue, he has attached to the language an equitable property. This property consists in this, that men can neither lie nor use deceitful words without stammering or blushing, by which means the innately bad are easily known.

As thus our language opens the way to happiness and blessedness, and thus helps to guard against evil inclinations, it is rightly named the language of the gods, and all those by whom it is held in honour derive honour from it. But what has happened? As soon as among our half brothers and sisters deceivers arose, who gave themselves out as servants of the good, it soon became otherwise. The deceitful priests and the malignant princes, who always clung together, wished to live according to their own inclinations, without regard to the laws of right. In their wickedness they went

tajodished send hja to gvngen ånd håvon ôthera tåla forsvnnen, til thju hja hêmlik machte sprêka in åjenwårtha fon alrek ôtherum, vr alle bosa thinga ånd vr alle vnwêrthlika thinga svnder thåt stemlêth hjam vrrêda mocht nach skåmråd hjara gelåt vrderva. Men hwat is thêrut bern. Êvin blyd as-t sêd thêra goda krûdum fon vnder ne grvûd ut vntkêmth, thåt avbêr sêjed is thrvch goda ljuda by helle dêi, êven blyd brength tyd tha skådlika krûda an-t ljucht, thêr sêjed send thrvch bosa ljuda in-t forborgne ånd by thjustrenesse.

Tha lodderiga mangertne ånd tha vnmånlika knåpa thêr mitha vvla presterum ånd forstum horadon vntlvkadon tha nya tåla an hjara bola, thêrwisa send hja forth kvmen êmong tha folkrum, til thju hja god-is tåle glåd vrjetten håve. Wilst nw wêta hwat thêr of wrden is? Nv stemlêth ner gelåt hjara bosa tochta navt longer mar vrrêdon, nv is düged fon ut hjara midden wêken, wisdom is folgth ånd frydom is mith gvngen, êndracht is sok råkt ånd twispalt heth sin stêd innommen, ljafde is fljucht ånd hordom sith mith nyd an têfel, ånd thêr êr rjuchtfêrdichhêd welde, welth nv thåt swêrd. Alle send slåvona wrden, tha ljuda fon hjara hêra, fon nyd, bosa lusta ånd bigyrlikhêd. Hêde hja nvmår êne tåle forsvnnen, müglik was-t thån jet en lith god gvngen. Men hja håvon alsa fêlo tåla utfonden as thêr ståta send. Thêrthrvch mêi thåt êne folk thåt ôre folk êvin min forstån as thju kv thene hvnd ånd thi wolf thåt skêp. Thit mügath tha stjurar bitjuga. Thach dånå is-t nv wêi kvmen, thåt alle slåvona folkar månlik ôthara lik ôra månniska biskoja ånd thåt hja to straffe hjarar vndigerhêd ånd fon hjara vrmêtenhêd, månlik ôthera alsa long biorloge ånd bikampa moton til thju alle vrdilgad send.

so far as to invent other languages, so that they might speak secretly in anybody's presence of their wicked and unworthy affairs without betraying themselves by stammering, and without showing a blush upon their countenances. But what has that produced? Just as the seed of good herbs which has been sown by good men in the open day springs up from the ground, so time brings to light the evil seed which has been sown by wicked men in secret and in darkness.

The wanton girls and effeminate youths who consorted with the immoral priests and princes, taught the new language to their companions, and thus spread it among the people till God's language was clean forgotten. Would you know what came of all this? how that stammering and blushing no longer betrayed their evil doings;—virtue passed away, wisdom and liberty followed; unity was lost, and quarrelling took its place; love flew away, and unchastity and envy met round their tables; and where previously justice reigned, now it is the sword. All are slaves—the subjects of their masters, envy, bad passions and covetousness. If they had only invented one language things might possibly have still gone on well; but they invented as many languages as there are states, so that one people can no more understand another people than a cow a dog, or a wolf a sheep. The mariners can bear witness to this. From all this it results that all the slave people look upon each other as strangers; and that as a punishment of their inconsiderateness and presumption, they must quarrel and fight till they are all destroyed.

Hyr is nv min Rêd.

Bist thv alsa gyrich that thu irtha allêna erva wilste, alsa achst thv nimmer måre nên ôre tåle ovir thina wêra ni kvma to lêtane as god-is tåle, ånd thån achst thv to njodane, til thju thin åjn tåle fry fon uthêmeda klinka bilyweth. Wilst thv thåt er svme fon Lydas bern ånd fon Findas bern resta, så dvath stv êvin alsa. Thju tåle thêra Ast Skênlandar is thrvch tha wla Mågjara vrbrûd; thju tåle thêra Kaltana folgar is thrvch tha smûgrige Gole vrderven. Nv send wi alsa mild wêst vmbe tha witherkvmande Hellêna folgar wither in vs midden to nêmande, men ik skrom ånd ben sêrelik ange, thåt hja vs mild-sa vrjelda skilun mith vrbrûding vsra rêne tåle.

Fül håvon wi witherfåren, men fon alle burgum, thêr thrvch arge tyd vrhomlath send ånd vrdiligad, heth Irtha Fryasburch vnforleth bihalden; åk mêi ik thêr by melda thåt Fryas jeftha god-is tåle hir evin vnforleth bihalden is.

Hyr to Texland most mån thus skola stifta, fon alle ståtum thêr et mitha alda sêdum halda, most-et jongk folk hyr hinne senden wrde, åfterdam mochton thêra utlêred wêre tha ôra helpa thêr to honk vrbêide. Willath tha ôra folkar ysre wêron fon thi sella ênd thêrvr mith thi sprêka ånd thinga, så moton hja to god-iståle wither kêra. Lêrath hja god-iståle så skilun tha worda fry-så ånd rjucht-hå to hjara inkvma, in hjara brêin skilet thån bijina to glimmande ånd to glorande til thju ella to-nę logha warth. Thissa logha skil alle balda forsta vrtêra ånd alle skinfråna ånd smûgriga prestera.

Tha bêinde ånd fêrhêmande sendabodon hêdon nocht fon vr thåt skrift, thach thêr ne kêmon nêne skola. Thå stifte Adel selva skola, åfter him dêdon tha ôra forsta lik hy. Jêrlikis gvngon Adel ånd Ifkja tha skola skoja. Fandon hja thån êmong tha inhêmar ånd uthêmar seliga thêr ekkorum

Here is my Counsel.

If you wish that you alone should inherit the earth, you must never allow any language but God's language to pass your lips, and take care that your own language remains free from outlandish sounds. If you wish that some of Lyda's children and some of Finda's children remain, you must do the same. The language of the East Schoonlanders has been perverted by the vile Magyars, and the language of the followers of Kaltana has been spoiled by the dirty Gauls. Now, we have been weak enough to admit among us the returned followers of Hellenia, but I anxiously fear that they will reward our weakness by debasing our pure language.

Many things have happened to us, but among all the citadels that have been disturbed and destroyed in the bad time, Irtha has preserved Fryasburgt uninjured; and I may remark that Frya's or God's language has always remained here untainted.

Here in Texland, therefore, schools should be established; and from all the states that have kept to the old customs the young people should be sent here, and afterwards those whose education is complete can help those who remain at home. If foreigners come to buy ironwares from you, and want to talk and bargain, they must come back to God's language. If they learn God's language, then the words, " to be free " and "to have justice," will come to them, and glimmer and glitter in their brains to a perfect light, and that flame will destroy all bad princes and hypocritical dirty priests.

The native and foreign messengers were pleased with that writing, but no schools came from it. Then Adel established schools himself. Every year Adel and Ifkja went to inspect the schools. If they found a friendly feeling

frjundskip bâradon, så lêton bêde gråte blidskip blika. Hêdon svme seliga ekkorum frjundskip sworen, alsa lêton hja alra mannalik to manlik ôrum kvma, mith gråte ståt lêton hja thån hjara nôma in en bok skriva, thrvch hjam thåt bok thêra frjundskip hêten, åfter dam warth fêrst halden. Al thissa plêga wrde dên vmbe tha asvndergana twyga fon Fryas stam wither et sêmene to snôrane. Men tha famna thêr Adel ånd Ifkja nydich wêron, sêidon that hja-t niwerth ôre vr dêdon as vmb en gode hrop, ånd vmb bi grådum to weldana in ovir ênis ôther man his ståt.

By min tåt sinra skriftum håv ik ênen brêf funden, skrêvin thrvch Ljudgêrth thene Gêrtmån,* bihalva svmlika sêka thêr min tåt allêna jelde, jêf ik hyr thåt ôthera to thåt besta.

Pang-ab, thåt is fyf wåtera ånd hwêr neffen wi wech kvme, is-ne runstråme fon afsvnderlika skênhêd, ånd fif wåtera hêten vmb thet fjuwer ôra runstråma thrvch sine mvnd in sê floja. Êl fere åstwarth is noch ne gråte runstråme thêr hêlige jeftha fråna Gong-ga hêten. Twisk thysum runstråmne is-t lônd thêra Hindos. Bêda runstrama runath fon tha håga bergum nêi tha delta del. Tha berga hwanå se del stråme sind alsa håch thet se to tha himel låja. Thêrvmbe wårth-et berchta Himellåja berchta hêten. Vnder tha Hindos ånd ôthera ut-a lôndum sind welka ljuda mank thêr an stilnise by malkorum kvma. Se gelåvath thet se vnforbastere bern Findas sind. Se gelåvath thet Finda fon ut-et Himmellåja berchta bern is, hwanå se mith hjara bern nêi tha delta jeftha lêgte togen is. Welke vnder tham gelåvath thet se mith hjra bern vppet skum thêr hêlige Gongga del gonggen is. Thêrvmbe skolde thi runstråme hêlige Gongga hêta. Mår tha prestera thêr ut en ôr lônd wech kvma lêton thi ljuda vpspêra ånd vrbarna, thêrvmbe

---

* Zie bl. 164.

existing between the natives and foreigners, they were extremely pleased. If there were any who had sworn friendship together, they assembled the people, and with great ceremony let them inscribe their names in a book which was called the Book of Friendship, and afterwards a festival was held. All these customs were kept up in order to bring together the separate branches of Frya's race; but the maidens who were opposed to Adel and Ifkja said that they did it for no other reason than to make a name for themselves, and to bring all the other states under their subjection.

Among my father's papers I found a letter from Liudgert the Geertman. Omitting some passages which only concern my father, I proceed to relate the rest.

Punjab, that is five rivers, and by which we travel, is a river of extraordinary beauty, and is called Five Rivers, because four other streams flow into the sea by its mouth. Far away to the eastward is another large river, the Holy or Sacred Ganges. Between these two rivers is the land of the Hindoos. Both rivers run from the high mountains to the plains. The mountains in which their sources lie are so high that they reach the heavens (laia), and therefore these mountains are called Himmellaia. Among the Hindoos and others out of these countries there are people who meet together secretly. They believe that they are pure children of Finda, and that Finda was born in the Himmellaia mountains, whence she went with her children to the lowlands. Some of them believe that she, with her children, floated down upon the foam of the Ganges, and that that is the reason why the river is called the Sacred Ganges. But the priests, who came from another country, traced out these people and had them burnt, so that they

---

* See page 164.

ne thurvath se far hjara sêk nit ôpentlik ut ni kvma. In thet lônd sind ôlle prestera tjok ånd rik. In hjara chårka werthat ôllerlêja drochtenlika byldon fvnden, thêr vnder sind fêlo golden mank. Biwesta Pangab thêr sind tha Yra jeftha wranga, tha Gedrostne jeftha britne, ånd tha Orjetten jeftha vrjetne. Ol thisa nôma sind-ar thrvch tha nydige prestera jêven, thrvchdam hja fon ar fljuchte, vmb sêda ånd gelâv, bi hjara kvmste hêdon vsa ethla hjara selva åk an tha åstlika ower fon Pangab del set, men vmb thêra prestera wille sind se åk nêi thêr wester ower fåren. Thêrthrvch håvon wi tha Yra ånd tha ôthera kenna lêrth. Tha Yra ne sind nêne yra mâr gôda minska thêr nêna byldon to lêta nach ônbidda, åk willath se nêna chårka nach prestar doga, ånd êvin als wi-t fråna ljucht fon Fåsta vpholda, êvin så holdon se ôllerwechs fjur in hjara hûsa vp. Kvmth môn efter êl westlik, ôlså kvmth môn by tha Gedrostne. Fon tha Gedrostne. Thisa sind mith ôra folkrum bastered ånd sprêkath ôlle afsvnderlika tåla. Thisa minska sind wêrentlik yra bonar, thêr ammer mith hjara horsa vp overa fjelda dwåla, thêr ammer jâgja ånd râwa ånd thêr hjara selva als salt-åtha forhêra an tha omhêmmande forsta, ther wille hwam se alles nither håwa hwat se birêka müge.

Thet lônd twisk Pangab ånd ther Gongga is like flet as Fryaslônd an tha sê, afwixlath mith fjeldum ånd waldum, fruchtbâr an alle dêlum, mâr thet mach nit vrletta that thêr bi hwila thûsanda by thûsanda thrvch honger biswike. Thisa hongernêde mach thêrvmbe nit an Wr.alda nach an Irtha wyten nit wertha, mâr allêna an tha forsta and prestera. Tha Hindos sind ivin blode ånd forfêred from hjara forstum, als tha hindne from tha wolva sind. Thêrvmbe håvon tha Yra ånd. ôra ra Hindos hêten, thêt hindne bitjoth. Mâr fon hjara blodhêd wårth afgrislika misbruk måkth. Kvmat thêr fêrhêmande kåpljud vmb kêren to kåpjande, alsa warth alles to jeldum

do not dare to declare openly their creed. In this country all the priests are fat and rich. In their churches there are all kinds of monstrous images, many of them of gold. To the west of the Punjab are the Yren (Iraniers), or morose (Drangianen), the Gedrosten (Gedrosiers), or runaways, and the Urgetten, or forgotten. These names are given by the priests out of spite, because they fled from their customs and religion. On their arrival our forefathers likewise established themselves to the east of the Punjab, but on account of the priests they likewise went to the west. In that way we learned to know the Yren and other people. The Yren are not savages, but good people, who neither pray to nor tolerate images; neither will they suffer priests or churches; but as we adhere to the light of Fasta, so they everywhere maintain fire in their houses. Coming still further westward, we arrive at the Gedrosten. Regarding the Gedrosten: They have been mixed with other people, and speak a variety of languages. These people are really savage murderers, who always wander about the country on horseback hunting and robbing, and hire themselves as soldiers to the surrounding princes, at whose command they destroy whatever they can reach.

The country between the Punjab and the Ganges is as flat as Friesland near the sea, and consists of forests and fields, fertile in every part, but this does not prevent the people from dying by thousands of hunger. The famines, however, must not be attributed to Wr-alda or Irtha, but to the princes and priests. The Hindoos are timid and submissive before their princes, like hinds before wolves. Therefore the Yren and others have called them Hindoos, which means hinds. But their timidity is frightfully abused. If strangers come to purchase corn, everything is turned

måkth. Thrvch tha prestera ni warth et nit wêrth, hwand thisa noch snoder ånd jyriger als alle forsta to samene, wytath êl god, thet al-et jeld endlik in hjara bûdar kvmth. Buta ånd bihalva thet tha ljuda thêr fül fon hjara forsta lyda, moton hja åk noch fül fon thet fenynige ånd wilde kwik lyda.. Thêr send store elefante thêr by êle keddum hlåpa, thêr bihwyla êle fjelda kêren vrtrappe ånd êle thorpa. Thêr sind bonte ånd swarte katta, tigrum hêten, thêr så gråt als gråte kalvar sind, thêr minsk ånd djar vrslynne. Bûta fêlo ôra wriggum sind thêr snåka fon af tha gråte êner wyrme ål to tha gråte êner båm. Tha gråteste kennath en êle kv vrslynna, mår tha lythste sind noch frêsliker als tham. Se holdon hjara selva twisk blom ånd fruchta skul vmb tha minska to bigåna tham thêr of plokja wille. Is môn thêr fon byten, så mot môn stårva, hwand åjen hjara fenyn heth Irtha nêna krûda jêven, ôlsånåka tha minska hjara selva håvon skildich måkt an afgodie. Forth sind thêr ôllerlêja slacht fon håchdiska nyndiska ånd adiska, ôl thisa diska sind yvin als tha snåka fon of ne wyrme til-ne båmstame gråt, nêi that hja gråt jof frêslik sind, sind hjara nôma, thêr ik alle nit noma ni ken, tha aldergråtesta ådiska sind algåtter hêten, thrvchdam se yvin grûsich bitte an thet rotte kwik, that mith-a stråma fon boppa nêi tha delta dryweth as an thet lêvande kwik, that se bigåna müge. An tha westsyde fon Pangab, wånå wi wech kvme ånd hwer ik bern ben, thêr blojath ånd waxath tha selva frûchta ånd nochta as an tha åstsyde. To fåra wrdon er åk tha selva wrigga fonden, mår vsa êthla havon alle krylwalda vrbårnath ånd alsånåka åfter et wilde kwik jåged, that ther fê mår resta. Kvmtk man êl westlik fon Pangab, then finth man neffen fette etta åk

into money, and this is not prevented by the priests, because they, being more crafty and rapacious than all the princes put together, know very well that all the money will come into their pockets. Besides what the people suffer from their princes, they suffer a great deal from poisonous and wild beasts. There are great elephants that sometimes go about in whole flocks and trample down cornfields and whole villages. There are great black and white cats which are called tigers. They are as large as calves, and they devour both men and beasts. Besides other creeping animals there are snakes from the size of a worm to the size of a tree. The largest can swallow a cow, but the smallest are the most deadly. They conceal themselves among the fruits and flowers, and surprise the people who come to gather them. Any one who is bitten by them is sure to die, as Irtha has given no antidote to their poison, because the people have so given themselves up to idolatry. There are, besides, all sorts of lizards, tortoises, and crocodiles. All these reptiles, like the snakes, vary from the size of a worm to the trunk of a tree. According to their size and fierceness, they have names which I cannot recollect, but the largest are called alligators, because they eat as greedily the putrid cattle that float down the stream as they do living animals that they seize. On the west of the Punjab where we come from, and where I was born, the same fruits and crops grow as on the east side. Formerly there existed also the same crawling animals, but our forefathers burnt all the underwood, and so diligently hunted all the wild animals, that there are scarcely any left. To the extreme west of the Punjab there is found rich clay land

dorra gêstlanda thêr vnendlik skina, bihwila ofwixlath mith ljaflika strêka, hwêran thet åg forbonden bilywet. Vnder tha fruchta fon min land sind fêlo slachta mank, thêr ik hyr nit fvnden håv. Vnder allerlêja kêren is er åk golden mank, åk goldgêle aple, hwêrfon welke så swêt as hûning sind, ånd welka sa wrang as êk. By vs werthat nochta fonden lik bern-håveda så gråt, thêr sit tsys ånd melok in, werthat se ald så måkt man ther ôlja fon, fon tha bastum måkt mån tåw ånd fon tha kernum måkt mån chelka ånd ôr geråd. Hyr inna walda håv ik krup ånd ståkbêja sjan. By vs sind bêibåma als jow lindabåma, hwêrfon tha bêja fül swêter ånd thêrwåra gråter as ståkbêja sind. Hwersa tha dêga vppa sin olderlôngste sind ånd thju svnne fon top skinth, then skinth se linrjucht vppa jow hole del. Is mån then mith sin skip êl fêr sûdlik faren, ånd mån thes meddêis mith sin gelåt nêi-t åsten kêred, så skinth svnne åjen thine winstere syde lik se ôwers åjen thine fêre syde dvath. Hyrmitha wil ik enda, mår after min skrywe skil-et thi licht nog falla, vmb tha lêgenaftiga teltjas to müge skiftane fon tha wara tellinga.—Jow Ljudgêrt.

Thet Skrift fon Bêden.

Mine nôm is Bêden, Hachgåna his svn. Konerêd min êm is nimmer bostigjath ånd alsa bernlås sturven. My heth mån in sin stêd koren. Adel thene thredde kåning fon thjuse nôme heth thju kêse godkêrth, mites ik him as mina måstre bikenna wilde. Buta thåt fvlle erv minre êm heth-er mi en êle plek grvnd jêven thåt an mina erva pålade, vnder fårwêrde that ik thêrvp skolde månniska stålla ther sina ljuda nimmerthe skolde.*

---

* Hier ontbreken in het H. S. twintig bladzijden (misschien meer), waarin Beeden geschreven heeft ovir dien koning Adel III. (Bij onze kronijk schrijvers Ubbo genoemd.)

as well as barren heaths, which seem endless, occasionally varied lovely spots on which the eye rests enchanted. Among the fruits there are many that I have not found here. Among the various kinds of corn some is as yellow as gold. There are also golden apples, of which some are as sweet as honey and others as sour as vinegar. In our country there are nuts as large as a child's head. They contain cheese and milk. When they are old oil is made from them. Of the husks ropes are made, and of the shells cups and other household utensils are made. I have found in the woods here bramble and holly berries. In my country we have trees bearing berries, as large as your lime-trees, the berries of which are much sweeter and three times as large as your gooseberries. When the days are at the longest, and the sun is in the zenith, a man's body has no shadow. If you sail very far to the south and look to the east at midday, the sun shines on your left side as it does in other countries on the right side. With this I will finish.. It will be easy for you, by means of what I have written, to distinguish between false accounts and true descriptions.—Your Luidgert.

The Writing of Beeden.

My name is Beeden, son of Hachgana. My uncle, not having married, left no children. I was elected in his place. Adel, the third king of that name, approved of the choice, provided I should acknowledge him as master. In addition to the entire inheritance of my uncle, he gave me some land which joined my inheritance, on condition that I would settle people there who should never ·his people*

---

* Here there are wanting in the manuscript twenty pages (perhaps more), in which Beeden has written about the King, Adel the Third, called Ubbo by the writers of our chronicles.

thêrvmbe wil ik thet hir-ne sted forjune.

BRÊF FON RIKA THJU ALDFAM, VPSEID TO STAVEREN BY-T JOLFÊRSTE.

Jy alle hwam his êthla mith Friso hir kêmon, min êrbydnesse to jo. Alsa jy mêne, send jy vnskeldich an afgodie. Thêr nil ik jvd navt vr sprêka, men jvd wil ik jo vppen brek wysa, thât fê bêtre sy. Jy wêtath jeftha jy nêtath navt, ho Wr.alda thusand glornôma heth, thach thât wêtath jy alle thât hy warth Alfêder hêten, ut êrsêke thât alles in ut him warth ånd waxth to fêding sinra skepsela. T-is wêr, thât Irtha warth bihwyla åk Alfêdstre hêten, thrvchdam hju alle früchd ånd nochta bêrth, hwermitha månnisk ånd djar hjara selva fêde. Thach ne skolde hju nêne früchd ner nocht navt ne bêra, bydam Wr.alda hja nêne krefta ne jêf. Ak wiva ther hjara bern måma lêta an hjara brosta, werthat fêdstra hêten. Thâ ne jêf Wr.alda thêr nên melok in, sa ne skoldon tha bern thêr nêne bâte by finda. Sâ thât by slot fon reknong Wr.alda allêna fêder bilywet. Thât Irtha bihwyla warth Alfêdstre heten, ånd êne måm fêdstre, kån jeta thrvch-ne wende, men thât-ne mån him lêt fêder hête vmbe thât er tât sy, thât strid with-åjen alle rêdnum. Thâ ik wêt wânât thjus dwêshêd wêi kvmth. Hark hyr, se kvmth fon vsa lêtha, ånd såhwersa thi folgath werthe, sâ skilun jy thêrthrvch slâvona wertha to smert fon Frya ånd jowe hâgmod to.ne straf. Ik skil jo melda ho-t by tha slâvona folkar to gvngen is, thêr åfter mêi jy lêra. Tha poppa kåningar tham nêi wilkêr lêva, stêkath Wr.alda nêi thêre krône, utn yd that Wr.alda Alfêder hêt, sa wildon hja fêdrum thêra folkar hêta. Nw wêt allera mannalik thåt-ne kêning navt ovir-ne waxdom

therefore I will allow it a place here.

LETTER OF RIKA THE OUDMAAGD, READ AT STAVEREN AT THE JUUL FEAST.

My greeting to all of you whose forefathers came here with Friso. According to what you say, you are not guilty of idolatry. I will not speak about that now, but will at once mention a failing which is very little better. You know, or you do not know, how many titles Wr-alda has; but you all know that he is named universal provider, because that everything comes and proceeds from him for the sustenance of his creatures. It is true that Irtha is named sometimes the feeder of all, because she brings forth all the fruits and grains on which men and beasts are fed; but she would not bear any fruit or grain unless Wr-alda gave her the power. Women who nourish their children at their breasts are called nurses, but if Wr-alda did not give them milk the children would find no advantage; so that, in short, Wr-alda really is the nourisher. That Irtha should be called the universal nourisher, and that a mother should be called a feeder, one can understand, figuratively speaking; but that a father should be called a feeder, because he is a father, goes against all reason. Now I know whence all this folly comes. Listen to me. It comes from our enemies; and if this is followed up you will become slaves, to the sorrow of Frya and to the punishment of your pride. I will tell you what happened to the slave people; from that you may take warning. The foreign kings, who follow their own will, place Wr-alda below the crown. From envy that Wr-alda is called the universal father, they wish also to be called fathers of the people. Now, everybody knows that kings do not regulate

ne welth, ånd thåt im sin fêding thrvch thåt folk brocht warth, men thach wildon hja fvlherdja by hjara formêtenhêd. Til thju hja to-ra dol kvma machte, alsa håvon hja thet forma navt fvldên wêst mith tha frya jefta, men håvon hja thåt folk êne tins vplêid. Fori thene skåt, tham thêrof kêm, hêradon hja vrlandiska salt-åtha, tham hja in-om hjara hova lêidon. Forth namon hja alsa fêlo wiva, as-ra luste, ånd tha lithiga forsta ånd hêra dêdon al-ên. As twist ånd tvyspalt åfternêi inna hûshaldne glupte ånd thêr-vr klåchta kêmon, thå håvon hja sêid, ja-hweder mån is thêne fêder fon sin hûshalden, thêrvmbe skil-er thêr åk bås ånd rjuchter ovir wêsa. Thå kêm wilkêr ånd êvin as tham mitha månnum in ovir tha hûshaldne welde, gvng er mit tha kåningar in ovir hjara ståt ånd folkar dvan. Thå tha kåningar et alsa wyd brocht hêdon, thåt hja fêderum thêra folkar hête, thå gvngon hja to ånd lêton byldon åfter hjara dåntne måkja, thissa byldon lêton hja inna tha cherka stalla nêst tha byldon thêra drochtne ånd thi jena tham thêr navt far bûgja nilde, warth ombrocht jeftha an kêdne dên. Jow êthla ånd tha Twisklandar håvon mitha poppa forsta ommegvngen, dåna håvon hja thjuse dwêshêd lêred. Tha navt allêna thåt svme jower mån hjara selva skeldich måkja an glornôma råw, åk mot ik my vr fêlo jower wiva biklågja. Werthat by jo mån fvnden, tham mith Wr.alda an ên lin wille, thêr werthat by jo wiva fvnden, thêr et mêi Frya wille. Vmbe thåt hja bern bêred håve, lêtath hja hjara selva modar hêta. Tha hja vrjettath, that Frya bern bêrde svnder jengong ênis mån. Jå navt allêna thåt hja Frya ånd tha êremodar fon hjara glor-rika nôma biråwa wille, hwêran hja navt nåka ne müge, hja dvath alên mitha glornôma fon hjara nêsta. Thêr send wiva thêr hjarar selva lêtath frovva hêta,

the productiveness of the earth; and that they have their sustenance by means of the people, but still they will persist in their arrogance. In order to attain their object they were not satisfied from the beginning with free gifts, but imposed a tax upon the people. With the tax thus raised they hired foreign soldiers, whom they retained about their courts. Afterwards they took as many wives as they pleased, and the smaller princes and gentry did the same. When, in consequence, quarrels and disputes arose in the households, and complaints were made about it, they said every man is the father (feeder) of his household, therefore he shall be master and judge over it. Thus arose arbitrariness, and as the men ruled over their households the kings would do over their people. When the kings had accomplished that, they should be called fathers of the people, they had statues of themselves made, and erected in the churches beside the statues of the idols, and those who would not bow down to them were either killed or put in chains. Your forefathers and the Twisklanders had intercourse with the kings, and learned these follies from them. But it is not only that some of your men have been guilty of stealing titles, I have also much to complain of against your wives. If there are men among you who wish to put themselves on a level with Wr-alda, there are also women who wish to consider themselves equals of Frya. Because they have borne children, they call themselves mothers; but they forget that Frya bore children without having intercourse with a man. Yes, they not only have desired to rob Frya and the Eeremoeders of their honourable title (with whom they cannot put themselves upon an equality), but they do the same with the honourable titles of their fellow-creatures. There are women who allow themselves to be called ladies,

afsken hja wête thåt thjuse nôme allêna to forsta wiva hêreth. Ak lêtath hja hjara toghater fåmna hêta, vntankes hja wête, thåt nêne mangêrt alsa hêta ne mêi, wåra hju to êne burch hêrth. Jy alle wånath thåt jy thruch thåt nôm råwa bêtre werthe, thach jy vrjettath thåt nyd thêr an klywet ånd thåt elk kwåd sine tuchtrode sêjath. Kêrath jy navt ne wither, så skil tid thêr waxdom an jêva, alsa stêrik thåt mån et ende thêr of navt bisjå ne mêi. Jow åfterkvmanda skilun thêr mith fêterath wertha, hja ne skilun navt ne bigripa hwånat thi slåga wêi kvme. Men afskên jy tha fåmna nêne burch bvwe ånd an lot vrlête, thach skilun thêr bilywa, hja skilun fon ut wald ånd holum kvma, hja skilun jow åfterkvmande biwysa thåt jy thêr willens skildech an send. Thån skil mån jo vrdema, jow skina skilun vrfêth fon ut-a grêvum rysa, hja skilun Wr.alda, hja skilun Frya ånd hjara fåmna anhropa, thå nimman skil-er åwet an bêtra ne müge, bifåre thåt Jol in op en ore hlåphring trêth, men thåt skil êrist bêra as thrê thûsand jêr vrhlåpen send åfter thisse êw.

ENDE FON RIKAS BRÊF.

---

* Hier eindigde het schrijven van Beeden. In het H. S. ontbreken twee bladzijden volgens de paginatuur. Maar zonder twijfel ontbreekt er meer. De afgebroken aanhef van het volgende wijst aan, dat de aanvang van het volgende geschrift verloren gegaan is en daarmede ook de aanduiding van den naam des schrijvers, die een zoon of kleinzoon van Beeden kan geweest zijn.

although they know that that only belongs to the wives of princes. They also let their daughters be called maagden, although they know that no young girls are so called unless they belong to a citadel. You all fancy that you are the better for this name-stealing, but you forget that jealousy clings to it, and that every wrong sows the seed of its own rod. If you do not alter your course, in time it will grow so strong that you cannot see what will be the end. Your descendants will be flogged by it, and will not know whence the stripes come. But although you do not build citadels for the maidens and leave them to their fate, there will still remain some who will come out of woods and caves, and will prove to your descendants that you have by your disorderliness been the cause of it. Then you will be damned. Your ghosts will rise frightened out of their graves. They will call upon Wr-alda, Frya, and her maidens, but they shall receive no succour before the Juul shall enter upon a new circuit, and that will only be three thousand years after this century.

THE END OF RIKA'S LETTER.

---

* Here the writing of Beeden ends. In the manuscript two successive pages are missing according to the paging, but no doubt there are more wanting. The abrupt opening of what follows shows that the beginning of the following writing has been lost, and, in consequence, also the notification of the name of the writer, who may have been a son or a grandson of Beeden.

thêrvmbe wil ik thåt forma vr swarte Adel skriva. Swarte Adel wêre thene fjurde kening åfter Friso. Bi sin jüged heth-er to Texland lêred, åfternêi heth-er to Ståveren lêred, ånd forth heth-er thrvch ovir alle ståta fåren. Thå thåt er fjuwer ånd tvintich jêr wêre, heth sin tåt måked thåt-er to Asega-åskar kêren is. Thå-er ênmel åskar wêre, åskte hi altid in-t fårdêl thêra årma. Tha rika, sêd-er, plêgath ênoch vnrjuchta thinga thrvch middel fon hjara jeld, thêrvmbe ågon wi to njvdane thåt tha årma nêi vs omme sjan. Thrvch thå-s ånd ôra rêdne wêr-i thene frjund thêra årma ånd thêra rika skrik. Alsa årg is-t kvmen thåt sin tåt him nêi tha ågum sach. Thå sin tåt fallen was, ånd hy vppa tham-his sêtel klywed, thå wild-er êvin god sin ambt bihalda, lik as tha keningar fon-t åsta plêgath. Tha rika nildon thåt navt ne dåja, men nw hlip allet ôra folk to håpe, ånd tha rika wêron blyde that hja hêl-hûd-is fon thêre acht of kêmon. Fon to ne hê-rade mån nimmar måra ovir êlika rjucht petårja. Hi dumde tha rika ånd hi strykte tha årma, mith hwam his helpe hi alle sêkum åskte, thêr-er bistek vp hêde. Kening Askar lik-er immer hêten warth, wêre by sjugun irthfêt lônge, så gråt sin tôl wêr, wêron åk sina krefta. Hi hêde-n hel forstån, så thåt-er alles forstånde, hwêrwr that sprêken warth, thach in sin dvan ne macht mån nêne wisdom spêra. Bi-n skên ônhlite hêd-er êne glade tonge, men jeta swarter as sin hêr is sine sêle fvnden. Thå that-er ên jêr kening wêre, nêdsêkte hi alle knåpa fon sin ståt, hja skoldon jerlikis vppet kåmp kvma ånd thêr skin-orloch måkja. In-t êrost hêde-r thêr spul mith, men to tha lersta warth-et så menêrlik, that ald ånd jong ut alle wrdum wêi kêmon to frêjande jef hja machte mith dva. Thå hi-t alsa fêre brocht hêde, lêt-er wêrskola stifta. Tha rika kêmon to bårane ånd sêidon, that

therefore I will first write about black Adel. Black Adel was the fourth king after Friso. In his youth he studied first at Texland, and then at Staveren, and afterwards travelled through all the states. When he was twenty-four years old his father had him elected Asega-Asker. As soon as he became Asker he always took the part of the poor. The rich, he said, do enough of wrong by means of their wealth, therefore we ought to take care that the poor look up to us. By arguments of this kind he became the friend of the poor and the terror of the rich. It was carried so far that his father looked up to him. When his father died he succeeded, and then he wished to retain his office as well, as the kings of the East used to do. The rich would not suffer this, so all the people rose up, and the rich were glad to get out of the assembly with whole skins. From that time there was no more talk of equality. He oppressed the rich and flattered the poor, by whose assistance he succeeded in all his wishes. King Askar, as he was always called, was seven feet high, and his strength was as remarkable as his height. He had a clear intellect, so that he understood all that was talked about, but in his actions he did not display much wisdom. He had a handsome countenance and a smooth tongue, but his soul was blacker than his hair. When he had been king for a year, he obliged all the young men in the state to come once a year to the camp to have a sham fight. At first he had some trouble with it, but at last it became such a habit that old and young came from all sides to ask if they might take part in it. When he had brought it to this point, he established military schools. The rich complained that their

hjara bern nw nên lêsa nach skryva navt ne lêrade. Askar ne melde-t navt, men as thêr kirt åfter wither skin-orloch halden warth, gvng-er vppen vpstal stonda, ånd kêtha hlûd. Tha rika sind to my kvmen to bârana, thåt hjara knåpa nên lêsa nach skryva noch lêra, ik n.åv thêr nawet vp sêith, thach hir wil ik mine mênong sedsa, ånd an tha mêna acht bithinga lêta. Thå alrek nw nêisgyrich nêi him vpsach, sêid-er forther, nêi min bigrip mot mån hjud thåt lêsa ånd skriva tha fåmna ånd alda lichta vrlêta. Ik n-il nên kwåd sprêka vr vsa êthla, ik wil allêna sega, vndera tyda hwêrvp thrvch svme så herde bogath warth, håvon tha burchfåmna twyspalt inovir vsa lånda brocht, ånd tha Modera für ånd nêi ne kvndôn twyspalt navt wither to-t land ut ne dryva. Jeta årger, thahwila hja kålta ånd petårade vr nådelåsa plêga, send tha Gola kvmen ånd håvon al vsa skêna sûdarlanda råweth. Hêmisdêga send hja mith vsa vrbrûda brotharum ånd hjara salt-åthum al overa Skelda kvmen, vs rest thus to kjasane twisk-et bêra fon juk jef swêrd. Willath wi fry bilywå, alsa ågon tha knåpa thåt lêsa ånd skryva får-hôndis åfterwêi-n to lêtane ånd in stêde that hja invppa mêide hwip ånd swik spêle, moton hja mith swêrd ånd spêr spêla. Seud wi in alle dêla ofned ånd tha knåpa stor enoch vmb helmet ånd skild to bêrane ånd tha wêpne to hôntêrane, then skil ik my mith jower helpa vppa thene fjand werpa. Tha Gola mêieath then tha nither-lêga fon hjara helpar ånd salt-åthum vppa vsa fjeldum skryva mith-et blod, thåt ût hjara wudum drjupth. Håvon wi thene fyand ên mel far vs ût drêven, alsa moton wi thêrmith forth gvnga, alhwenne thêr nên Gola ner Slåvona nach Tartara måra fon Fryas erv to vrdryvane send. Tha-s rjucht, hrypon tha måsta ånd tha rika ne thvradon hjara mvla navt êpen ne dva. Thjus tosprêke hêd

children no longer learned to read and write. Askar paid no attention to it; but shortly afterwards, when a sham fight was held, he mounted a throne and spoke aloud: The rich have come to complain to me that their boys do not learn to read and write. I answered nothing; but I will now declare my opinion, and let the general assembly decide. While they all regarded him with curiosity, he said further: According to my idea, we ought to leave reading and writing at present to the maagden and wise people. I do not wish to speak ill of our forefathers; I will only say that in the times so vaunted by some, the Burgtmaagden introduced disputes into our country, which the mothers were unable, either first or last, to put an end to. Worse still, while they talked and chattered about useless customs the Gauls came and seized all our beautiful southern country. Even at this very time our degenerate brothers and their soldiers have already come over the Scheldt. It therefore remains for us to choose whether we will carry a yoke or a sword. If we wish to be and to remain free, it behoves our young men to leave reading and writing alone for a time; and instead of playing games of swinging and wrestling, they must learn to play with sword and spear. When we are completely prepared, and the boys are big enough to carry helmet and shield and to use their weapons, then, with your help, I will attack the enemy. The Gauls may then record the defeat of their helpers and soldiers upon our fields with the blood that flows from their wounds. When we have once expelled the enemy, then we must follow it up till there are no more Gauls, Slaves, or Tartars to be driven out of Fryä's inheritance. That is right, the majority shouted, and the rich did not dare to open their mouths.

er sekur to fara forsonnen ånd vrskriva lêten, hwand sêwendis fon thêre selvare dêi wêron tha ofskriftum thêra hwel in twintich honda ånd thi alle wêron ênishlûdende. Afternêi bifel-er tha skipmanna, hja skoldon dubbele fårstêwene måkja lêta, hwêran mån êne stêlen krånboga macht fåstigja. Thêra thêr åfterwêi bilêv warth bibot, kvn imman swêra that-er nêne midle navt nêde, alsa moston tha rika fon sin gå-t bitalja. Hjud skil mån sjan hwêr vppa al thåt bå hêi ûthlåpen is. An-t north-ende fon Britanja thåt fvl mith håga bergum is, thêr sit en Skots folk, vr-et måradêl ût Fryas blod sproten, vr-a êne helte send hja ût Kåltana-folgar, vr-et ôra dêl ût Britne ånd bannane, thêr by grådum mith tyd fon-ût-a tinlônum thêr hinna fljuchte. Thêr ut-a tinlôna kêmon, håvath algadur vrlandiska wiva jeftha fon vrlandis tuk. Thi alle send vnder-et weld thêra Golum, hjara wêpne send woden boga ånd spryta mith pintum fon herthis-hornum åk fon flintum. Hjara hûsa send fon sådum ånd strê ånd svme hêmath inna hola thêra bergum. Skêpon thêr hja råwed håve, is hjara ênge skåt. Mong tha åfter-kvmanda thêra Kåltanafolgar håvath svme jeta ysera wêpne, thêr hja fon hjara êthlum urven håve. Vmbe nw god forstån to werthande, môt ik min telling vr thåt Skotse folk resta lêta, ånd êwet fon tha hêinda Krêkalanda skriva. Tha hêinda Krêkalanda håvon vs to fara allêna to hêrath, men sunt vnhüglika tidum håvon ra thêr åk åfterkvmanda fon Lyda ånd fon Finda nitherset, fon tha lersta kêmon to tha lersta en êle håpe fon Trôje. Trôje alsa heth êne stêde hêten, thêr et folk fon tha fêre Krêkalanda innomth ånd vrhomelt heth. Thå tha Trôjana to tha hêinda Krêkalandum nestled wêron, tha håvon hja thêr mith tid ånd flit êne sterke stêd mith wålla ånd burgum bvwed, Rome, that is

He must certainly have thought over this address and had it written out, for on the evening of the same day there were copies in at least twenty different hands, and they all sounded the same. Afterwards he ordered the ship people to make double prows, upon which steel crossbows could be fixed. Those who were backward in doing this were fined, and if they swore that they had no means, the rich men of the village were obliged to pay. Now we shall see what resulted from all this bustle. In the north part of Britain there exists a Scotch people—the most of them spring from Frya's blood—some of them are descended from the followers of Keltana, and, for the rest, from Britons and fugitives who gradually, in the course of time, took refuge there from the tin mines. Those who come from the tin mines have wives, either altogether foreign or of foreign descent. They are all under the dominion of the Gauls. Their arms are wooden bows and arrows pointed with stag's-horn or flint. Their houses are of turf and straw, and some of them live in caves in the mountains. Sheep that they have stolen form their only wealth. Some of the descendants of Keltana's followers still have iron weapons, which they have inherited from their forefathers. In order to make myself well understood, I must let alone for a while my account of the Scotch people, and write something about the near Krekalanders (Italians). The Krekalanders formerly belonged to us only, but from time immemorial descendants of Lyda and Finda have established themselves there. Of these last there came in the end a whole troop from Troy. Troy is the name of a town that the far Krekalanders (Greeks) had taken and destroyed. When the Trojans had nestled themselves among the near Krekalanders, with time and industry they built a strong town with walls and citadels, named Rome, that is,

Rum, hêten. Thâ thât dên was, heth thât folk him selva thrvch lest ånd weld fon thât êle lånd mâster mâked. Thât folk thât anda sûdside thêre Middelsê hêmth, is fâr-et mâra dêl fon Fhonysja wêi kvmen. Tha Fhonysjar * send en bastred folk, hja send fon Fryas blod ånd fon Findas blod ånd fon Lyda his blod. Thât folk fon Lyda send thêr as slâvona, men thrvch tha vntucht thêr wyva håvon thissa swarte månniska al-et ôra folk bastered ånd brun vrfårvet. Thit folk ånd tham fon Rome kåmpath ôlån vmb-et mâsterskip fon tha Middelsê. Forth lêvath tham fon Roma an fjandskip with tha Fonysjar, ånd hjara prestera thêr-et rik allêna welda wille wr irtha, ne mügon tha Gola navt ne sjan. Thât forma håvon hja tha Fphonysjar Mis-selja ofnomen, dånå alle landa, thêr sûd-ward, westward ånd northward lidsa, åk et sûdardêl fon Britanja, ånd allerwêikes håvon hja tha Fonysjar prestera, that hêth tha Gola vrjågeth, dånå sind thusanda Gola nêi north Brittanja brit. Kirt vrlêden was thêr tha vreste thêra Golum sêten vppa thêre burch, thêr is kêthen Kêrenåk that is herne, hwanath hi sin bifêla jef an alle ôra Gola. Ak was thêr al hjara gold togadur brocht. Kêren herne jeftha Kêrenåk is êne stênen burch, thêr êr an Kålta hêrde. Thêrvmbe wildon tha fâmna fon tha åfterkvmande thêra Kåltana-folgar tha burch wither hâ. Alsa was thrvch tha fyanskip thêra fâmna ånd thêra Go-lum faithe ånd twist in ovir thât Berchland kvmen mith morth ånd brônd. Vsa stjûrar kêmou thêr fåken wol hålja, thât hja sellade fori tobirêde hûdum ånd linne. Askar was often mith wêst, an stilnesse hêd-er mith tha fâmna ånd mith svme forstum åtskip sloten, ånd him selva forbonden vmbe tha Gola to vrjågane ût Kêrenåk. As-er thêrnêi wither kêm jef hi tha forsta ånd wig-andliksta manna ysere helma ånd stêla boga. Orloch was mith kvmen ånd kirt åfter flojadon strâma blod by

---

* Fhonysiar, Carthagers.

Spacious. When this was done, the people by craft and force made themselves masters of the whole land. The people who live on the south side of the Mediterranean Sea, come for the most part from Phœnicia. The Phœnicians (Puniers or Carthaginians) are a bastard race of the blood of Frya, Finda, and Lyda. The Lyda people were there as slaves, but by the unchastity of the women these black people have degenerated the other people and dyed them brown. These people and the Romans are constantly struggling for the supremacy over the Mediterranean Sea. The Romans, moreover, live at enmity with the Phœnicians; and their priests, who wish to assume the sole government of the world, cannot bear the sight of the Gauls. First they took from the Phœnicians Marseilles—then all the countries lying to the south, the west, and the north, as well as the southern part of Britain—and they have always driven away the Phœnician priests, that is the Gauls, of whom thousands have sought refuge in North Britain. A short time ago the chief of the Gauls was established in the citadel, which is called Kerenac (Karnac), that is the corner, whence he issued his commands to the Gauls. All their gold was likewise collected there. Keeren Herne (chosen corner), or Kerenac, is a stone citadel which did belong to Kalta. Therefore the maidens of the descendants of Kaltana's followers wished to have the citadel again. Thus through the enmity of the maidens and the Gaul's, hatred and quarrelling spread ever the mountain country with fire and sword. Our sea people often came there to get wool, which they paid for with prepared hides and linen. Askar had often gone with them, and had secretly made friendship with the maidens and some princes, and bound himself to drive the Gauls out of Kerenac. When he came back there again he gave to the princes and the fighting men iron helmets and steel bows. War had come with him, and soon blood was streaming down

---

* *Phonsiar* are Carthaginians.

tha hellinga thêra bergum del. Thâ Askar mênde that kans him tolâkte, gvng-er mith fjuwertich skêpum hin ånd nam Kêrenåk ånd thene vreste thêra Golum mith al sine gold. Thåt folk wêrmith hi with tha salt-åthum thêra Golum kåmped hêde, hêd-er ût-a Saxanamarkum lvkt mith lofte fon grâte hêra-râve ånd but. Thus warth tha Gola newet lêten. Afternêi nam-er twâ êlanda to berch far sinum skêpum, ånd hwånath hi lêter ûtgvng vmb alle Fonysjar skêpa ånd stêda to biråwane thêr hi bigåna kv. Tha er tobek kêm brocht-i tomet sex hvndred thêra storeste knåpum fon thåt Skotse berchfolk mith. Hi sêide that hja him to borgum jêven wêren, til thju hi sêkur wêsa machte thåt tha eldra him skolde trow bilywa, men-t was jok, hi hild ra as lifwêre et sina hova, thêr hja allera distik les krêjon in-t ryda ånd in-t hôndtêra fon allerlêja wêpne. Tha Denamarkar tham hjara selva sunt lông boppa alle ôra stjûrar stoltlike sêkåmpar hête, hêdon så ringe navt fon Askar sina glorrika dêdum navt ne hêred, jef hja wrdon nydich thêr vr, thêrmête, that hja wilde orloch brensa over-ne sê ånd over sina landa. Sjan hyr, ho hi orloch formitha machte. Twisk tha bvwfala thêre vrhomelde burch Stavja was jeta êne snode burchfåm mith svme fåmna sêten. Hjra nôme was Rêintja ånd thêr gvng en grâte hrop fon hira wishêd ût. Thjus fåm bâd an Askar hjra helpe vnder bithing, that Askar skolde tha burch Stavja wither vpbvwa lête. As-er him thêr to forbonden hêde, gvng Rêintja mith thrim fåmna nêi Hals,[*] nachtis gvng hju rêisa ånd thes dêis kêthe hju vppa alle markum ånd binna alle mêidum. Wralda sêide hju hêde hja thrvch thongar tohropa lêta that allet Fryas folk moston frjunda wertha, lik sustar ånd brothar tâmed, owers skolde Findas folk kvma ånd ra alle fon irtha vrdilligja. Nêi thongar wêron Fryas sjvgun wåkfåmkes hja anda drâme forskinnen, sjvgun nachta åfter ekkôrum.

---

[*] Hals, Holstein.

the slopes of the mountains. When Askar thought a favourable opportunity occurred, he went with forty ships and took Kerenac and the chief of the Gauls, with all his gold. The people with whom he fought against the soldiers of the Gauls, he had enticed out of the Saxenmarken by promises of much booty and plunder. Thus nothing was left to the Gauls. After that he took two islands for stations for his ships, from which he used later to sally forth and plunder all the Phœnician ships and towns that he could reach. When he returned he brought nearly six hundred of the finest youths of the Scotch mountaineers with him. He said that they had been given him as hostages, that he might be sure that the parents would remain faithful to him; but this was untrue. He kept them as a bodyguard at his court, where they had daily lessons in riding and in the use of all kinds of arms. The Denmarkers, who proudly considered themselves sea-warriors above all the other sea-people, no sooner heard of the glorious deeds of Askar, than they became jealous of him to such a degree, that they would bring war over the sea and over his lands. See here, then, how he was able to avoid a war. Among the ruins of the destroyed citadel of Stavia there was still established a clever Burgtmaagd, with a few maidens. Her name was Reintja, and she was famed for her wisdom. This maid offered her assistance to Askar, on condition that he should afterwards rebuild the citadel of Stavia. When he had bound himself to do this, Reintja went with three maidens to Hals (Holstein). She travelled by night, and by day she made speeches in all the markets and in all the assemblies. Wr-alda, she said, had told her by his thunder that all the Frya's people must become friends, and united as brothers and sisters, otherwise Finda's people would come and sweep them off the face of the earth. After the thunder Frya's seven watch-maidens appeared to her in a dream seven nights in succession. They had

---

* *Hals* is Holstein.

Hja hêde seith boppa Fryas landum swabbert ramp mith juk ånd kêdne omme. Thêrvmbe moton alle folkar thêr ût Frya sproten send hjara tonôma wêi werpa ånd hjara selva allêna Fryas bern jeftha folk hêta. Forth moton alle vpstonda ånd et Findas folk fon Fryas erv dryva. Nillath hja thåt navt ne dva, alsa skilun hja slâvona benda vmbe hjara halsa krêja, alsa skilun tha vrlandaska hêra hjara bern misbruka ånd frytra lêta, til thju thåt blod sygath inna jowre grêva. Thân skilun tha skinna jowre ethla jo kvma wekja ånd jo bikyvja vr jo lefhêd ånd vndigerhêd. Thåt dvme folk, thåt thrvch todvan thêra Mâgyara al an sa fül dwêshêd wenth was, lâvadon alles hwat hju sêide ånd tha måmma klimdon hjara bern åjen hjara brosta an. Thâ Rêintja thene kening fon Hals ånd alle ôthera manniska to êndracht vrwrocht hede, sand hju bodon nêi Askar ånd tâg selva alingen thene Balda sê. Dânâ gvng hju by tha Hlith-hâwar, althus hêten vmbe that hja hjara fyanda immer nêi thet ônhlite hâwe. Tha Hlithhâwar send britne ånd bannene fon vs åjn folk thåt inna tha Twisklanda sit ånd omme dwarelt. Hjara wyva hâvon hja mêst algadur fon tha Tartara râwed. Tha Tartara sênd en dêl fon Findas slachte ånd althus thrvch tha Twisklandar hêten vmbe thåt hja nimmerthe nên frêtho wille, men tha månniska alti ût tarta to strydande. Forth gvng hju åftera Saxnamarka tweres thrvch tha ôra Twisklanda hin, allerwêikes thåt selva ûtkêtha. Nêi twam jêr om wêron, kêm hju allingen thêre Rêne to honk. By tha Twisklandar hede hju hjara selva as Moder ûtjân ånd sêid thåt hja mochton as fry ånd franka månniska wither kvma, men thån mosten hja ovir tha Rêne gvngga ånd tha Gola folgar ût Fryas sûdarlandum jâgja. As hja thåt dêde, sa skolde hjra kêning Askar overa Skelda gvngga ånd thêr thåt land ofwinna. By tha Twisklandar send fêlo tjoda plêga fon tha Tartarum ånd Mâgjara binna glupt, men åk fül send

said, Disaster hovers over Frya's land with yoke and chains; therefore all the people who have sprung from Frya's blood must do away with their surnames, and only call themselves Frya's children, or Frya's people. They must all rise up and drive Finda's people out of Frya's inheritance. If you will not do that, you will bring the slave-chains round your necks, and the foreign chiefs will ill-treat your children and flog them till the blood streams into your graves. Then shall the spirits of your forefathers appear to you, and reproach your cowardice and thoughtlessness. The stupid people who, by the acts of the Magyars, were already so much accustomed to folly, believed all that she said, and the mothers clasped their children to their bosoms. When Reintja had brought the king of Holstein and the others to an agreement, she sent messengers to Askar, and went herself along the Baltic Sea. From there she went to the Lithauers (Face-hewers), so called because they always strike at their enemy's face. The Lithauers are fugitives and banished people of our own race, who wander about in the Twisklanden. Their wives have been mostly stolen from the Tartars. The Tartars are a branch of Finda's race, and are thus named by the Twisklanders because they never will be at peace, but provoke people to fight. She proceeded on beyond the Saxsenmarken, crossing through the other Twisklanders in order always to repeat the same thing. After two years had passed, she came along the Rhine home. Among the Twisklanders she gave herself out for a mother, and said that they might return as free and true people; but then they must go over the Rhine and drive the Gauls out of Frya's south lands. If they did that, then her King Askar would go over the Scheldt and win back the land. Among the Twisklanders many bad customs of the Tartars and Magyars have crept in, but likewise many of our

thêr fon vsa sêdum bilêwen. Thêr thrvch håvath hja jeta fåmna thêr tha bern lêra ånd tha alda rêd jeva. Bit-anfang wêron hja Rêintja nydich, men to tha lesta wårth hju thrvch hjam folgath ånd thjanjath ånd allerwêikes bogath, hwêr-et nette ånd nêdlik wêre.

Alsa ringen Askar fon Rêintja hjra bodon fornom ho tha Juttar nygath wêron, sand hi bistonda bodon fon sinant wegum nêi tha kåning fon Hals. Thåt skip, wêrmith tha bodon gvngon, was fvl lêden mith fåmna syrhêdum ånd thêr by wêr en golden skild, hwêrvppa Askar his dånte kunstalik was utebyld. Thissa bodon mosten frêja jef Askar thes kåning his toghter Frêthogunsta to sin wif håve machte. Frêthogunsta kêm en jêr lêter to Ståveren, bi hjara folgar wêre åk ênen Mågy, hwand tha Juttar wêron sunt lông vrbrud. Kirt åfter that Askar mith Frêthogunsta bostigjath was, wårth thêr to Ståveren êne scherke bvwad, inna thju scherke wrdon tjoda drochten lykanda byldon stålth mith gold trvch wrochtne klåthar. Ak is er biwêrath that Askar thêr nachtis ånd vntydis mith Frêthogunsta får nitherbuwgade. Men så fül is sêkur, thju burch Stavia ne wårth navt wither vpebvwed. Rêintja was al to bek kvmen, ånd gvng nydich nêi Prontlik thju Moder et Texland bårja. Prontlik gvng to ånd sand allerwêikes bodon thêr ûtkêthon, Askar is vrjêven an afgodie. Askar dêde as murk-i-t navt, men vnwarlingen kêm thêr êne flåte ût Hals. Nachtis wrdon tha fåmna ût-êre burch drywen, ånd ogtins kvn mån fon thêre burch allêna êne glandere håpe sjan. Prontlik ånd Rêintja kêmon to my vmb skul. Thå ik thêr åfternêi vr nêi tochte, lêk it my to, that it kwådlik får min ståt bidêja kvste. Thêrvmbe håvon wi to sêmne êne lest forsonnen, thêr vs alle båta most. Sjan hyr ho wi to gvngen send. Middel in-t Krylwald biasten Ljvwerde lêith vsa fly jeftha wêra, thêr mån allêna thrvch dwarlpåda mêi nåka. In vppa thjus burch hêd ik sunt lônge

laws have remained. Therefore they still have Maagden, who teach the children and advise the old. In the beginning they were opposed to Reintja, but at last she was followed, obeyed, and praised by them where it was useful or necessary.

As soon as Askar heard from Reintja's messengers how the Jutlanders were disposed, he immediately, on his side, sent messengers to the King of Hals. The ship in which the messengers went was laden with women's ornaments, and took also a golden shield on which Askar's portrait was artistically represented. These messengers were to ask the King's daughter, Frethogunsta, in marriage for Askar. Frethogunsta came a year after that to Staveren. Among her followers was a Magy, for the Jutlanders had been long ago corrupted. Soon after Askar had married Frethogunsta, a church was built at Staveren. In the church were placed monstrous images, bedecked with gold-woven dresses. It is also said that Askar, by night, and at unseasonable times, kneeled to them with Frethogunsta; but one thing is certain, the citadel of Stavia was never rebuilt. Reintja was already come back, and went angrily to Prontlik the mother, at Texland, to complain. Prontlik sent out messengers in all directions, who proclaimed that Askar is gone over to Idolatry. Askar took no notice of this, but unexpectedly a fleet arrived from Hals. In the night the maidens were driven out of the citadel, and in the morning there was nothing to be seen of the citadel but a glowing heap of rubbish. Prontlik and Reintja came to me for shelter. When I reflected upon it, I thought that it might prove bad for my state. Therefore, we hit upon a plan which might serve us all. This is the way we went to work. In the middle of the Krijlwood, to the east of Liudwerd, lies our place of refuge, which can only be reached by a concealed path. A long time ago I had

jonga wâkar stald, thêr alle êne grins an Askar hêde, ånd alle ôra månniska dånath halden. Nv wast bi vs åk al sa wyd kvmen, thåt fêlo wyva ånd åk manna al patêrade vr spoka, witte wyva ånd uldermankes, lik tha Dênamarkar. Askar hêde al thissa dwåshêde to sin båta anwenth ånd thåt wildon wi nv åk to vsa båta dva. Bi-ne thjustre nacht brocht ik tha fåmna nêi thêre burch ånd dånå gongen hia mith hjara fåmna in thrvch tha dwarlpåda spokka in wttta klåthar huled, så that thêr afternêi nên månnisk måra kvma ne thvrade. Tha Askar mênde thåt-er thu hônda rum hêde, lêt-i tha Mågjara vnder allerlêja nôma thrvch ovir sina ståta fåra ånd bûta Grênegå ånd bûta mina ståt ne wrdon hja nårne navt ne wêrath. Nêi that Askar alsa mith tha Juttar ånd tha ôra Dênamarkar forbonden was, gvngon hja alsêmina råwa; thach that neth nêne gode früchda båred. Hja brochton allerlêja vrlandiska skåta to honk. Men just thêr thrvch nildon thåt jong folk nên ambacht lêra, nach vppa tha fjeldum navt ne werka, så that hi to tha lersta wel slåvona nimma moste. Men thit was êl al åjen Wralda his wille ånd åjen Fryas rêd. Thêrvmbe kv straf navt åfterwêga ne bilywa. Sjan hyr ho straffe kvmen is. Ênis hêdon hja to sêmine êne êle flåte wnnen, hju kêm fon ûta Middelsê. Thjus flåte was to lêden mith purpera klåthar ånd ôra kostelikhêd, thêr alle fon of Phonisja kêmon. Thåt wraka folk thêre flåte wårth bisûda thêre Sêjene an wal set, men thåt stora folk wårth halden. Thåt most ra as slåvona thianja. Tha skêneste wrdon halden vmbe vppet land to bilywane ånd tha lêdliksta ånd swartste wrdon an bord halden vmbe vppa tha benka to rojande. Av-t Fly wårth tha bodel dêlath, men svnder hjara wêta wårth åk hjara straf dêlath. Fon tha månniska thêr vppa tha vrlandiska skepum stalt wêron, wêron sex thrvch bukpin felth. Mån tochte thåt et eta ånd drinka vrjêven wêre,

established a garrison of young men who all hated Askar, and kept away all other people. Now it was come to such a pitch among us, that many women, and even men, talked about ghosts, white women, and gnomes, just like the Denmarkers. Askar had made use of all these follies for his own advantage, and we wished to do the same. One dark night I brought the Maagden to the citadel, and afterwards they went with their serving-maids dressed in white along the path, so that nobody dare go there any more. When Askar thought he had his hands free, he let the Magyars travel through his states under all kinds of names, and, except in my state, they were not turned away anywhere. After that Askar had become so connected with the Jutlanders and the Denmarkers, they all went roving together; but it produced no real good to them. They brought all sorts of foreign treasures home, and just for that reason the young men would learn no trades, nor work in the fields; so at last he was obliged to take slaves; but that was altogether contrary to Wr-alda's wish and to Frya's counsel. Therefore the punishment was sure to follow it. This is the way in which the punishment came. They had all together taken a whole fleet that came out of the Mediterranean Sea. This fleet was laden with purple cloths and other valuables that came from Phœnicia. The weak people of the fleet were put ashore south of the Seine, but the strong people were kept to serve as slaves. The handsomest were retained ashore, and the ugly and black were kept on board ship as rowers. In the Fly the plunder was divided, but, without their knowing it, they divided the punishment too. Of those who were placed in the foreign ships six died of colic. It was thought that the food and

thêrvmbe wârth alles ovir bord jompth. Men bûkpin reste ånd allerwêikes, hwêr slâvona jeftha god kêm, kêm âk bûkpin binna. Tha Saxmanna brochten hju ovir hjara marka, mith tha Juttar for hju nêi Skênland ånd alingen thêre kâd fon tha Balda-sê, mith Askar his stjûrar for hju nêi Britanja. Wi ånd tham fon Grênegâ ne lêton nên god ner minniska ovir vsa pâla navt ne kvma, ånd thêrvmbe bilêwon wi fon tha bûkpin fry. Ho fêlo månniska bûkpin wêirâpth heth, nêt ik navt to skrywane, men Prontlik thêr et åfternêi fon tha ôra fâmna hêrde, heth my meld, thât Askar thûsandmel mâra frya månniska ût sina stâtum hulpen heth, as er vvla slâvona inbrochte. Tha pest far god wyken was, tha kêmon tha fri wrden Twisklandar nêi thêre Rêne, men Askar nilde mith tha forstum fon thât vvla vr basterde folk navt an êne lyne navt ne stonda. Hi nilde navt ne dåja, that hja skoldon hjara selva Fryas bern hêta, lik Rêintja biboden hêde, men hi vrjet thêrbi that-i selva swarte hêra hêde. Emong tha Twisklandar wêron thêr twâ folkar, thêr hjara selva nêne Twisklandar hêton. Thât êne folk kêm êl fêr ût-et sûdâsten wêi, hja hêton hjara selva Allemanna. Thissa nôma hêdon hja hjara selva jêven, thâ hja jeta svnder wiva inna tha walda as bannane ommedwarelde. Lêtar håvon hja fon-et slâvona folk wiva râvath, êvin sa tha Hlithâwar, men hja håvon hjara nôme bihalden. Thât ôra folk, thât mâra hêinde ommedwarelde, hêton hjara selva Franka, navt vmbe that hja fry wêron, men Frank alsa hêde thene êroste kåning hêten, tham him selva mith hulpe fon tha vrbrûda fâmna to ervlik kåning ovir sin folk mâkad hêde. Tha folkar tham an him påladon, hêton hjara selva Thjoth-his svna, that is folkhis svna, hja wêron Frya månniska bilêwen, nêidam hja nimmer ênen kåning ner forste nach mâster bikånnna nilde, as thene jenge tham by mêna willa was kêren vppa thêre mêna acht. Askar hêde

drink were poisoned, so it was all thrown overboard, but the colic remained all the same. Wherever the slaves or the goods came, there it came too. The Saxsenmen took it over to their marches. The Jutlanders brought it to Schoonland and along the coasts of the Baltic Sea, and with Askar's mariners it was taken to Britain. We and the people of Grênegâ did not allow either the people or the goods to come over our boundaries, and therefore we remained free from it. How many people were carried off by this disease I cannot tell; but Prontlik, who heard it afterwards from the maidens, told me that Askar had helped out of his states a thousand times more free-men than he had brought dirty slaves in. When the pest had ceased, the Twisklanders who had become free came to the Rhine, but Askar would not put himself on an equality with the princes of that vile degenerate race. He would not suffer them to call themselves Frya's children, as Reintja had offered them, but he forgot then that he himself had black hair. Among the Twisklanders there were two tribes who did not call themselves Twisklanders. One came from the far south-east, and called themselves Allemannen. They had given themselves this name when they had no women among them, and were wandering as exiles in the forests. Later on they stole women from the slave people like the Lithauers, but they kept their name. The other tribe, that wandered about in the neighbourhood, called themselves Franks, not because they were free, but the name of their first king was Frank, who, by the help of the degenerate maidens, had had himself made hereditary king over his people. The people nearest to him called themselves Thiothhis sons—that is, sons of the people. They had remained free, because they never would acknowledge any king, or prince, or master except those chosen by general consent in a general assembly. Askar had

al fon Rêintja fornommen, that tha Twisklandar forsta mêst alti in fiandskip ånd faitha wêron. Nw stald-i hjam to fåra, hjå skolde ênen hêrtoga fon sin folk kjasa vmbe that-er ang wêre seid-er that hja skolde mit manlik ôtherum skoldon twista ovir-et måsterskip. Ak sêid-er kvndon sina forsta mith-a Golum sprêka. Thåt sêid-er wêre åk Moder his mêne. Thå kêmon tha forsta thêra Twislandar to ekkôrum ånd nêi thrija sjugun etmelde kêron hja Alrik to-ra hertoga ut. Alrik wêre Askar his nêva, hi jef him twên hvndred skotse ånda hvndred thêra storosta Saxmanna mith to lifwêra. Tha forsta moston thrija sjvgun fon hjara svnum nêi Ståveren senda to borg hjarar trow. To nv was alles nêi winsk gvngen, men thå mån ovire Rêne fara skolde, nildon thene kåning thêra Franka navt vnder Alrikis bifêla navt ne stonda. Thêrthrvch lip alles an tha tys. Askar thêr mênde thåt alles god gvng, lande mith sina skêpa anna tha ôre syde thêre Skelda, men thêr was was man long fon sin kvmste to ljucht ånd vppa sin hod. Hja moston alsa ring fljuchta as hja kvmen wêron, ånd Askar wrde selva fath. Tha Gola niston navt hwa hja fensen hêde, ånd alsa warth hi åfternêi ûtwixlath fori ênnen håge Gol, thêr Askar his folk mith forath hêde. Thawila thåt-et alles bêrade, hlipon tha Mågjara jeta dryster as to fåra ovir vsa bûra ra landa hinna. By Egmvda hwêr to fåra tha burch Forâna ståu hêde, lêton hja êne cherka bvwa jeta grâter ånd rikar as Askar to Ståveren dên hêde. Afternêi sêidon hja that Askar thju kåse vrlêren hêde with tha Gola, thrvchdam et folk navt låwa navt nilde, that Wodin hjam helpa kvste, ånd that hja him thêrvmbe navt anbidda nilde. Forth gvngon hja to ånd skåkton jonga bern tham hja by ra hildon ånd vpbrochten in tha hemnissa fon hjara vrbruda lêre. Wêron thêr månniska tham

[Het overige ontbreekt.]

already learned from Reintja that the Twisklander princes were almost always at war with each other. He proposed to them that they should choose a duke from his people, because, as he said, he was afraid that they would quarrel among themselves for the supremacy. He said also that his princes could speak with the Gauls. This, he said, was also the opinion of the mother. Then the princes of the Twisklanders came together, and after twenty-one days they chose Alrik as duke. Alrik was Askar's nephew. He gave him two hundred Scotch and one hundred of the greatest Saksmannen to go with him as a bodyguard. The princes were to send twenty-one of their sons as hostages for their fidelity. Thus far all had gone according to his wishes; but when they were to go over the Rhine, the king of the Franks would not be under Alrik's command. Thereupon all was confusion. Askar, who thought that all was going on well, landed with his ships on the other side of the Scheldt; but there they were already aware of his coming, and were on their guard. He had to flee as quickly as he had come, and was himself taken prisoner. The Gauls did not know whom they had taken, so he was afterwards exchanged for a noble Gaul whom Askar's people had taken with them. While all this was going on, the Magyars went about audaciously over the lands of our neighbours. Near Egmuda, where formerly the citadel Forana had stood, they built a church larger and richer than that which Askar had built at Staveren. They said afterwards that Askar had lost the battle against the Gauls, because the people did not believe that Wodin could help them, and therefore they would not pray to him. They went about stealing young children, whom they kept and brought up in the mysteries of their abominable doctrines. Were there people who

[Here the manuscript ends abruptly.]

LaVergne, TN USA
19 April 2010
179792LV00003B/98/A